Envision It! | Visual Skills Handbook

Author's Purpose

To Persuade

To Inform

To Entertain

To Express Emotion

An author's purpose is the reason an author has for writing.

Cause and Effect

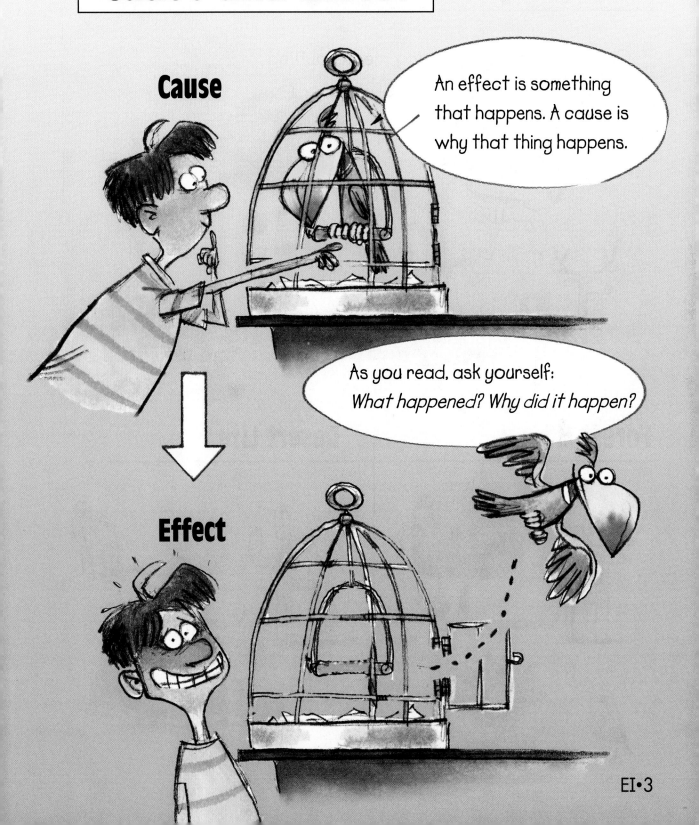

EI·3

Classify and Categorize

Classifying or categorizing means putting things that are related into groups.

Forest Life

Desert Life

Compare and Contrast

As you read, think about what is alike and what is different.

Alike	Different

Draw Conclusions

Combine what you already know with new information to draw conclusions.

What I know:

Riding uphill can make you tired.
Sometimes your face scrunches up when you work hard.
Exercise can make you feel warm.

Conclusion:

The girl is becoming hot and tired.

Fact and Opinion

A statement of fact can be proven true or false.
A statement of opinion tells someone's ideas or feelings.

Generalize

Main Idea and Details

What is the selection all about? What details support the main idea?

Graphic Sources

Where Spider Monkeys Live

North America

South America

Map

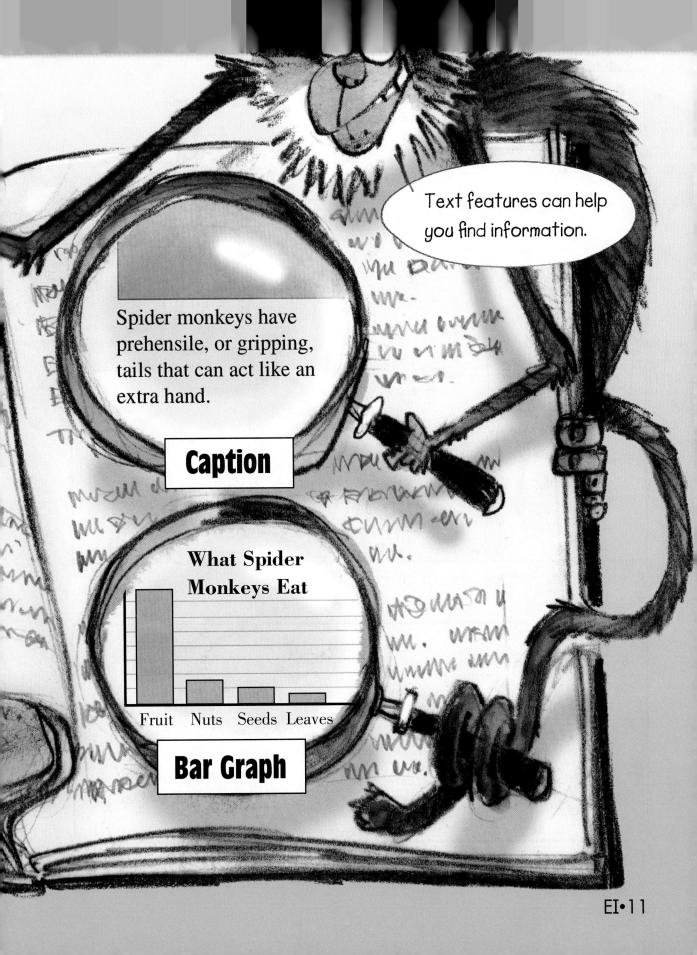

Literary Elements

Characters

A character is a person or animal in a story.

Setting

The setting is the time and place in which a story happens.

Plot

A story's plot is the important events that happen.
The plot starts with a problem and ends with a solution.

Theme

The theme is the big idea of a story.

Sequence

The sequence of a selection is the order of events.

First

Next

Last

Steps in a Process

Envision It! | Visual Strategies Handbook

Background Knowledge

Important Ideas

Inferring

Monitor and Clarify

Predict and Set Purpose

Questioning

Story Structure

Summarize

Text Structure

Visualize

TEKS
3.2.C, RC-3.C.1,
RC-3.F.1

Background Knowledge

Background knowledge is what you already know about a topic based on your reading and personal experience. Make connections to people, places, and things from the real world. Use background knowledge before, during, and after reading to monitor and adjust comprehension.

To use background knowledge
- with fiction, preview the title, author's name, and illustrations
- with nonfiction, preview chapter titles, headings, graphics, captions, and other text features
- think about what you already know

Let's **Think** About **Reading!**

When I use background knowledge, I ask myself
- Does this character remind me of someone?
- How is this story or text similar to others I have read?
- What else do I know about this topic from what I've read or seen?

Important Ideas

Important ideas are essential facts in a nonfiction selection. Important ideas include details that provide clues to the author's purpose.

To identify important ideas
- read all titles, headings, and captions
- look for words in italics, bold print, or bulleted lists
- look for signal words and phrases: *for example, most important,* and others
- use photographs, illustrations, diagrams, or maps
- note how the text is organized— cause and effect, question and answer, or other ways

The caption under the photograph gives more information about wolves.

Let's Think About Reading!

When I identify important ideas, I ask myself
- What information is included in bold, italics or other special lettering?
- What details support important ideas?
- Are there signal words and phrases?
- What do illustrations, photos, diagrams, and charts show?
- How is the text organized?
- Why did the author write this?

Inferring

When we **infer** we use background knowledge with clues in the text to come up with our own ideas about what the author is trying to present.

To infer

- identify what you already know
- combine what you know with text clues to come up with your own ideas

Let's Think About Reading!

When I infer, I ask myself

- What do I already know?
- Which text clues are important?
- What is the author trying to present?

Monitor and Clarify

We **monitor comprehension** to make sure our reading makes sense. We **clarify** to find out why we haven't understood. Then we fix up problems to adjust comprehension.

To monitor and clarify

- use background knowledge as you read
- try different strategies: reread, ask questions, or use text features and illustrations

Let's **Think** About **Reading!**

When I monitor and clarify, I ask myself
- Do I understand what I'm reading?
- What doesn't make sense?
- What strategies can I try here?

Predict and Set Purpose

We **predict** to tell what might happen next in a story. The prediction is based on what has already happened. We **set a purpose** to guide our reading.

To predict and set a purpose
- preview the title, author's name, and illustrations or photos
- identify why you're reading
- use what you already know to make predictions
- check your predictions to confirm them

Let's Think About Reading!

When I predict and set a purpose, I ask myself
- What do I already know?
- What do I think will probably happen?
- What is my purpose for reading?

Questioning

Questioning is asking good questions about important text information. Questioning takes place before, during, and after reading.

To question
- read with a question in mind
- stop, think, and record your questions as you read
- make notes when you find information
- check your understanding and ask questions to clarify

Let's Think About Reading!

When I question, I ask myself
- Have I asked a good question with a question word?
- What questions help me make sense of my reading?
- What does the author mean?

EI•23

Story Structure

Story structure is the arrangement of a story from beginning to end. You can use this information to summarize, or retell, the plot.

To identify story structure
- note what happens at the beginning, middle, and end of the story
- use this information to summarize, or retell, the story

Let's Think About Reading!

When I identify story structure, I ask myself
- What happens in the beginning, middle, and end?
- How can I use this information to summarize?
- How might this affect future events?

Summarize

We **summarize**, or retell, to check our understanding of what we've read. A summary is a brief statement. It's no more than a few sentences.

To summarize fiction
- tell what happens in the story
- include the goals of the characters
- tell how characters try to reach goals and if they are successful

To summarize nonfiction
- tell the main idea of the selection
- think about text structure
- think about how the selection is organized

…and that's how Lewis and Clark helped create new communities.

Let's Think About Reading!

When I summarize, I ask myself
- What is the story or selection mainly about?
- In fiction, what are the characters' goals? Are they successful?
- In nonfiction, how is this information organized?

Text Structure

We use **text structure** to look for how the author has organized the text; for example, cause and effect, problem and solution, sequence, or compare and contrast. Analyze text structure before, during, and after reading to locate information.

To identify text structure

- before reading, preview titles, headings, and illustrations
- during reading: notice the organization
- after reading: recall the organization and summarize the text

> This article uses sequence to explain how soil is formed.

Let's Think About Reading!

When I identify text structure, I ask myself

- What clues do titles, headings, and illustrations provide?
- How is information organized?
- How does the organization help my understanding?

Visualize

We **visualize** to form pictures in our minds about what is happening in a story or article. This helps us monitor our comprehension.

To visualize fiction

- combine what you already know with words and phrases from the text to form pictures in your mind
- use your senses to put yourself in the story or text

Let's Think About Reading!

When I visualize, I ask myself

- What do I already know?
- Which words and phrases help me form pictures in my mind?
- How can my senses put me in the story?

EI•27

Program Authors

Peter Afflerbach

Camille Blachowicz

Candy Dawson Boyd

Elena Izquierdo

Connie Juel

Edward Kame'enui

Donald Leu

Jeanne R. Paratore

P. David Pearson

Sam Sebesta

Deborah Simmons

Alfred Tatum

Sharon Vaughn

Susan Watts Taffe

Karen Kring Wixson

 **PEARSON**

Glenview, Illinois • Boston, Massachusetts • Chandler, Arizona •
Upper Saddle River, New Jersey

We dedicate Reading Street to
Peter Jovanovich.

His wisdom, courage,
and passion for education
are an inspiration to us all.

Accelerated Reader

About the Cover Artist
When Leo Timmers was young he liked to putter with tape and shoeboxes to make animals, boats, and cars. Now, Leo is an illustrator and loves to draw and paint pictures of animals, boats, and cars. Some say his paintings look like they could jump off the page! Leo lives in Belgium.

PEARSON

ISBN-13: 978-0-328-45539-3
ISBN-10:   0-328-45539-3
2 3 4 5 6 7 8 9 10 V063 14 13 12 11 10
CC1

Dear Texas Reader,

Are you enjoying your trip down *Scott Foresman Reading Street*? We hope you are ready for more reading adventures. This book is about being unique, about cultures, and about freedom. You will read about the world record breakers on planet Earth. You will meet a girl who leaves her best friend behind when she moves to a new country. You will read about the Statue of Liberty and about two ants who run away. At each intersection, you will learn something new. But you will also have many chances to use what you learned before. We hope you have fun in the process.

Buckle up and enjoy the trip!

Sincerely,
The Authors

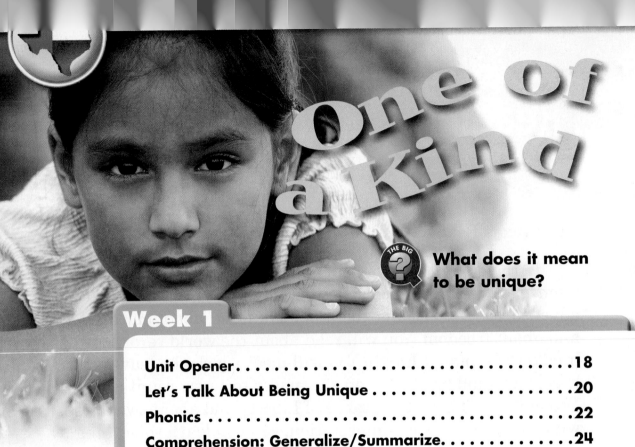

One of a Kind

What does it mean to be unique?

Week 1

Let's **Think** About Reading!

biography • social studies

4

Week 6

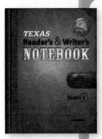

Unit 4

Envision It! **A TEKS Comprehension Handbook**

**Envision It! Visual Skills
Handbook EI•1–EI•16**

**Envision It! Visual Strategies
Handbook EI•17–EI•27**

Words! **Vocabulary Handbook W•1–W•15**

What happens when two ways of life come together?

CULTURES

Week 1

Let's **Think** About **Reading!**

realistic fiction • social studies

Week 2

Week 3

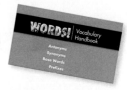

A TEKS Comprehension Handbook

Envision It! Visual Skills Handbook EI•1–EI•16

Envision It! Visual Strategies Handbook EI•17–EI•27

Words! **Vocabulary Handbook W•1–W•15**

FREEDOM

What does freedom mean?

Week 2

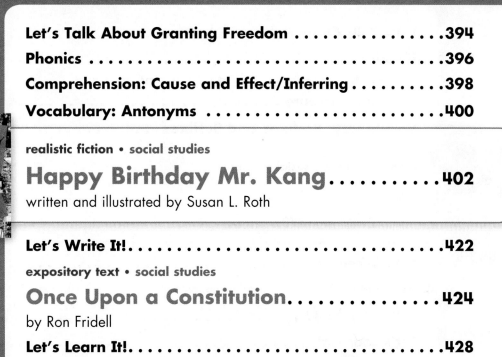

Week 3

Unit 6 Contents

Week 6

Interactive Review

Reader's and Writer's Notebook

Unit 6

 **Envision It!** A TEKS Comprehension Handbook

Envision It! Visual Skills Handbook EI1–EI16

Envision It! Visual Strategies Handbook EI17–EI27

Words! Vocabulary Handbook W1–W15

Don Leu
The Internet Guy

Right before our eyes, the nature of reading and learning is changing. The Internet and other technologies create new opportunities, new solutions, and new literacies. New reading comprehension skills are required online. They are increasingly important to our students and our society.

Those of us on the Reading Street team are here to help you on this new, and very exciting, journey.

See It!

- **Big Question Video**

- **Concept Talk Video**

- **Envision It! Animations**

- **eReaders**

- **Interactive Sound-Spelling Cards**

butterfly

b

Hear It!

- **eSelections**

- **Grammar Jammer**

- **Vocabulary Activities**

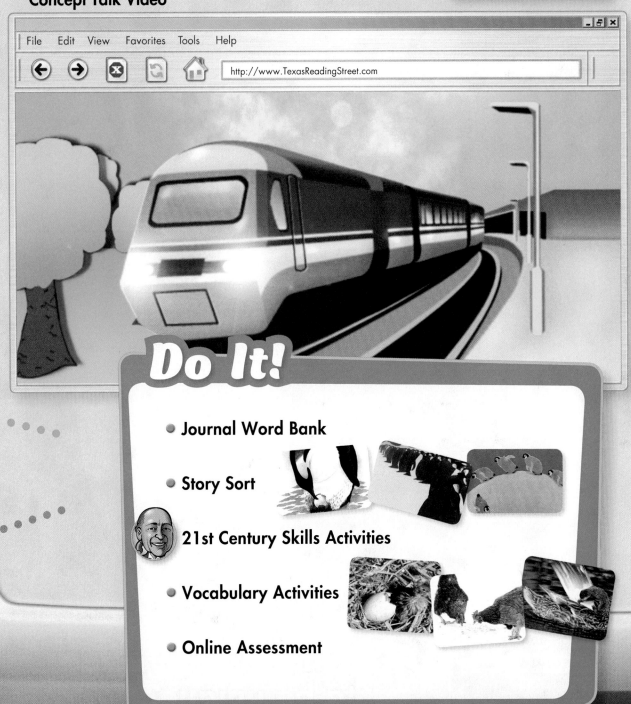

Do It!

- Journal Word Bank

- Story Sort

- 21st Century Skills Activities

- Vocabulary Activities

- Online Assessment

One of a Kind

TEXAS
Reading Street Online
www.TexasReadingStreet.com
- Big Question Video
- eSelections
- Envision It! Animations
- Story Sort

What does it mean to be unique?

Let's **Think** About Reading!

The Man Who Invented Basketball: James Naismith and His Amazing Game BIOGRAPHY

  How do talents make someone unique?

Paired Selection
My Turn at Bat: The Story of My Life AUTOBIOGRAPHY

 Hottest, Coldest, Highest, Deepest
EXPOSITORY TEXT

What makes nature's record holders unique?

Paired Selection
Paul Bunyan and the Great Lakes LEGEND

 Rocks in His Head BIOGRAPHY

Why is it valuable to have unique interests?

Paired Selection
Marvelous Marble Mania PERSUASIVE TEXT

 America's Champion Swimmer: Gertrude Ederle BIOGRAPHY

What unique traits does it take to be the first to do something?

Paired Selection
Women Athletes ONLINE DIRECTORIES

 Fly, Eagle, Fly! FOLK TALE

What behaviors are unique to different animals?

Paired Selection
Purple Coyote TRICKSTER TALE

TEKS

3.29.A.3 Make pertinent comments.
3.31.A.1 Participate in teacher-led
discussions by posing questions
with appropriate detail. **3.31.A.2**
Participate in teacher-led discussions by
answering questions with appropriate
detail. **Also 3.29.A.1, 3.31.A.3.**

Oral Vocabulary

Let's Talk About

Being Unique

- Share ideas about how special skills and talents make people unique.

- Make and listen to comments about ways people are unique.

- Pose and answer questions about what we can learn from the talents of others.

READING STREET ONLINE
CONCEPT TALK VIDEO
www.TexasReadingStreet.com

20

Phonics

🔊 Irregular Plurals

Words I Can Blend

knives
women
geese
children
fish

Sentences I Can Read

1. We used knives to slice the bread.

2. The women fed crumbs to the flock of geese.

3. How many fish did the children catch?

I Can Read!

A family of mice lived in a hole under the porch next door. For their entire lives these mice had been afraid of men and women.

One day they peeked out and saw several pairs of large feet near the entrance to their home. Their teeth began to chatter from fear.

A voice said, "Do not fear, little mice. We are the wives who live nearby. We baked extra loaves of bread today and brought some to share with you and the sheep and deer who roam in the field."

You've learned

🔄 Irregular Plurals

TEKS

3.8.A.2 Summarize the plot's main events. **RC-3.E.1** Summarize information in text, maintaining meaning. **RC-3.E.2** Summarize information in text, maintaining logical order. **Also 3.8.A.1, 3.8.A.3.**

Envision It! | Skill Strategy

Skill

Strategy

READING STREET ONLINE
ENVISION IT! ANIMATIONS
www.TexasReadingStreet.com

Comprehension Skill

🎯 Generalize

- When you read, you can sometimes make a general statement about what you have read.

- A general statement tells how some things are mostly alike or all alike.

- Use what you learned about generalizing as you read "Batting the Ball." Use the text and a graphic organizer like the one below to make a generalization.

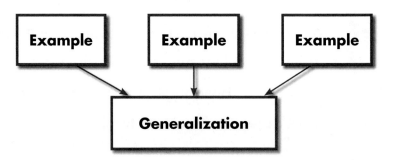

Comprehension Strategy

🎯 Summarize

Active readers sum up what happens as they read a story. When you sum up, remember to tell only the important events in the order that they happened, maintaining the meaning of the story and what the characters learned. This will help you remember what you are reading.

Batting the Ball

Betsy went to a new school at the beginning of third grade. At recess, Betsy wanted to play baseball. The teacher told Betsy that she could not play with a hard baseball, because someone might get hurt. The playground rule was that only soft balls were allowed.

Skill Can you make a generalization about school playgrounds using the details from the first paragraph?

Betsy laughed. "But I am a baseball player," she said. Betsy did not understand why she could only play with a soft ball.

A few days later, another third-grader brought a hard baseball to school. Betsy was eager to show off her baseball skills. She loved the feel of the bat as it hit the hard ball.

When it was Betsy's turn to bat, she stepped up to home plate. The pitcher threw the ball, and it curved around. The ball hit Betsy in the shoulder and she fell to the ground.

"Ouch!" Betsy cried. The teacher ran over to see what had happened. Betsy stood up, rubbing her shoulder. "I think we should use a soft ball," she said to the teacher.

"What good thinking!" the teacher said, replacing the baseball with a soft ball.

Strategy Summarize the story. What is the order of events? What are the results of Betsy's actions?

Your Turn!

Need a Review? See the *Envision It! Handbook* for help with generalizing and summarizing.

Let's Think About..

Ready to Try It? As you read *The Man Who Invented Basketball,* use what you learned about generalizing and summarizing to understand the text.

TEKS

3.4.B.1 Use context to determine the relevant meaning of unfamiliar words.

Envision It! | Words to Know

basketball

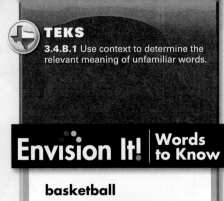

freeze

guard

disease

popular

sports

study

terrible

READING STREET ONLINE
VOCABULARY ACTIVITIES
www.TexasReadingStreet.com

Vocabulary Strategy for

Unfamiliar Words

Context Clues Unfamiliar words are words you haven't seen before. Context clues in the nearby words and sentences can help you figure out the meaning of these new words. Writers often define or explain unfamiliar words in context to help you understand what you are reading.

1. Read the words and sentences around the word you don't know. Sometimes the author tells you what the word means.

2. If not, use the words and sentences to predict a meaning for the word.

3. Try that meaning in the sentence. Does it make sense?

Read "Carlos Catches Sports Fever" on page 27. Use context clues to help you understand the meanings of the Words to Know.

Words to Write Reread "Carlos Catches Sports Fever." Do you have a sport you like to play or watch? Write about the sport you are interested in. Use as many words from the Words to Know list as you can.

Carlos Catches Sports Fever

Ever since his parents could remember, Carlos had been a sports fanatic. He would study about his favorite players, especially basketball's most popular player: Michael Jordan. Carlos was hoping to become the greatest point guard in the history of the sport. He spent hours practicing shooting hoops in his driveway. Carlos's uncle had installed a pole, basketball hoop, and backboard so that Carlos could play all the time.

Carlos practiced in all kinds of weather, even in January. Carlos just put on extra layers of clothing and extra socks so his toes wouldn't freeze. His mother kept telling him to come inside before he caught a terrible cold. But Carlos didn't want to stop playing. He knew that Michael Jordan had become the best basketball player in history because he was so dedicated to the game. Like Michael Jordan, Carlos had the basketball "disease," but he didn't want a cure!

Your Turn!

⏸ **Need a Review?** For additional help with using context clues to find the meanings of unfamiliar words, see *Words!*

▶ **Ready to Try It?**
Read *The Man Who Invented Basketball* on pp. 28–41.

The Man Who Invented Basketball

JAMES NAISMITH AND HIS AMAZING GAME

by Edwin Brit Wyckoff

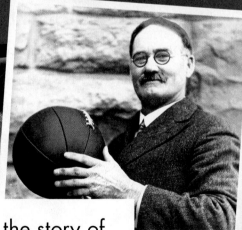

BASKET BALL
Filed March 5, 1928

Fig.3.

Fig.5.

Fig.1.

Fig.4.

Inventor
L Pierce

Question of the Week
How do talents make someone unique?

Let's **Think** About **Reading!**

TOUGH LOVE AND A TOUGH LIFE

Winter in Canada can be very hard. Icy wind sweeps down from the north. Rivers freeze solid. Crossing them can be scary and dangerous.

James Naismith turned eleven in 1872. He was old enough to know where the river near his home became safe, solid ice. But he took a shortcut he had never tried before. His team of horses pulled his wagon onto the frozen river. Their feet pounded the ice. Then one heavy hoof slammed through the sheet of ice. James jumped off the wagon and landed in the water. Grabbing the horses by their reins, he pulled hard. Slowly he forced them to the other side of the river.

James looked around. He saw his uncle Peter Young watching him from behind some trees. But his uncle had not helped him. Uncle Peter wanted James to learn to solve problems by himself and not to take foolish chances. It was a tough lesson.

Let's Think About...

Read the second paragraph. What do you think the biography will be about? Support your prediction with evidence from the text. **Predict**

30

James grew up near Almonte, Ontario, in Canada.

James was born on November 6, 1861, near Almonte, Ontario, which is in Canada. When he was almost nine, his father, John Naismith, came down with deadly typhoid fever. So they would not catch the disease, James, his sister, Annie, and brother, Robbie, were taken to their grandmother's home. A few days later, their father died. Two weeks later, their mother, Margaret, died of the same disease. A short time later, their grandmother Annie Young died of old age.

That left Uncle Peter to take care of the children in Bennie's Corners, near Almonte. The village had a schoolhouse, a blacksmith shop, a store, and lots of other kids to play with.

The children had lots of fun with very little money. When James needed ice skates, he made them. Then he raced out onto the frozen swimming hole like a champion skater.

Let's Think About...

How would you describe the early part of James Naismith's childhood? Use information from the text and maintain a logical order.

Summarize

Let's **Think** About...

Can you visualize how to play the game of duck on a rock? **Visualize**

Let's **Think** About...

How do you think James will use duck on a rock years later in his life? **Predict**

The best game in town was called duck on a rock. One player, the guard, would put a rock about the size of his fist on top of a great big rock near the blacksmith shop. The other boys threw stones at the "duck" to knock it off the big rock. If they missed, they had to pick up their stones before the guard could tag them. It sounds easy, but it is not. The pitch could be soft, but it had to be perfectly aimed. When a player missed the duck, there was a lot of running, shouting, and laughing. James would remember duck on a rock years later when it would be very important to him.

James and his friends used this big rock to play their favorite game, duck on a rock.

THE DROPOUT

James was great at sports. He also worked hard on the family farm. He did not work hard at school, though, and his grades were never very good. He wanted to grow up fast and be a man with a job. When he was fifteen, he left school and worked as a lumberjack.

He cut down trees for almost five years. Then he decided to change his life.

James had a plan. He wanted to go back to high school and finish fast. His next step would be college. In 1883, James entered McGill University in Montreal, Canada.

When James was home for a visit, his brother, Robbie, had a terrible pain in his side. They all thought it was just a stomachache. It was actually a very bad infection. Robbie died a few hours later. A doctor could have helped him. Knowing Robbie might have been saved stayed in James's mind every day of his life.

In 1887, James graduated from McGill University after studying Hebrew and philosophy. Hebrew is an ancient language that many ministers study. Philosophy teaches people to think about life. James had a lot to think about.

Let's Think About...

How would you summarize some of the things James had to think about? Support your answer with information from the text.

Summarize

THE MINISTER PLAYS HARDBALL

For James, the next step was studying to become a minister at McGill's Presbyterian College. There was much to learn, and he studied day and night. His friends tried to get him to play sports. They told him it would sharpen his mind and toughen up his body. He said no and kept on studying.

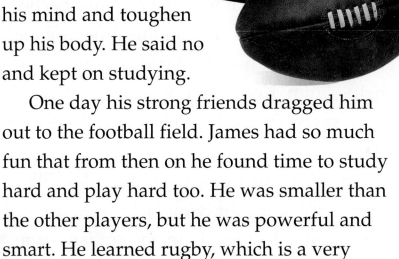

One day his strong friends dragged him out to the football field. James had so much fun that from then on he found time to study hard and play hard too. He was smaller than the other players, but he was powerful and smart. He learned rugby, which is a very rough game. He loved lacrosse, which can be even rougher.

One Saturday James got two black eyes in a wild game of lacrosse. The next day was Sunday, and he had to give a sermon in the church. James, the student minister, looked out from behind those two black eyes. He may have looked kind of funny, but he finished the sermon he had written.

Let's **Think** About...

What words and phrases create a graphic visual image on this page?
Visualize

In 1890, James became a Presbyterian minister. But he did not want to give sermons in a church. He thought he could help teens live better lives if he talked to them while teaching them sports. His first sports job was at the International YMCA Training School, which is now Springfield College. So he moved from Canada to Springfield, Massachusetts, in the United States.

James Naismith believed that the fun and action of sports could improve the lives of young people.

As a student teacher, James was very good at the job of teaching baseball, field hockey, football, and rugby, which are great games during spring, summer, and fall. Winter was a problem. The men had to come indoors and exercise, which was not much fun. They were so bored that some of them wanted to quit the YMCA training school. James was told to invent an exciting indoor game. It had to be ready in two weeks. That was the deadline.

Let's Think About...

Summarize the section "The Minister Plays Hardball." Be sure to maintain the meaning of the section title in your summary.

Summarize

INVENTING FUN

James struggled with the problem for twelve days. The game had to be fast and fun. It could not be risky, like football or rugby, with teams of men banging into the gym walls.

That good old game from his childhood, duck on a rock, flashed into his head. He remembered how using a soft pitch was the best way to aim for the "duck." James's eyes lit up. He shouted out loud, "I've got it!"

There was no time to invent new gear. Two peach baskets were used as goals. James explained the strange rules. Two teams of men dragged themselves onto the gym floor, grumbling. They took a soccer ball and started playing. The grumbling soon stopped. Cheers and shouts filled the gym. The date was December 21, 1891. Basketball was born. Soon teams formed in gyms all around town.

Let's **Think** About...

What parts of the games and sports James knew well went into basketball?

Summarize

Peach baskets were used as basketball goals before nets.

In schools across the United States, students began to play basketball. Women began playing, too.

A young woman named Maude Sherman was on one of the first women's teams. James and Maude soon became friends, and then fell in love. They married on June 20, 1894. James and Maude would have five children together.

In a few years, basketball started being played more like it is played today. The peach baskets had changed to rope baskets. Backboards were added. Dribbling became popular because players were not allowed to hold the ball very long without throwing it. When the ball bounced off the floor as a player raced down the court, it sounded like a fast drumbeat. James thought dribbling was a great idea.

Let's Think About...

How were James's first basketball games different from later ones?

Summarize

Let's **Think** About...

Were your predictions correct so far? What do you think will happen next in James's life?
Predict

In 1895, James and Maude moved to Denver, Colorado. There James became director of physical education at the largest YMCA in the country.

He was always working on his plan for the future. He remembered his brother dying horribly without help from a doctor. He had seen athletes have terrible accidents. He wanted to be a doctor and help people.

There was no stopping James when he had a plan. He became a student at Gross Medical College in Denver. He would work all day at the YMCA and then study to be a doctor after work and on weekends. James graduated as a medical doctor in 1898. That year he got the job of assistant physical director at the University of Kansas. By 1909 James was working there as a minister, a professor, and a medical doctor.

James Naismith could have made lots of money by selling sports equipment. He could have used his fame to pose for ads selling products. He refused the offers. He just wanted to do his job as a teacher, minister, and sports doctor.

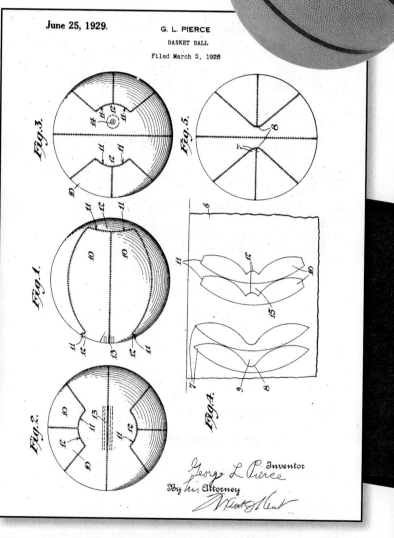

George L. Pierce invented the basketball used today. Here is his sketch for the patent.

NAISMITH'S ORIGINAL THIRTEEN RULES OF BASKETBALL, 1891

1. The ball may be thrown in any direction.

2. It can be batted with hands, but not with the fist.

3. No running with the ball.

4. Hold the ball only with the hands.

5. No holding, pushing, hitting, or tripping the other team's players.

6. Follow the rules or a foul will be declared.

7. Make three fouls and the other team is given a goal.

8. A goal is made when the ball goes into the basket.

9. When the ball goes out of bounds, the first person to touch it, or the umpire, will throw it onto the court.

10. The umpire is the judge of the players. He can call fouls.

11. The referee is the judge of the ball. He decides on goals.

12. Game time is two fifteen-minute halves.

13. The team with the most goals in that time is the winner.

Let's **Think** About...

Use the rules to imagine how the game was played in 1891. How was the game different then?
Visualize

TIME LINE

- **1861** Born on November 6, Almonte, Ontario, Canada.

- **1870** Parents die; moves to Bennie's Corners, Ontario.

- **1887** Graduates from McGill University in Montreal, Quebec, Canada.

- **1890** Becomes a Presbyterian minister.

- **1891** Invents basketball; first game is played December 21.

- **1894** Marries Maude Sherman on June 20.

- **1895** Becomes director of physical education at YMCA in Denver, Colorado.

- **1898** Graduates as a medical doctor

- **1909** Is professor, minister, and doctor at the University of Kansas.

- **1917** Helps American soldiers in World War I as a military chaplain.

- **1925** Becomes United States citizen.

- **1936** Is honored at Olympic Games in Berlin, Germany.

- **1939** Dies on November 28 in Lawrence, Kansas.

Let's Think About...

Which of the events in the time line are supported by facts and details in the biography?

 Summarize

41

TEKS

3.9.A.1 Explain the difference in point of view between a biography and autobiography. **Also 3.2.B.4, 3.2.B.6, 3.2.B.8. 3.2.B.9, RC-3.E.1, RC-3.E.2.**

Envision It! Retell

READING STREET ONLINE
STORY SORT
www.TexasReadingStreet.com

Think Critically

1. On page 36, the author writes about James Naismith coming up with the idea for basketball in only two weeks. Have you ever quickly solved a hard problem? Why was James Naismith's idea for basketball right for the problem?

   Text to Self

2. Is the selection written in first or third person? Why was it written that way? How would the selection be different if it were an autobiography instead of a biography? **Think Like an Author**

3. On page 38, what generalization does the author make about Naismith? What clue word does the author use? Is the generalization well-supported?

   Generalize

4. What important events in Naismith's life led to him becoming a teacher and coach? What important events led to him becoming a doctor? **Summarize**

5. **Look Back and Write** Look back through the selection to find for facts and details about the character of James Naismith. Write about what traits helped him become a success in his life. Provide evidence to support your answer.

    **TEST PRACTICE** Extended Response

Edwin Brit Wyckoff

Edwin Brit Wyckoff is the co-creator of the first children's interactive television program *Winky Dink and You*, which originally ran on Saturday mornings from 1953 until 1957. He has also made hundreds of films, videos, and educational programs in a variety of medias. Mr. Wyckoff lives in both New York City and Washington, D.C.

Mr. Brit Wyckoff is the author of several books about inventors including *Electric Guitar Man: The Genius of Les Paul; Ferris Wheel!: George Ferris and His Amazing Invention; Heart Man: Vivien Thomas, African-American Heart Surgery Pioneer; Laser Man: Theodore H. Maiman and His Brilliant Invention;* and *The Teen Who Invented Television: Philo T. Farnsworth and His Awesome Invention.*

Here is another book by Edwin Brit Wyckoff.

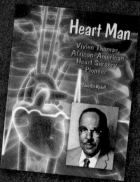

Heart Man: Vivien Thomas, African-American Heart Surgery Pioneer

Reading Log

Use the *Reader's and Writer's Notebook* to record your independent reading.

TEKS

3.21.A.1 Write persuasive essays for appropriate audiences that establish a position. **3.21.A.2** Write persuasive essays for appropriate audiences that use supporting details.

Let's Write It!

Key Features of a Persuasive Essay

- takes a position on a subject
- tries to influence the reader's opinion
- provides details to support the position
- may urge the reader to take action

READING STREET ONLINE
GRAMMAR JAMMER
www.TexasReadingStreet.com

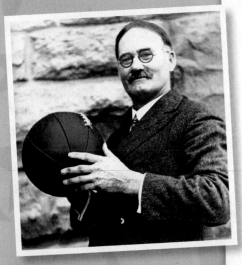

Persuasive

Persuasive Essay

A persuasive essay tries to get readers to agree with an opinion or to do something. The student model on the next page is an example of a persuasive essay.

Writing Prompt *The Man Who Invented Basketball* is about Joseph Naismith, who invented the game of basketball. Write an essay about your favorite sport or game, persuading someone to play it.

Writer's Checklist

Remember, you should ...

✓ state your position.

✓ include details that support your position.

✓ use words that appeal to the reader's emotions.

✓ end by restating your position.

44

Bocce Ball

Bocce ball is the best sport ever! I've been playing since I could walk, so I should know. One of the best things about bocce ball is that it can be played almost anywhere. My family and I play in the yard, at the park, at the beach, and when **we** go camping. It's lots of fun for everyone!

The equipment for bocce ball is easy to find and isn't expensive, so almost anyone can afford it. The rules are easy to learn too. People of all ages can play, so you can play with your neighbors, your friends, your little sister, or your grandparents! I think everyone should play bocce ball because it is the best, cheapest, and most fun game.

Genre A **persuasive essay** supports a position with details.

Singular and plural pronouns are used correctly.

Writing Trait Conventions Conjunctions such as *and, so,* and *because* make writing clearer.

Conventions

Singular and Plural Pronouns

Remember Pronouns are words that take the place of nouns. **Singular pronouns** are words that take the place of singular nouns. **Plural pronouns** take the place of plural nouns.

TEKS

3.2.B.6 Locate facts about other texts. **3.2.B.8** Locate details about other texts. **3.2.B.9** Support answers with evidence from text. **3.9.A.1** Explain the difference in point of view between a biography and autobiography.

Social Studies in Reading

Genre
Autobiography

- An autobiography is the story of a person's life written by the person who lived it.

- Autobiographies are written in the first person, using *I, me,* and *my.*

- The events in an autobiography are actual events and experiences in a person's life.

- As you read, think about the difference in point of view between the autobiography and the biography sections of "My Turn at Bat."

MY TURN AT BAT
The Story of My Life

Ted Williams with John Underwood

Baseball great Ted Williams was born in 1918. His mother, May Venzer, was a Salvation Army worker. She was part Mexican and part French. His father, Samuel Stuart Williams, was a soldier, U.S. marshal, and photographer. He was part Welsh and part Irish.

Their son, Ted, came to have several nicknames, including "Teddy Ballgame," "The Splendid Splinter," and "The Kid."

Ted recalls his childhood:

Wilber Wiley was my first real boyhood pal. Wilber had a job delivering the *Evening Tribute*, and when he'd get through about an hour before dark, we'd go to the playground, just the two of us, and hit, hit, hit, and throw, throw, throw.

The playground director was a man named Rodney Luscomb, and Rod Luscomb was my first real hero. I know when I walked up to the rostrum in Cooperstown the day they inducted me into the Hall of Fame Rod Luscomb was one of the people on my mind, one of the people I felt made it possible. That should tell you something about how much a coach can mean to a kid.

I suppose the first strong influence I had to continue in baseball, to make it my life's work, was my coach at Herbert Hoover High in San Diego, a wonderful man named Wos Caldwell.

I'll never forget one day I hit a ball they say went 450 feet, between the right and center fielders. I fell down rounding third—a big skinny kid, all arms and legs—and I got thrown out at home plate.

San Diego was a ballplayer's town, year-round, and by the time I was a pitcher at Herbert Hoover High I was hooked. As a pitcher-outfielder, I batted .583 and .406 my last years in high school, .430 for three years.

Let's **Think** About...

What words indicate that this section is written in the first person point of view?
Autobiography

Ted recalls his baseball career:

I signed my first professional contract with the San Diego Padres at age 17 and discovered the joys of paychecks and train rides. I never had so much fun.

In 1937, the Padres sold Ted to the Boston Red Sox. In 1938, at the Red Sox's farm club in Minneapolis, Williams led the league in hitting. He moved up to the Red Sox team the next year.

Let's **Think** About...

In this paragraph, John Underwood describes Ted's career. How is this different from Ted's own account in the paragraphs before and after?

Autobiography

That spring I was a nuisance to everybody, asking questions about hitting … I quizzed every player on the team, and they all had something to say, and the weight of the evidence pretty much proved out. I can't imagine anyone having a better, happier first year in the big leagues. I used to send Rod Luscomb diagrams showing how the parks were laid out and where I had hit my home runs, telling him how happy I was. I hit a home run in every park, completing the list in Yankee Stadium on the last day.

BASEBALL HISTORY TIME LINE

Sept. 28, 1941 - Williams goes 6-for-8 in a doubleheader and finishes with a .406 average.

1947 - Williams wins the Triple Crown by batting .343 with 32 homers and 114 RBIs.

1948 - Williams wins the American League batting title with a .369 average.

1949 - Williams drives in a career-high 159 runs. He leads the league with career-high 150 walks and wins the American League MVP award.

1951 - Williams hits .318 with 30 homers and 126 RBIs. He scores 109 runs for the season.

July 23, 1955 - Williams hits a 450-foot home run onto the right-field roof at Comiskey Park.

July 29, 1958 - Williams hits the 17th and final grand slam of his career in an 11–8 win over Detroit.

Sept. 28, 1960 - The final game of Ted Williams' baseball career as a player.

July 25, 1966 - Williams is inducted into the Hall of Fame.

Let's **Think** About...

Why is a time line a good graphic source to use in a biography or autobiography?

Autobiography

In 1941, only his third season in the majors, Williams chased a .400 batting average.

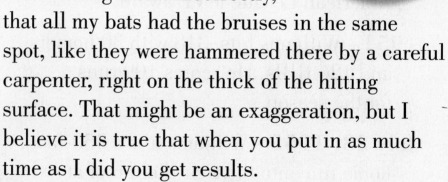

TED WILLIAMS
BOSTON RED SOX

Let's **Think** About...

How is the point of view in this paragraph different from the point of view in *The Man Who Invented Basketball*? What evidence from the texts supports your answer?
Autobiography

Rod Luscomb used to say that in seven years on the playground I never broke a bat hitting a ball incorrectly, that all my bats had the bruises in the same spot, like they were hammered there by a careful carpenter, right on the thick of the hitting surface. That might be an exaggeration, but I believe it is true that when you put in as much time as I did you get results.

A hitter can't just go up there and swing. He's got to think. Listen, when I played I knew the parks, the mounds, the batters' boxes, the backgrounds. I studied the pitchers. I knew what was going on at that plate. It used to kill me to strike out, but when I struck out I knew what it was that got me and what I was going to try to do about it.

Baseball Hall of Fame

A man has to have goals—for a day, for a lifetime—and that was mine, to have people say, "There goes Ted Williams, the greatest hitter who ever lived."

Ted Williams

LF 1939-1942, 1946-1960
Class of 1966

Theodore Samuel Williams
Born: August 30, 1918, San Diego, CA
Died: July 5, 2002, Crystal River, FL
Bats: Left   **Throws:** Right

Played for: Boston Red Sox
(1939-1942, 1946-1960)
Elected to Hall of Fame by Baseball Writers: 1966
282 votes of 302 ballots cast (93.38%)

Hitting Stats

AVG	G	AB	R	H	HR	RBI	SB	SLG
.344	2292	7706	1798	2654	521	1839	24	.634

Let's **Think** About...

Using the baseball card on this page, locate facts and details about Ted Williams's life. What other texts might you use to gather information about Ted Williams?
Autobiography

Let's **Think** About...

Reading Across Texts How are James Naismith and Ted Williams alike? How are they different?

Writing Across Texts Create a Venn diagram to compare and contrast the careers of James Naismith and Ted Williams.

TEKS

3.3.A.1 Read aloud grade-level appropriate text with fluency. **3.3.A.2** Read aloud grade-level appropriate text with comprehension. **3.30.A.1** Speak coherently about the topic under discussion. **3.30.A.2** Speak coherently, employing eye contact, speaking rate, volume, enunciation, and the conventions of language to communicate ideas effectively. **3.4.B.1** Use context to determine the relevant meaning of unfamiliar words. Also **3.29.A.1, 3.29.A.2, 3.29.A.3, 3.31.A.4, 3.31.A.5, 3.31.A.6.**

Let's Learn It!

READING STREET ONLINE
ONLINE STUDENT EDITION
www.TexasReadingStreet.com

Vocabulary

Unfamiliar Words

Context Clues Use context clues to find the meanings of unfamiliar words while you are reading. The words or sentences around the unfamiliar word may provide its meaning.

Practice It! Choose a book from your classroom library or a book you are reading from your school library. Write down any unfamiliar words that you find. Use context clues to determine the meanings of the words. Check the dictionary to see if you are correct.

Fluency

Accuracy

It is important to read with accuracy so you can understand the text. Reading each word as it is written on the page makes this possible. Listen to yourself as you read to make sure what you are reading makes sense.

Practice It! With a partner, practice reading aloud page 31 from *The Man Who Invented Basketball*. Have your partner make a list of any words you read incorrectly. Look back at each word. Reread the page again. Did your accuracy improve?

52

Listening and Speaking

Work productively with others and acknowledge their contributions.

Presentation

The purpose of oral reports about a topic is to inform. Reports can also be used to entertain, to persuade, or to express an opinion.

Practice It! With a group, prepare an oral report on how James Naismith invented basketball. Use the information from the story and outside research. When you present, use photos, sounds, or props to make your report more interesting.

Tips

Listeners ...

- Listen attentively and respond to the topic.
- Think about how visual and sound aids influence the message.

Speakers ...

- Determine your purpose for speaking.
- Speak coherently about the topic.

Teamwork ...

- Give suggestions that build on others' ideas.
- Ask and answer questions with detail.

TEKS

3.29.A.2 Ask relevant questions.
3.29.A.3 Make pertinent comments.
3.31.A.3 Participate in teacher-led
discussions by providing suggestions
that build upon the ideas of others.
Also 3.30.A.2.

Oral Vocabulary

Let's Talk About

Nature's Record Holders

- Ask relevant questions about natures's record holders.

- Comment on nature's unique environments.

- Offer suggestions for how we might protect unique places in nature.

READING STREET ONLINE
CONCEPT TALK VIDEO
www.TexasReadingStreet.com

55

TEKS

3.1.B.1.iv Use common syllabication patterns to decode words including *r*-controlled vowels.

Envision It! | **Sounds to Know**

fern
er

pearls
ear

girl
ir

score
ore

artist
ar

orchestra
or

worm
or

curtains
ur

Phonics

r-Controlled Vowels

Words I Can Blend

ferment

carpool

circus

purchase

support

Sentences I Can Read

1. We saw the bread ferment when we watched it rise.

2. Our group will carpool to the circus.

3. This purchase will support a good cause.

Last fall our class took a field trip to a farm in the country. We carpooled early in the morning so there would be more time to learn. In the first barn we visited, we learned how apples turn into apple cider. The apple cider we tasted had a great flavor.

The second barn had dairy cows. We learned how milk ferments into yogurt.

After that, we carved pumpkins, and I spilled pumpkin seeds down my shirt. We were introduced to a herd of cattle and watched hawks soar overhead.

Our last stop was with some furry kittens that were adorable. We had a wonderful time!

You've learned

 *r*-Controlled Vowels

TEKS

3.2.B.6 Locate facts about other texts. **3.15.B.1** Locate specific information in graphic features of text. **3.15.B.2** Use specific information in graphic features of text. **Also 3.2.A.1, 3.2.A.2, 3.13.D.2, 3.13.D.3.**

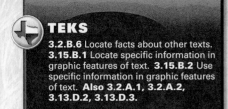

Envision It! | Skill Strategy

Skill

Strategy

Comprehension Skill

Graphic Sources

- Graphic sources are ways of showing information visually, or in a way you can see.

- Charts, diagrams, maps, and graphs are examples of graphic sources, or features.

- Graphic sources can help you predict what the reading will be about.

- Use what you learned about graphic sources to read "Largest U.S. Cities." Then use the text and the bar graph to make a new graph showing how the population of New York City compares to Los Angeles, Chicago, and Houston combined.

Comprehension Strategy

Important Ideas

Before you read a selection or story, look for the important ideas in titles, topic sentences, key words, charts, or photos and other illustrations. While you read, stop and ask, "What is this text all about?" Important ideas summarize a selection or tell what it is all about. Try to find the most important idea in each paragraph and verify your predictions.

Largest U.S. Cities

New York

Los Angeles

Chicago

Houston

Millions of people in the United States live in cities. The number of people who live in a city is called its population.

The U.S. city with the most people living in it is New York City. Los Angeles, California, comes in second. Chicago, Illinois, is the third largest city with Houston, Texas, closely following. New York City, however, has almost as many people as Los Angeles, Chicago, and Houston put together!

Strategy What are two important ideas in the text?

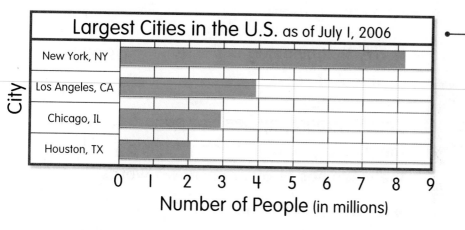

Largest Cities in the U.S. as of July 1, 2006

City	Number of People (in millions)
New York, NY	
Los Angeles, CA	
Chicago, IL	
Houston, TX	

0 1 2 3 4 5 6 7 8 9

Skill Look at the bar graph. What facts can you learn from the graph?

Your Turn!

Need a Review? See the *Envision It! Handbook* for help with graphic sources and important ideas.

Ready to Try It? As you read *Hottest, Coldest, Highest, Deepest*, use what you learned about graphic sources and important ideas.

HOTTEST
COLDEST
HIGHEST
DEEPEST

TEKS

3.4.E.1 Alphabetize a series of words to the third letter. **3.4.E.2** Use a dictionary or glossary to determine meanings of unknown words.

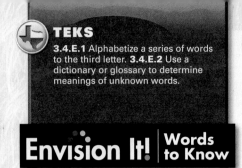

Envision It! Words to Know

erupted

outrun

tides

average
depth
deserts
peak
waterfalls

Vocabulary Strategy for

Unknown Words

Dictionary/Glossary You can use a dictionary or glossary to find the meaning of an unknown word. The words in a dictionary or glossary are in alphabetical order.

Follow these steps with *deepest, deserts,* and *depth* from "Geography Bee."

1. Turn to the section for the words' first letter in the glossary or dictionary.

2. Look at the first three letters in the word. Put them in alphabetical order, and then find and read the entry for each word.

3. Decide which meaning you think fits in the sentence if there is more than one meaning listed.

4. Try that meaning in the sentence to see if it makes sense.

Read "Geography Bee" on page 61. Use the glossary or a dictionary to help you find the meanings of other unknown words.

Words to Write Reread "Geography Bee." Write four geography bee questions about your state. Then find and write the answers. Use words from the Words to Know list.

Geography Bee

Have you heard of a geography bee? You probably know what a spelling bee is. In a spelling bee, people take turns spelling difficult words. The person who spells the most words correctly wins. In a geography bee, people answer questions about places on Earth.

The questions in a geography bee will never have a yes or no answer. For example, this question would not be used in a geography bee: Can a person outrun the tides at the Bay of Fundy?

To answer the questions in a geography bee, you must know facts about continents, countries, states, and physical features of the world, such as deserts or oceans.

Here are some sample questions for you to try: When was the last time Mount St. Helen's erupted? What is the hottest spot on Earth? Which is the highest of all the waterfalls on Earth? Which mountain peak is the tallest in the world? What is the average summer temperature at the South Pole? What is the depth of the deepest point of Marianas Trench?

Your Turn!

❚❚ **Need a Review?** For additional help with using a dictionary or glossary to find unknown words, see *Words!*

▶ **Ready to Try It?** Read *Hottest, Coldest, Highest, Deepest* on pp. 62–75.

HOTTEST
COLDEST
HIGHEST
DEEPEST

HOTTEST
COLDEST
HIGHEST
DEEPEST

BY STEVE JENKINS

Genre

Expository text gives information about the real world. Look for numbers and diagrams that help you understand the facts.

Question of the Week
**What makes nature's
record holders unique?**

If you could visit any spot on Earth, where would you go? What if you wanted to see some of the most amazing natural wonders in the world?

There are deserts that haven't seen rain for hundreds of years and jungles where it pours almost every day. There are places so cold that even in the summer it's below freezing and spots where it's often hot enough to cook an egg on the ground. There are mountains many miles high and ocean trenches that are even deeper. You can find rivers thousands of miles long and waterfalls thousands of feet high.

Where are the very hottest and coldest, windiest and snowiest, highest and deepest places on Earth? Travel the world and visit the planet's record holders.

U.S. **2,750 miles wide**

Nile **4,145 miles**

Amazon River **4,007 miles**

Chiang Jiang **3,964 miles**

Mississippi-Missouri **3,710 miles**

The Nile, in Africa, is the **longest** river in the world. It is 4,145 miles long.

The Amazon River, in South America, is not as long—4,007 miles—but it is considered mightier because it carries half of all the river water in the world. The Chiang Jiang (Yangtze), in Asia (3,964 miles), and the Mississippi-Missouri, in the United States (3,710 miles), are the world's third and fourth longest rivers.

65

Lake Baikal, in Russia, is the world's **oldest** and **deepest** lake. The lake was formed about 25 million years ago. In one spot it is 5,134 feet deep.

The largest freshwater lake in the world is Lake Superior, one of the Great Lakes in North America (31,700 square miles), but Lake Baikal (5,500 square miles) contains more water than any other lake on Earth—more than all five Great Lakes combined.

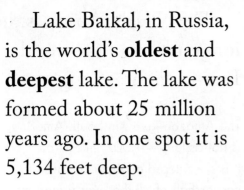

Lake Baikal
5,134 ft.

Empire State
Building
1,250 ft.

Mount Everest is the **highest** mountain in the world. Its peak is 29,028 feet above sea level.

Mount Everest is considered the **highest** mountain—above sea level—in the world, but it's not really the **tallest.** Measured from its base on the floor of the ocean, Mauna Kea, in Hawaii, is 33,476 feet tall. Only the top 13,796 feet of Mauna Kea are above sea level.

The **hottest** spot on the planet is Al Aziziyah, Libya, in the Sahara, where a temperature of over 136°F has been recorded.

The hottest temperature ever recorded in the United States is 134.6°F, in Death Valley, California.

136°F
134.6°F

98.6°F
Body temp.

68°F
Room temp.

32°F
Water freezes

The **coldest** place on the planet is Vostok, Antarctica. A temperature of 129°F below zero was recorded there.

It is so cold at the South Pole that the average summer temperature is –58°F. The coldest temperature ever recorded in the United States is –80°F, at Prospect Creek Camp, Alaska.

The **wettest** place on Earth is Tutunendo, Colombia, where an average of 463 inches of rain falls every year.

Mount Wai-ale-ale, on the island of Kauai in Hawaii, has the most rainy days—350 a year. On the island of La Réunion, in the Indian Ocean, more than 61 inches of rain fell in a single day.

69

The **driest** place is the Atacama Desert, in Chile, where no rain has fallen for the last 400 years.

Any place that receives less than 10 inches of precipitation a year is considered a desert. The driest place in the United States is Death Valley, California, where only about 1½ inches of rain fall every year.

72 in. Adult man

10 in.
Desert precipitation

1½ in.
Death Valley average annual precipitation

The **windiest** spot on Earth is atop Mount Washington, in New Hampshire. A wind speed of 231 miles per hour has been recorded there.

It is also very windy near the tops of the world's highest mountains, the Himalayas. Many of these peaks are tall enough to reach the jet stream, a narrow, strong air current that is found above 28,000 feet.

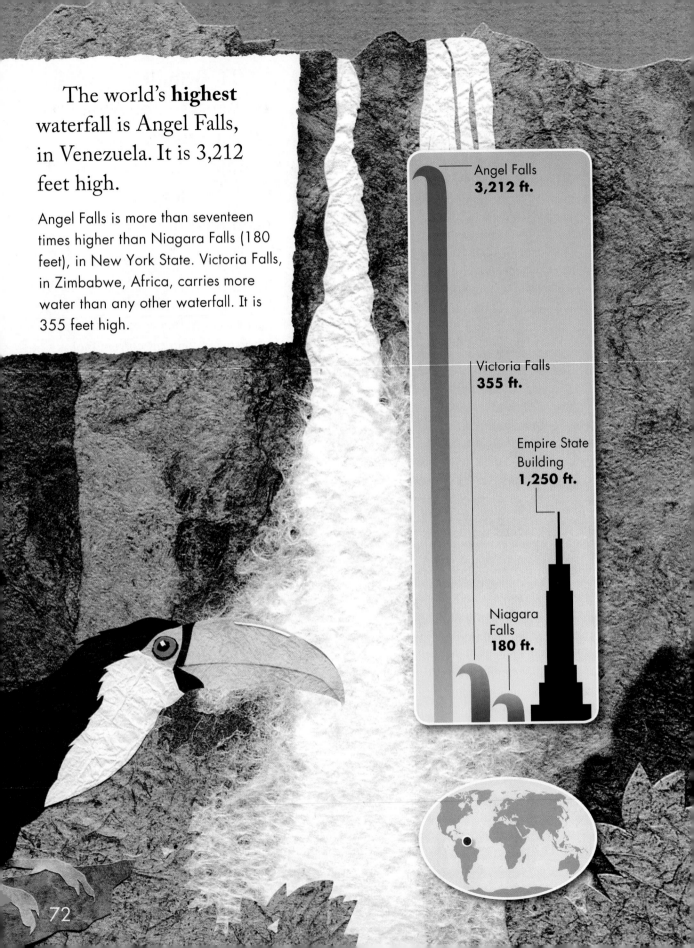

The world's **highest** waterfall is Angel Falls, in Venezuela. It is 3,212 feet high.

Angel Falls is more than seventeen times higher than Niagara Falls (180 feet), in New York State. Victoria Falls, in Zimbabwe, Africa, carries more water than any other waterfall. It is 355 feet high.

Angel Falls
3,212 ft.

Victoria Falls
355 ft.

Empire State Building
1,250 ft.

Niagara Falls
180 ft.

The **deepest** spot in the ocean is the Marianas Trench, in the Philippines. It is 36,202 feet deep.

The average depth of the world's oceans is about 3 miles, or 16,000 feet. The lowest spot on dry land is the shore of the Dead Sea, 1,100 feet below sea level.

The world's **most active** volcano is Sangay, in Ecuador. Since 1937 it has erupted once every 24 hours on average. It once erupted more than 400 times in a single day.

Other very active volcanoes include Colima, in Mexico (it has erupted regularly since 1560); Aso, in Japan (erupting since 533); and Mount Etna, in Italy (erupting regularly since 1500 B.C.).

73

The **most extreme tides** occur in the Bay of Fundy, in Nova Scotia, Canada. There the water level rises and falls more than 50 feet every 6 hours.

The tide here comes in so fast that it can overtake a person trying to outrun it.

100 ft.
Mt. Rainier record
1-year snowfall

6 ft.
Adult man

3 ft.
Typical annual
New York City
snowfall

The **snowiest** place on Earth is Mount Rainier, in Washington State. One year, more than 1,200 inches of snow fell there.

Mount Rainier is covered in snow the whole year. Some of the snow has formed glaciers, masses of ice that slowly move down the mountain under their own weight.

Envision It! | Retell

Think Critically

1. Which environment would you most like to visit? In which environment would you most like to live? Explain your answers. **Text to World**

2. Why did the author show a man and the Empire State Building on some of the pages? How were these graphic features helpful in locating facts from the selection? **Think Like an Author**

3. Which graphic source from the selection was most helpful to you? How was it helpful? **Graphic Sources**

4. How does the selection's title help you understand the most important ideas on each page? **Important Ideas**

5. **Look Back and Write** Mount Everest is the highest mountain, but Mauna Kea is the tallest mountain. Look back at page 67. Write the reason that the tallest and the highest mountain are not the same. Provide evidence to support your answer.

TEST PRACTICE Extended Response

STEVE JENKINS

Steve Jenkins has always liked science and art. As a child he kept spiders and lizards and liked to draw and paint. His father was a scientist. "We did a lot of projects together," he said. "We wrote a little book about animals."

In his books, Mr. Jenkins tries to make science fun. "Kids have a natural interest in animals and things like volcanoes," he said. He wrote *Hottest, Coldest, Highest, Deepest* partly because his son was always asking him those kinds of questions.

The pictures in Mr. Jenkins's books are not drawings or paintings. They are called collages. His collages are made by cutting different kinds of paper and pasting them in layers.

Read more books by Steve Jenkins.

The Top of the World: Climbing Mount Everest

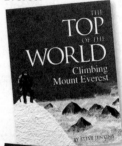

What Do You Do With a Tail Like This?

Reading Log
Use the Reader's and Writer's Notebook to record your independent reading.

TEKS
3.18.A.1 Write imaginative stories that build the plot to a climax. **3.18.A.2** Write imaginative stories that contain details about the characters. **3.18.A.3** Write imaginative stories that contain details about the setting.

Let's Write It!

Key Features of a Story

- characters, events, and settings are made up
- plot events make sense
- details may or may not be like real life

READING STREET ONLINE
GRAMMAR JAMMER
www.TexasReadingStreet.com

Story

A **story** is fictional writing that has characters, events, and settings that are made up. The student model on the next page is an example of a story.

Writing Prompt Write an imaginative story in which one character tells a riddle to another.

Writer's Checklist

Remember, you should . . .

☑ include details about the characters and setting.

☑ have a beginning, middle, and end.

☑ be sure to include a riddle in your story.

☑ build the plot to a climax.

Riddles in Outer Space

From **my** spaceship, **I** like to explore the Milky Way with my brother Bo. Yesterday **we** left **our** planet, Planet X, and visited planet Earth. I flew close to spectacular spots I had read about because I wanted **us** to get a good look at **them**.

On the way home, Bo asked, "Remember the riddles Grandma used to tell us? Let's think of riddles about Earth!"

"**Me** first," I said. "I am the driest place on Earth. I am— "

". . . the desert," Bo replied. "My turn . . . I am the windiest spot on Earth."

"Mt. Washington," I answered.

Just then, Planet X came into view.

"Visiting Earth was fun," said Bo. "But it's great to get back to the pink shiny planet we call home."

Writing Trait Conventions
Complex sentences are made up of an independent and at least one dependent clause.

Subject and object pronouns are used correctly.

Genre A **story** is made up by its author.

Conventions

Subject and Object Pronouns

Remember A pronoun used as the subject of a sentence is called a **subject pronoun.** A pronoun used after an action verb or as the object of a preposition is called an **object pronoun.**

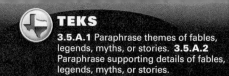

TEKS

3.5.A.1 Paraphrase themes of fables, legends, myths, or stories. **3.5.A.2** Paraphrase supporting details of fables, legends, myths, or stories.

Science in Reading

Genre
Legend

- A legend is a story told from generation to generation until someone writes it down.

- Legends may be based on truth but are mostly fiction.

- Legends often are about great heroes who carry out bigger-than-life actions, and they usually are set in real locations.

- The themes of legends are usually based on what a culture values, or finds important.

- Read the legend "Paul Bunyan and the Great Lakes." What details from the text make this story a legend?

PAUL BUNYAN and the GREAT LAKES

retold by Don Abramson

The first thing most people noticed about Paul Bunyan was that he was big. Now, when I say "big," I mean HUGE, GIGANTIC! Everything he did, he did big.

He could walk a mile by taking just a few steps. His clothes had to be specially made, of course. Twenty tailors had to sew together the canvas sails from five or six sailing ships to make one of his shirts.

The second thing people noticed was that he was usually accompanied by his pet ox, Babe. Babe was big too. He had to be, to keep up with Paul. Babe was as strong as he was big. Paul could hitch Babe up to one end of a winding, curving road, and Babe could pull it straight. Oh, and did I mention that Babe was bright blue?

Let's Think About...

What details about Babe tell me that this legend is not a true story? **Legend**

Babe wasn't just a pet. He was a working animal. That was useful because Paul was a lumberjack. Paul decided to hire a crew of lumberjacks. He had to build a lumber camp to give his crew a place to live. He found a nice spot and set the men to building, using lumber they had cut down themselves.

A camp needs a good supply of drinking water, so Paul dug out a huge reservoir to catch rainwater and to hold water from a number of rivers that emptied into it. People called it Lake Ontario, after some Native American words that mean "great lake." That worked fine for a while, but Babe could drink half the lake himself every morning before breakfast. So Paul dug another reservoir, and then another. They were also given Native American names: Lake Erie and Lake Huron.

Let's Think About...

What is the setting of this legend?
Legend

82

Paul's lumber camp was growing too, and he had more men and more animals than ever before. So he dug Lake Michigan and then, finally, Lake Superior. Now he had a really good water supply.

As I said, Paul did everything BIG!

Let's **Think** About...

According to this legend, how were the Great Lakes made? **Legend**

Let's **Think** About...

What is the theme of the story? What details support the theme? **Legend**

Let's **Think** About...

Reading Across Texts *Hottest, Coldest, Highest, Deepest* tells interesting facts about real places on Earth. How is this legend about Paul Bunyan similar and different?

Writing Across Texts Choose one place described in *Hottest, Coldest, Highest, Deepest*. Make up a short story in which Paul Bunyan makes the amazing feature of that setting.

TEKS

3.4.E.3 Use a dictionary or glossary to determine syllabication of unknown words. **3.4.E.4** Use a dictionary or glossary to determine pronunciation of unknown words. **3.16.A.1** Understand how communication changes when moving from one genre of media to another. **3.29.A.1** Listen attentively to speakers. **3.30.A.1** Speak coherently about the topic under discussion. **Also 3.3.A.1, 3.3.A.2, 3.4.E.2, 3.30.A.2, 3.31.A.4, 3.31.A.5, 3.31.A.6.**

Let's Learn It!

READING STREET ONLINE
ONLINE STUDENT EDITION
www.TexasReadingStreet.com

Vocabulary

Unknown Words

Dictionary/Glossary You can use a dictionary or glossary to look up the definition of unknown words. Find out how to pronounce the word by using the pronunciation key and looking at each syllable.

 Find two or three unknown words from *Hottest, Coldest, Highest, Deepest.* Look up their definitions, syllable divisions, and pronunciations in a dictionary or glossary. Rewrite each definition in your own words.

Fluency

Appropriate Phrasing

Remember to pause when you come to a comma, a dash, and before and after reading information in parentheses.

Practice It! With your partner, practice reading *Hottest, Coldest, Highest, Deepest,* page 66. Remember to pause for a comma, a dash, and before and after information in parentheses.

Media Literacy

Work productively and follow etiquette for conversation.

Weather Forecast

In a weather forecast, an announcer tells about the weather in an area and the expected weather for the next few days.

Practice It! Prepare a weather forecast for a TV news program. Use newspapers, Web sites, and TV and radio broadcasts for ideas. Include elements unique to TV in your presentation. Then discuss how communication changes when moving from one genre of media to another.

Tips

Listening ...

- Listen to identify the speaker's credibility and effectiveness.

Speaking ...

- Make eye contact with your audience by looking at the camera.
- Speak clearly and loudly.

Teamwork ...

- Ask and answer questions about communication and digital media.

TEKS

3.29.A.1 Listen attentively to speakers. **3.29.A.2** Ask relevant questions. **3.29.A.3** Make pertinent comments. **3.31.A.3** Participate in teacher-led discussions by providing suggestions that build upon the ideas of others.

Oral Vocabulary

Let's Talk About

Unique Interests

- Work together to pose and answer questions about unique interests.

- Make and listen to comments about why unique interests are valuable.

- Suggest ways one can develop unique interests.

READING STREET ONLINE
CONCEPT TALK VIDEO
www.TexasReadingStreet.com

87

TEKS

3.1.A.iv Decode multisyllabic words in context and independent of context by applying common spelling patterns including using knowledge of common prefixes. **Also 3.1.A.v.**

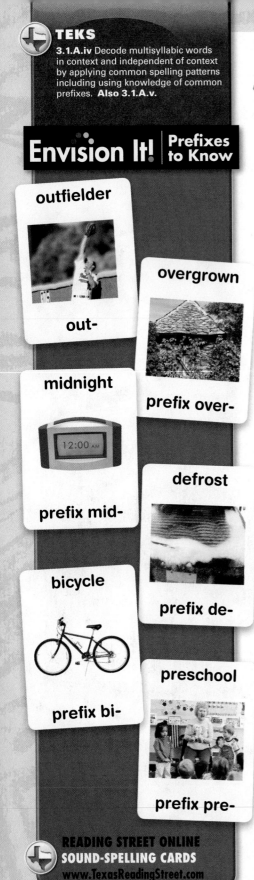

Envision It! | Prefixes to Know

outfielder

out-

overgrown

prefix over-

midnight

prefix mid-

defrost

prefix de-

bicycle

prefix bi-

preschool

prefix pre-

READING STREET ONLINE
SOUND-SPELLING CARDS
www.TexasReadingStreet.com

Phonics

Affixes: Prefixes *pre-, mid-, over-, out-, bi-, de-*

Words I Can Blend

midway

preheated

decomposed

outweigh

overheard

bimonthly

Sentences I Can Read

1. Midway through the recipe, I preheated the oven.

2. The decomposed leaves outweigh the freshly fallen leaves.

3. I overheard that our bimonthly meeting was canceled.

88

I Can Read!

Ever since I was in preschool, midsummer has been my favorite time of year. I don't worry about oversleeping because I can get up whenever I want.

I ride my bicycle from midmorning through midafternoon. Mom calls me in at midday to eat lunch and drink some water. She wants to make sure I don't get dehydrated.

My biggest challenge is trying to outrun my dog when we race with each other. Mom says summer is when I outgrow most of my clothes. All that fresh air is good for me.

You've learned

- Prefixes *pre-, mid-, over-, out-, bi-, de-*

TEKS

3.13.B.1 Draw conclusions from facts presented in text. **3.13.B.2** Support assertions with textual evidence. **RC-3.D.1** Make inferences about text. **RC-3.D.2** Use textual evidence to support understanding. **Also 3.2.B.6, 3.2.B.8, 3.2.B.9.**

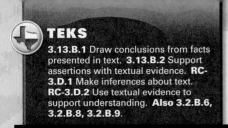

Envision It! | Skill Strategy

Skill

Strategy

READING STREET ONLINE
ENVISION IT! ANIMATIONS
www.TexasReadingStreet.com

Comprehension Skill

Fact and Opinion

- A fact can be proved true or false.

- An opinion gives someone's thoughts or feelings about something. An opinion cannot be proved true or false.

- Use what you learned about fact and opinion and the chart below as you read "Looking at Rocks." Then choose one fact from your chart. Use a reference source to prove the fact true or false.

Facts	Opinions

Comprehension Strategy

Inferring

When you infer, you combine your background knowledge with ideas in the text to come up with your own idea about what the author is trying to present. Active readers infer the ideas, morals, lessons, and themes of a written work.

LOOKING AT ROCKS

Looking at rocks is fun and interesting. Some rocks look the same all over. They are made of one thing. However, most rocks do not look the same all over. Some have different colors. Some have sparkles. Others have shiny spots. The colors and sparkles and shine come from the different materials mixed together in the rock.

Skill What opinion is expressed in this paragraph? What words tell you that it is an opinion?

If you like looking at rocks, you can get a job working with rocks when you grow up. Some scientists look at rocks to find out about people from long ago. Other scientists look at rocks to find oil. Some rock scientists help builders make buildings safe. Others try to predict when an earthquake will happen or a volcano will erupt.

Strategy How do you think rock scientists can help builders make safe buildings?

Rocks can tell us many things. Take a look!

Your Turn!

Need a Review? See the *Envision It! Handbook* for help with fact and opinion and inferring.

Ready to Try It? As you read *Rocks in His Head*, use what you've learned about fact and opinion and inferring to understand the text.

TEKS

3.4.B.2 Use context to distinguish among multiple-meaning words.

chores

labeled

stamps

attic

board

customer

spare

**READING STREET ONLINE
VOCABULARY ACTIVITIES**
www.TexasReadingStreet.com

Vocabulary Strategy for

Multiple-Meaning Words

Context Clues You may read a word you know but whose meaning does not make sense in the sentence. The word may have more than one meaning. For example, *bug* means "an insect" and "to annoy."

1. Try the meaning of the word that you know. Does it make sense in the sentence?

2. If it does not make sense, perhaps it has another meaning. Can you figure out another meaning from the context?

3. Try the new meaning in the sentence. Does it make sense?

Read "More Than a Hobby" on page 93. Look for words that might have more than one meaning. Remember to use nearby words to figure out the correct meaning.

Words to Write Reread "More Than a Hobby." What kind of shop would you like to open? Write about your shop. Use words from the Words to Know list in your answer.

More Than a Hobby

It starts out as a hobby. As a child, you collect stamps or toy cars or rocks. At first, collecting is an activity you do in your spare time or after doing your chores.

Perhaps you collect a few rocks here and a few rocks there. Then one day you realize that the shelves in your room are bulging with rocks. So you move them to the basement or the attic where there is more space.

As you get older, you learn more about rocks, and you talk with other rock collectors. You begin to think *Maybe this isn't just a hobby.*

Could it be a business?

So you open a rock shop. Every rock in the shop is labeled with information about the rock and how much it costs. This really impresses your very first customer, so he buys several rocks. You are on your way.

Over time, your small business grows large, and you become the chairman of the board. And it all started with a hobby.

Your Turn!

❚❚ **Need a Review?** For additional help with context clues and multiple-meaning words, see *Words!*

▶ **Ready to Try It?** Read *Rocks in His Head* on pp. 94–105.

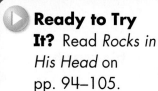

ROCKS IN HIS HEAD

by Carol Otis Hurst

illustrated by James Stevenson

Genre

A **biography** is the story of a real person's life, written by another person. As you read, think about how this author is connected to the person she wrote about.

Question of the Week
Why is it valuable to have unique interests?

95

Some people collect stamps. Some people collect coins or dolls or bottle caps. When he was a boy, my father collected rocks. When he wasn't doing chores at home or learning at school, he'd walk along stone walls and around old quarries, looking for rocks. People said he had rocks in his pockets and rocks in his head. He didn't mind. It was usually true.

When people asked what he wanted to be when he grew up, he'd say, "Something to do with rocks, I think."

"There's no money in rocks," someone said.

"Probably not," said my father.

When he grew up, my father decided to open a gas station. (People called them filling stations then.) My grandfather helped him build one on Armory Street in Springfield, Massachusetts.

They called the station the Antler Filling Station. My father carefully painted the name right over the doorway.

Inside the filling station was a desk with a cash drawer (which my father usually forgot to lock) and a table for his chess set.

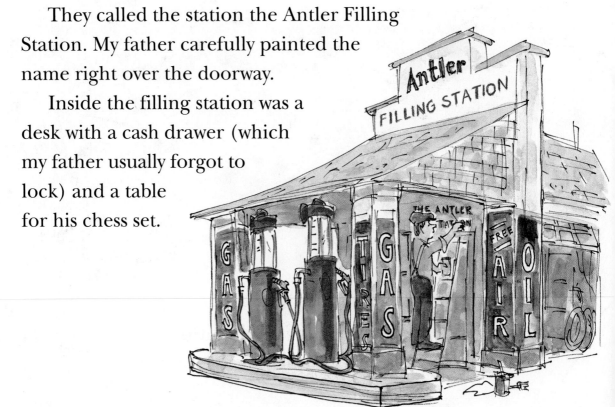

96

My father built narrow wooden shelves on the back wall and painted them white. People said, "What are those shelves for?"

He said, "I've got rocks in my head, I guess."

Then, one by one, he placed his rocks and minerals on those shelves. He carefully labeled each rock to show what kind it was and where it had come from.

In those days lots of rich people had automobiles, but then Henry Ford came out with the Model T.

That was a car many people could afford. My father had taken one apart and put it back together again and again until he knew every inch of the Model T. He thought that anyone who had spare parts for the Model T and could repair it so that it drove like new would do a good business. He bought some parts from dealers and found some parts in junkyards.

The pile of Model T parts sat just to the left of the lift. Soon, that pile of parts was bigger than the filling station.

People said, "If you think people are going to buy that junk, you've got rocks in your head."

"Maybe I have," he said. "Maybe I have."

But people did come to buy that junk. They came to buy gas, and they came to play chess, and they came to look at the rocks.

For a while my father was too busy for the chess games. He was pumping gas, changing tires, and fixing Model Ts.

"Where did you get this one?" a customer would say, holding up a rock.

"Found it in a slag pile in New Hampshire," he'd say. Or, "Traded for it with a fella from Nevada. Gave him some garnets from Connecticut."

"People in Nevada and Connecticut collect rocks like you do?" people would ask.

"Lots of folks have rocks in their heads," said my father. He'd dig into his pocket and take out a rock. "Take a look at this one."

Then the stock market fell. At first, people didn't think it would matter much to my father. After all, he had no money in the stock market.

"I may have rocks in my head," he said, "but I think bad times are coming."

And bad times did come. People couldn't afford to buy new cars or fix their old ones.

When business was slow, my father would play chess with some of his customers. When business was very slow, my grandfather would mind the filling station, and we'd pile as many of us kids as would fit into our Model T, and we'd hunt for more rocks with my father.

He had to build more shelves for the rocks, up the west wall of the station.

Then people stopped coming for gas. They stopped coming to play chess, and they even stopped coming to look at the rocks and minerals. They were all too busy looking for work.

One day my father picked up the chess set and carefully packed it in a big box. He took down each mineral, wrapped it in newspaper, and carefully placed it in a wooden box.

When his friends came with a truck to help us move, they said, "Watch out for those wooden boxes. He's got rocks in his boxes, now."

"Yessir," said my father. "That's just what I got in there. Take a look at this one."

The house we moved to was old and falling apart. My father said he'd have it fixed up in no time.

But before he started in on the repairs, we had to take those rocks up to the attic, where he'd already built tiny little wooden shelves.

My father did fix up the old house, and after he finished each repair, he went up to the attic with his rocks. He spent a lot of time reading about rocks, too.

"If you think those rocks are ever going to do you any good," said my mother, "you've got rocks in your head."

"Maybe I have," said my father. "Maybe I have." He reached into his pocket. "Take a look at this one."

My father spent a lot of time looking for any job he could find. Most jobs lasted only a day or two.

On rainy days when my father could find no other work, he'd take the bus to the science museum. They had a whole room full of glass cases containing many rocks. Sometimes he'd spend the whole day in that room.

One afternoon he looked up to see a lady standing beside him. "I've seen you here before," she said.

"I come here a lot," he said. "I guess I've got rocks in my head."

"Tell me what you're looking for," she said.

"I'm looking for rocks that are better than mine," he said.

"How many did you find?" she asked.

"Ten," he said.

The lady looked around at the hundreds of rocks, in all those glass cases. "Only ten?"

"Maybe eleven," he said.

He smiled. She did, too.

"You *have* got rocks in your head," she said. "I'm Grace Johnson, the director of this museum. These rocks have come from all over the world."

"So have mine," said my father. He reached into his pocket. "Take a look at this one," he said.

"Did you study rocks at college?" she asked.

"Couldn't afford to go to college," he said.

"Let me see the rest of your rocks," she said.

Mrs. Johnson got out her big Packard touring car, and my father got in. They drove to our house.

"Where are the rocks?" she asked.

"Up here," said my father, leading the way to the attic. "Watch your step."

Two hours later Mrs. Johnson said, "I can't hire you as a mineralogist. The board won't allow it. But I need a night janitor at the museum. Will you take the job?"

"Will I be cleaning rocks?" he asked.

"Sometimes," she said.

So my father took the job as night janitor at the museum. Before he went home, he'd open some of the mineral cases and scrub some of the rocks with a toothbrush until they sparkled like diamonds.

Mrs. Johnson came in early for work one morning and saw him carefully writing a new label for one of the rocks.

"What are you doing?" she asked.

"One rock was labeled wrong," he said. "I fixed it."

Mrs. Johnson smiled. "I've been talking to the board of directors. They know that I need a person here who knows as much about rocks as you do."

"What about the college education?" he asked.

She said, "I told them I need somebody with rocks in his head and rocks in his pockets. Are you it?"

"Maybe I am," said my father. "Maybe I am."

He reached into his pocket and took out a rock.
"Take a look at this one," he said.

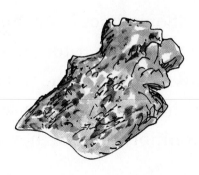

Talent with a Twist of the Tongue

The phrase "rocks in his head" is a play on words. Tongue twisters are also a type of word play. People all around the world enjoy these playful verses and they exist in every language. Below are three well-known tongue twisters. As you read, think about what makes this language playful.

Try to say these three tongue twisters as fast as you can:

She sells sea shells by the sea shore.
The shells she sells are surely seashells.
So if she sells shells on the seashore,
I'm sure she sells seashore shells.

Peter Piper picked a peck of pickled peppers.
Did Peter Piper pick a peck of pickled peppers?
If Peter Piper picked a peck of pickled peppers,
where's the peck of pickled peppers Peter Piper picked?

How much wood would a woodchuck chuck
if a woodchuck could chuck wood?
He would chuck, he would, as much as he could,
and chuck as much wood as a woodchuck would
if a woodchuck could chuck wood.

Envision It! Retell

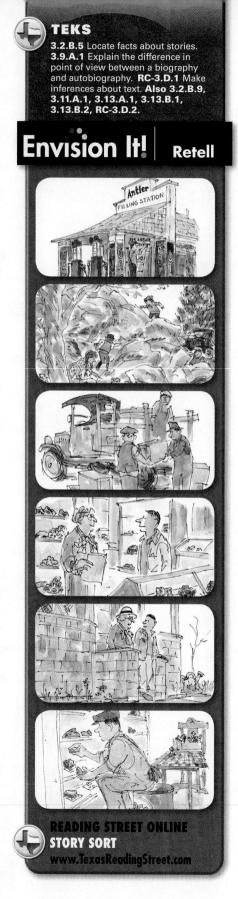

Think Critically

1. What is the difference in point of view between a biography and autobiography? How is this biography different from the autobiography by Ted Williams? **Text to Text**

2. The author tells you that her father has rocks in his head. Is she making fun of him? Is she proud of him? How can you tell? **Think Like an Author**

3. What facts did you learn about the jobs the author's father had? Which job do you think the father liked best? Why? Which job would you like best? Why? **Fact and Opinion**

4. Using facts and details from this selection, what can you infer about the people who work in museums? How has this information changed your view of people and things that are unique? **Inferring**

5. **Look Back and Write** Look back at pages 96–98. Use facts and details from the selection to write what the father collected and why. Provide evidence to support your answer.

TEST PRACTICE Extended Response

Carol Otis Hurst

Rocks in His Head was **Carol Otis Hurst's** first book. It is the true story of her father. "He collected rocks from the time he was a small boy. He kept at it throughout his life, not caring that others thought it was a waste of time." Ms. Hurst says her father loved to learn new things. "He'd be thrilled to think kids at school were reading a story about him."

James Stevenson

James Stevenson has written and illustrated more than one hundred children's books. More than thirty of them have won awards.

He wrote his first children's book with his eight-year-old son. "Tell me a story and we'll make a book," he told his son James. "He stood at my desk and told a story. I wrote it down and then did the pictures." They called the book *If I Owned a Candy Factory*. It was published in 1968.

Read more books about unique people.

Beethoven Lives Upstairs by Barbara Nichol

Snowflake Bentley by Jacqueline Briggs Martin

Use the Reader's and Writer's Notebook to record your independent reading.

Reading Log

TEKS

3.18 Write literary texts to express ideas and feelings about real or imagined people, events, and ideas. **Also: 3.22.A.1.vi, 3.23.B.1.i, 3.23.B.1.ii, 3.23.B.1.iii.**

Narrative

Biography

A **biography** is the story of a real person's life written by another person. The student model on the next page is an example of a biography.

Writing Prompt *Rocks in His Head* describes a person with a collection. Think about a friend or family member who has an interesting collection. Now write a short biography of that person's life.

Key Features of a Biography

- tells a true story about a real person

- may cover part or all of the subject's life

- written in third person point of view

READING STREET ONLINE
GRAMMAR JAMMER
www.TexasReadingStreet.com

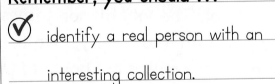

Writer's Checklist

Remember, you should ...

✓ identify a real person with an interesting collection.

✓ include details about your subject.

✓ write descriptively and clearly.

✓ use possessive pronouns correctly.

✓ capitalize any geographical names or places, historical periods, or official titles.

Grampa Ed's Cups

My grandfather, "Grampa Ed," has a collection of coffee cups. Grampa Ed loves to go to different places. He's been to Hawaii, Washington, D.C., Florida, California, France, Sweden, Denmark, and Mexico. Everywhere he goes he gets a coffee cup with the name of the place on it.

When I visit Grampa Ed, our favorite thing to do is have breakfast together. We use **his** cups in the morning when we have breakfast. Grampa Ed drinks coffee from **his** cup, but I drink hot chocolate or milk out of my cup. When he is drinking out of one of **his** special cups, he talks about the place listed on the cup and what he liked about it.

Genre A **biography** is a story about a real person.

Writing Trait Sentences Combining short, choppy sentences helps writing sound natural.

Possessive pronouns are used correctly.

Conventions

Possessive Pronouns

Remember Pronouns are words that take the place of nouns. **Possessive pronouns** show who or what owns or possesses something.

TEKS

3.14.A.1 Identify what the author is trying to persuade the reader to think or do. **RC-3.E.2** Summarize information in text, maintaining logical order. **Also 3.15.A.2, 3.15.A.3, 3.15.B.1, 3.15.B.2, RC-3.F.1, RC-3.F.2.**

Social Studies in Reading

Genre
Persuasive Text

- When an author's purpose is to persuade, the text will have facts or opinions to convince you to think or do something.

- An author can use "loaded words," or strong, opinionated words.

- The "bandwagon approach" is used to convince the reader that a large number of people are doing something and you should do it too.

- Read the article, "Marvelous Marble Mania." As you read, look for loaded words and the bandwagon approach.

Marvelous Marble Mania

by Robert Kausal

Look in your closet. Is it over filled with games that you never play anymore? Every year toy-makers come out with hundreds of new games. Many of these games can be fun to play for a few days, or weeks, but then the game pieces get scattered around the house, the batteries run down, or they just get super boring.

Sometimes the best games are the ones that have been around the longest. That's because they are fun, challenging, and easy to learn.

Knuckle Down · · · · · · · · · · · · · · ·

One of the oldest and most popular games in the world is played with marbles. You might be surprised to learn that marbles have been around for thousands of years. Children in Egypt played with marbles as far back as 4000 B.C.E.! Back then marbles were made out of clay. Today, most marbles are made of glass. Games with these multi-colored balls are played in places like Australia, India, Turkey, and yes, even the United States.

Let's **Think** About...

What persuasive device is the author using in this paragraph? Support your answer with evidence from the text. **Persuasive Text**

Here are some terms people use when playing marbles:

Keepsies: You get to keep all of the marbles you win. Also called "playing for keeps."

Knuckle down: When you begin a game, you touch your shooting knuckle to the ground.

Mibs: These are the target marbles in a game.

Quitsies: When you allow an opponent to quit the game whenever he or she wants. You can also call "No Quitsies."

Elephant Stomps: Allows a player to smash his or her marble into the ground, making it difficult to knock out.

111

Keepsies

Marbles are popular all over the world. That's because there are hundreds of games you can play with them. Some really fun games are Poison, Boss Out, Cherry Pit, Ringer, Nine Holes, and Black Snake. In the United States, kids and adults play Ringer in marble tournaments. The goal with most marble games is to "knuckle down" and shoot your opponents marbles out of the ring. It takes a lot of skill, but if you practice enough, you can play for keeps, or keepsies.

Don't Lose Your Marbles

Another reason that marbles are popular is because of their brilliant beauty. Marbles come in all colors, designs, and sizes. One handmade marble from the 1800s can be worth thousands of dollars! People still make handmade marbles today, but most are made by machine. Once you start collecting marbles, you will be amazed by how unique and beautiful they are. So what are you waiting for? Join the millions of people around the world who play marbles. It is fun, challenging, and easy to learn. And who knows, maybe some day your marbles will be worth lots of money too.

Let's **Think** About...

Does the author use any "loaded words" in this paragraph? What is he trying to get you to think or do? **Persuasive Text**

How to Play the Game Ringers

Thirteen mibs are arranged in the middle of a circle. The goal of the game is to shoot from outside the circle and knock the marbles out of the ring. If you knock out a mib and your marble is still in the circle, you can keep shooting. If your shooter goes outside the circle, you lose your turn. The first player to knock out seven mibs wins.

Let's **Think** About...

Summarize how to play Ringers, explaining the game in logical order in five or six steps. Then follow the directions when you play!
Persuasive Text

Let's **Think** About...

Look at the illustrations. How should you arrange the marbles?
Persuasive Text

Let's **Think** About...

Reading Across Texts What would a rock collection, like the one in *Rocks in His Head*, have in common with a marble collection?

Writing Across Texts Write a letter to a friend telling why you want to collect rocks or marbles, and why your friend should too.

113

TEKS

3.29.A.1 Listen attentively to speakers. **3.30.A.2** Speak coherently, employing eye contact, speaking rate, volume, enunciation, and the conventions of language to communicate ideas effectively. **3.31.A.4** Participate in student-led discussions by posing questions with appropriate detail. **3.31.A.5** Participate in student-led discussions by answering questions with appropriate detail. **Also 3.3.A.1, 3.3.A.2, 3.4.B.2, 3.22.A.1.vi, 3.29.A.2, 3.30.A.1.**

READING STREET ONLINE
ONLINE STUDENT EDITION
www.TexasReadingStreet.com

Vocabulary

Multiple-Meaning Words

Context Clues Multiple-meaning words are words that are spelled the same but have different meanings. Use context clues by looking at the words around a multiple-meaning word to figure out its meaning in the sentence.

Practice It! Make a list of four multiple-meaning words. Use each word in a sentence. Exchange papers with a partner and use context clues to figure out the meanings of the four words.

Fluency

Expression

Reading with expression makes a story more exciting. Stressing words differently, saying some words with more feeling than others, or changing your tone of voice for dialogue makes the story lively.

Practice It! With your partner, read aloud page 96. How should your tone of voice be different when reading dialogue than when reading a regular paragraph?

Listening and Speaking

Speak clearly and make eye contact with your subject.

Interview

In an interview, one person asks another person questions. Use formal language and remember to speak clearly, coherently, and with expression during an interview.

Practice It! Work in pairs to prepare an interview to present to the class. You might want to pretend the person being interviewed has an interesting job, and a reporter will interview him or her for a newspaper article. Prepare questions and conduct your interview in front of the class.

Tips

Listening ...

- Try to anticipate what the speaker will say next.
- Ask relevant questions in response.

Speaking ...

- Speak clearly and distinctly
- Use possessive pronouns correctly.

Teamwork ...

- Ask and answer questions with detail.
- Make the interview sound like a natural conversation.

TEKS

3.29.A.2 Ask relevant questions.
3.31.A.1 Participate in teacher-led discussions by posing questions with appropriate detail. **3.31.A.2** Participate in teacher-led discussions by answering questions with appropriate detail.

Oral Vocabulary

Let's Talk About

Being First

- Ask questions about bravery, imagination, and determination.

- Pose and answer questions about what it takes to be first at something.

- Discuss historical firsts.

READING STREET ONLINE
CONCEPT TALK VIDEO
www.TexasReadingStreet.com

TEKS

3.1.A.iv Decode multisyllabic words in context and independent of context by applying common spelling patterns including using knowledge of common prefixes. **Also 3.1.A.v.**

Envision It! | Suffixes to Know

painter
-er

lioness
-ess

violinist
-ist

sailor
-or

READING STREET ONLINE
SOUND-SPELLING CARDS
www.TexasReadingStreet.com

Phonics

Suffixes -er, -or, -ess, -ist

Words I Can Blend

teach**er**

invent**or**

act**ress**

art**ist**

visit**or**

Sentences I Can Read

1. My teacher told us about the great inventor Thomas Edison.

2. I don't have one favorite actress.

3. Last week a famous artist was a visitor at our school.

118

I Can Read!

I am kind of a dreamer. I often imagine what my life will be like when I grow up. Each day I imagine I am something different.

For example, one day I am a famous inventor, the next a writer or sailor. I love music, so sometimes I pretend I am a flutist or pianist in an orchestra. And, of course, sometimes I imagine life as a princess.

I guess this is all practice for when I decide what kind of work I will do, as an office worker, a doctor, or maybe even an actress.

You've learned

 Suffixes *-er, -or, -ess, -ist*

TEKS

3.2.B.2 Ask relevant questions about other texts. **3.2.B.4** Seek clarification about other texts. **3.2.B.6** Locate facts about other texts. **Also 3.2.B.9, 3.2.C.2, 3.2.C.3, RC-3.B.1, RC-3.B.2, RC-3.B.3, RC-3.C.1, RC-3.C.2.**

Envision It! | **Skill Strategy**

Skill

Strategy

Comprehension Skill

Fact and Opinion

- A statement of fact can be proved true or false.

- A statement of opinion cannot be proved true or false. It is a belief of judgement.

- Use what you learned about fact and opinion and a chart like the one below as you read "Swim!" Then write a short paragraph about swimmers.

Statement	Fact? How Can It Be Checked?	Opinion? What Are Clue Words?

Comprehension Strategy

Questioning

As you read, ask questions. Questioning helps you identify what you don't understand. Continue to read to find an answer to your question. You can ask literal questions about details in a selection. You can ask interpretive and evaluative questions that you have to think about and answer on your own.

Swim!

Exercise is important for good health. When people do not exercise, their muscles become soft and weak.

Swimming is one of the best ways to exercise. When swimming, you must move against the water. This makes muscles stronger. It takes more energy to move through water than it does through air. So swimming helps people lose fat. All this also helps your heart get and stay strong.

Many people get hurt playing soccer, football, or basketball. Not in swimming! It's one of the safest ways to exercise.

Swimming is also a great way to have fun while you exercise. You can cool off on a hot summer day and play water games with your friends. Swimming races are an exciting way to beat the heat.

If you do not know how to swim, you should learn how—now!

Skill What reference could you use to see whether these statements are true?

Strategy What questions can you ask about swimming as a way to have fun? How can you answer your questions?

Your Turn!

Need a Review? See *Envision It! Handbook* for help with fact and opinion and questioning.

Ready to Try It? As you read *America's Champion Swimmer: Gertrude Ederle*, use what you've learned about fact and opinion and questioning.

TEKS

3.4.B.2 Use context to distinguish among multiple-meaning words.

celebrate

current

medals

continued

drowned

stirred

strokes

Vocabulary Strategy for

Multiple-Meaning Words

Context Clues You may read a word that doesn't make sense in a sentence. The word may have another meaning. For example, *safe* can mean "free from harm" or "a metal box for storing money and valuables."

1. Try the meaning of the word that you know. Does it make sense in the sentence?

2. If not, perhaps the word has another meaning. Read on and look at the words around it to figure out another meaning.

3. Try the new meaning in the sentence. Does it make sense?

Read "Learn to Swim" on page 123. Look for words that can have more than one meaning. Use nearby words to figure out a new meaning.

Words to Write Reread "Learn to Swim." Think about another sport or activity you know. Write an article about it, including the rules for safety. Use words from the Words to Know list in your article.

LEARN TO SWIM

Some people swim for exercise, some swim in races, and some swim for fun. But no matter the reason, everyone should learn how to swim. People have drowned because they couldn't swim.

The first step is to learn to float, bob, and tread water. Then learn to swim the basic strokes—front crawl, backstroke, breaststroke, and sidestroke. These are different ways of moving through the water quickly.

Take your time when you're learning to swim. You're not trying to win medals in the Olympics. You do want to coordinate your arms, legs, and breathing.

Even after you know how to swim, never swim where there is no lifeguard. Ocean tides can pull you under, a river's current can sweep you away, and weather can cause problems too. One swimmer continued to swim after it started to rain. High winds stirred up the water. Luckily, a boater helped the swimmer back to shore.

So, celebrate the beginning of your life-long swimming adventure. Everyone into the pool!

Your Turn!

Need a Review? For additional help with context clues and multiple-meaning words, see *Words!*

Ready to Try It? Read *America's Champion Swimmer: Gertrude Ederle*, pp. 124–139.

AMERICA'S CHAMPION SWIMMER:

Gertrude Ederle

by David A. Adler

illustrated by Terry Widener

Genre

A biography gives facts about a real person's life. Why do you think the author wrote a biography about Gertrude Ederle?

Question of the Week
What unique traits does it take to be the first to do something?

In 1906 women were kept out of many clubs and restaurants. In most states they were not allowed to vote. Many people felt a woman's place was in the home.

But Gertrude Ederle's place was in the water.

Gertrude Ederle was born on October 23, 1906. She was the third of six children and was raised in New York City, where she lived in an apartment next to her father's butcher shop. Her family called her Gertie. Most everyone else called her Trudy.

Trudy spent her early years playing on the sidewalks of New York. It wasn't until she was seven that she had her first adventure in the water. While visiting her grandmother in Germany, Trudy fell into a pond and nearly drowned.

After that near disaster, Trudy's father was determined to teach her to swim. For her first lesson, he tied one end of a rope to Trudy's waist and held on to the other end. He put Trudy into a river and told her to paddle like a dog.

Trudy mastered the dog paddle. She joined her older sister Margaret and the other children in the water and copied their strokes. Soon Trudy swam better than any of them.

From that summer on, it was hard to keep Trudy out of the water. She *loved* to swim. At the age of thirteen she became a member of the New York Women's Swimming Association and took lessons there.

At fifteen Trudy won her first big race.

The next year, she attempted to be the first woman to swim the more than seventeen miles from lower Manhattan to Sandy Hook, New Jersey. When Trudy slowed down, her sister Margaret yelled, "Get going, lazybones!" And Trudy did. She finished in just over seven hours. And she beat the men's record.

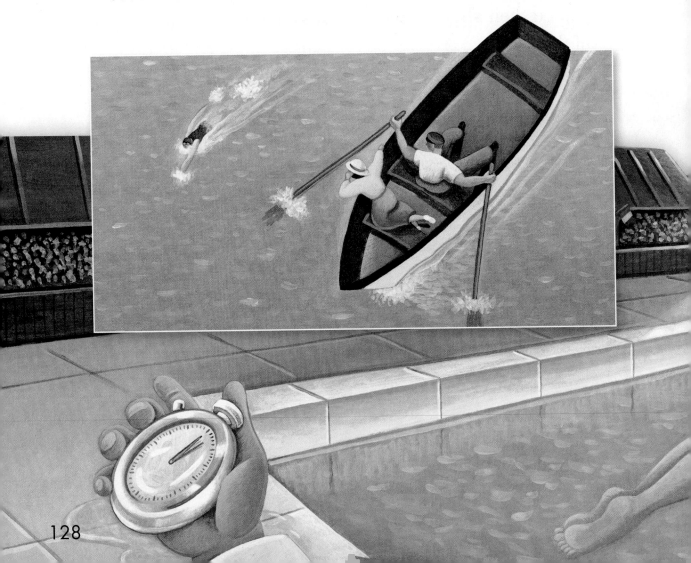

People were beginning to notice Gertrude Ederle. Newspapers described her as courageous, determined, modest, and poised. They called her the most perfect swimmer. Trudy's mother said she was "just a plain home girl."

In 1924 this "plain home girl" was good enough to make the U.S. Olympic team. Trudy won three medals at the games in Paris. Her team won more points than all the other countries' swimming teams combined.

By 1925 Trudy had set twenty-nine U.S. and world records. She was determined to take on the ultimate challenge: the English Channel. Many had tried to swim the more-than-twenty-mile-wide body of cold, rough water that separates England from France. But only five men—and no women—had ever made it all the way across.

Many people were sure Trudy couldn't do it. A newspaper editorial declared that Trudy wouldn't make it and that women must admit they would "remain forever the weaker sex."

It didn't matter to Trudy what people said or wrote. She was going to swim the Channel.

Early in the morning on August 18, 1925, Trudy stepped into the water at Cape Gris-Nez, France, the starting point for the swim. For almost nine hours she fought the strong current. Then, when Trudy had less than seven miles to go, her trainer thought she had swallowed too much water and pulled her, crying, from the sea.

Trudy did not give up her dream. She found a new trainer, and a year later, on Friday, August 6, 1926, she was ready to try again.

Trudy wore a red bathing cap and a two-piece bathing suit and goggles that she and her sister Margaret had designed. To protect her from the icy cold water, Margaret coated Trudy with lanolin and heavy grease. The greasing took a long time—too long for Trudy. "For heaven's sake," she complained. "Let's get started."

Finally, at a little past seven in the morning, she stepped into the water. "Gee, but it's cold," Trudy said.

Trudy's father, her sister Margaret, her trainer, and a few other swimmers were on board a tugboat named *Alsace*. The boat would accompany Trudy to make sure she didn't get lost in the fog and was safe from jellyfish, sharks, and the Channel's powerful currents. There was a second boat, too, with reporters and photographers on board.

As the *Alsace* bobbed up and down in the choppy water, Margaret wrote in chalk on the side of the boat, "This way, Ole Kid." She drew an arrow that pointed to England.

To entertain Trudy, Margaret and some of the others sang American songs, including "The Star-Spangled Banner" and "East Side, West Side." Trudy said the songs kept her "brain and spirit good."

At first the sea was calm.

Trudy swam so fast that her trainer was afraid she would tire herself out. He ordered her to slow down.

Trudy refused.

At about ten-thirty in the morning, Trudy had her first meal. She floated on her back and ate chicken and drank beef broth. A while later, she ate chocolate and chewed on sugar cubes. Then she swam on.

At about one-thirty in the afternoon, it started to rain. A strong wind stirred the water. For a while, Trudy would swim forward a few feet only to be pulled back twice as far.

By six o'clock the tide was stronger. The waves were twenty feet high. The rough water made the people aboard the *Alsace* and the news boat seasick.

Trudy's trainer was sure she couldn't finish the swim. He told her to give up.

"No, no," Trudy yelled over the sound of the waves. She kept swimming.

In the next few hours, the rain and wind became stronger and the sea rougher. At times the rough water pulled the boats away, out of Trudy's sight. She was scared. It was eerie being out there all alone.

Now Trudy began to have trouble kicking in the water. When the *Alsace* came close again, Trudy said her left leg had become stiff. Her trainer was frightened for her. He yelled, "You must come out."

"What for?" Trudy shouted, and kept swimming.

Trudy continued to fight the tide and the constant stinging spray of water in her face. She knew she would either swim the Channel or drown.

As Trudy neared Kingsdown, on the coast of England, she saw thousands of people gathered to greet her. They lit flares to guide her to shore.

At about nine-forty at night, after more than fourteen hours in the water, Trudy's feet touched land. Hundreds of people, fully dressed, waded into the water to greet her. When she reached the shore, her father hugged Trudy and wrapped her in a warm robe.

"I knew if it could be done, it had to be done, and I did it," Trudy said after she got ashore. "All the women of the world will celebrate."

Trudy swam the Channel in just fourteen hours and thirty-one minutes. She beat the men's record by almost two hours. In newspapers across the world, Trudy's swim was called history-making. Reporters declared that the myth that women are the weaker sex was "shattered and shattered forever."

Trudy sailed home aboard the SS *Berengaria*. After six days at sea, the ship entered New York Harbor.

Two airplanes circled and tipped their wings to greet Trudy. People on boats of all kinds rang their bells and tooted their horns to salute her. Foghorns sounded.

Trudy climbed into an open car for a parade up lower Broadway. An estimated two million people, many of them women, stood and cheered. They threw scraps of newspaper, ticker tape, pages torn from telephone books, and rolls of toilet paper.

When her car arrived at the New York city hall, Mayor Jimmy Walker praised Trudy for her courage, grace, and athletic prowess. "American women," he said, "have ever added to the glory of our nation."

President Calvin Coolidge sent a message
that was read at the ceremony. He called Trudy
"America's Best Girl." And she was. Gertrude
Ederle had become a beacon of strength to girls
and women everywhere.

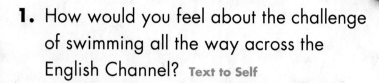

TEKS

3.13.A.1 Identify details or facts that support the main idea. **3.13.B.1** Draw conclusions from facts presented in text. **3.13.B.2** Support assertions with textual evidence. **Also 3.2.B.2, 3.2.B.6, 3.8.C.2, 3.9.A.1, RC-3.B.1, RC-3.B.2, RC-3.B.3.**

Envision It! | Retell

Think Critically

1. How would you feel about the challenge of swimming all the way across the English Channel? **Text to Self**

2. David Adler writes many biographies. Explain the difference in point of view between a biography and autobiography. How would this biography have been different if it were an autobiography? **Think Like an Author**

3. This biography is full of facts and also several statements of opinion. Write a sentence that tells your opinion of this biography. Support your opinion with evidence from the text.  **Fact and Opinion**

4. What questions do you have about swimmers who beat records and make history? Write a literal, an interpretive, and an evaluative question. **Questioning**

5. **Look Back and Write** Look back at the question on page 125. Write about Gertrude Ederle and how she surprised the world by being first. Provide evidence to support your answer.

   TEST PRACTICE | **Extended Response**

Meet the Author
DAVID ADLER

David Adler has written almost two hundred books! He was the first person to write a book about Gertrude Ederle. "I read every newspaper and magazine story I could find about her," he says. Some newspapers said a woman could never swim the English Channel.

Mr. Adler has five brothers and sisters. "My parents encouraged each of us to be an individual. As a child I was known as the family artist." Paintings and drawings he did then still hang in his parents' home.

"I've always been a dreamer," Mr. Adler says. He recently spoke with his fourth-grade teacher. She remembered the time she went to the principal. "What should I do with Adler?" she asked. "He's always dreaming."

"Leave him alone," the principal said. "Maybe one day he'll become a writer."

Read more books by David Adler.

The Babe and I

A Picture Book of Harriet Beecher Stowe

Use the Reader's and Writer's Notebook to record your independent reading.

141

TEKS

3.19.A.1 Write about important personal experiences. **3.23.C.1.i.1** Recognize punctuation marks including apostrophes in contractions. **Also:** **3.23.C.1.i.2, 3.23.D.1, 3.24.F.1.**

Narrative

Autobiography

An **autobiography** is the story of a person's life, written by the person who lived it. The student model on the next page is an example of an autobiography.

Writing Prompt Think about your own life and experiences. Now write an autobiography.

Let's Write It!

Key Features of an Autobiography

- tells the story of a person's own life

- may cover a person's whole life or only part of it

- written in first person

READING STREET ONLINE GRAMMAR JAMMER
www.TexasReadingStreet.com

Writer's Checklist

Remember, you should . . .

☑ tell about things that have happened to you.

☑ write about events in order.

☑ include details to make your writing more interesting.

☑ indent new paragraphs.

☑ use and spell contractions correctly.

Ski Fan

Learning to Ski

My parents always loved to ski. I started to ski when I was only 4 years old. My first hill was a gentle slope. I fell down many times, but I kept trying, and I got much better.

My First Race

I'll never forget my first race. I **should've** pushed off hard on my skis like the other racers. Instead I walked forward, clumsy like a bear. I came in last place. That **won't** happen again.

A Winner!

Last year, I won my first ski race. I pushed off hard and held my body tight as I shot down the hill. Only one skier was ahead of me. I **didn't** think I could pass him, but I did, and I got a first place ribbon!

Writing Trait Subheads help organize information.

Contractions are used correctly.

Genre An **autobiography** tells the story of a person's own life.

Conventions

Contractions

Remember A **contraction** is a word made by putting two words together. When words are joined in a contraction, an apostrophe is used to show where a letter or letters have been left out.

TEKS

3.16.A.1 Understand how communication changes when moving from one genre of media to another.
3.16.C.1 Compare written conventions used for digital media.

21st Century Skills
INTERNET GUY

Online Directories

Directories have large amounts of information. They organize things for you. Look for the link to the category you need. Then follow the links. Bookmark useful directories.

- Online directories group Web sites by topic. Online directories list topics as links on their homepage. If you click on a topic link, you will see a list of Web site links on that topic.

- Read "Women Athletes" to learn how to navigate in an online directory. Compare the language and conventions of an online directory to the language and conventions of a search engine and Web-based news article.

Women Athletes

Let's say you want to find out more about women athletes like Gertrude Ederle. You could go to an Internet online directory.

Here are some of the topics you might find listed there. The closest general topic is <u>Olympics</u>, so you click on this link.

File

http://www.url.here

ONLINE DIRECTORY

Today's Pictures
Space Images, Weather
Current News
Health, Technology
Sports
Olympics

File   Edit   View   Favorites   Tools   Help

http://www.url.here

ONLINE DIRECTORY

Olympic History
Olympic Events
Summer Olympics
Winter Olympics
Female Olympians
Male Olympians

The Olympic Games are a celebration of sports and athletes. The first Olympics were held in ancient Greece.

It takes you to a page of specific categories about this general topic. Here are some of them. You click on <u>Female Olympians</u>.

When you click on <u>Female Olympians</u>, you get a
list of Web sites. You decide to click on this one:

Notice how the formal
language used in the
summary lets you quickly
evaluate the Web site.

<u>Female Olympians</u>   Search

1. <u>**Wilma Rudolph:**</u> The 20th of 22 children, Rudolph
overcame many hardships to become an outstanding
African American female athlete.

2. <u>**Charlotte Cooper:**</u> The first woman gold medalist in
modern day

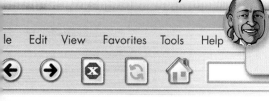

Here is what you get.

NAME: Wilma Glodean Rudolph

BIRTHDATE: June 23, 1940

BIRTHPLACE: Clarksville, Tennessee

FAMILY BACKGROUND:
Wilma weighed only 4 1/2 pounds when she was
born. Because of racial segregation laws, she and
her mother were not permitted into the local hospital.
Over the next few years, her mother nursed her to
health. Then Wilma got polio, a crippling
disease that had no cure at the time.
The doctor told Mrs. Rudolph that
Wilma would never walk. But after
hard work, Wilma was finally able
to walk with the aid of a metal leg
brace. By age twelve, she could walk
normally. It was then that she decided
to become an athlete.

Notice that this Web site
uses formal language and
text features to convey
and organize facts.

ACHIEVEMENTS: In high school, she became a basketball star. She set state records for scoring. She led her team to a state championship. Then she became a track star, going to her first Olympic Games in 1956. She won a bronze medal in the 4 x 4 relay.

On September 7, 1960, in Rome, Wilma became the first American woman to win three gold medals in the Olympics. She won the 100-meter dash and the 200-meter dash, and ran anchor on the 400-meter relay team.

If you wanted to see a video of Wilma, you could look for a documentary about her life.

 **for more practice**

Get Online!
www.TexasReadingStreet.com
Use online directories to find out about women athletes.

21st Century Skills Online Activity
Log on and follow the step-by-step directions for using online directories to find more about women athletes.

TEKS

3.3.A.1 Read aloud grade-level appropriate text with fluency. **3.3.A.2** Read aloud grade-level appropriate text with comprehension. **3.30.A.1** Speak coherently about the topic under discussion. **3.30.A.2** Speak coherently, employing eye contact, speaking rate, volume, enunciation, and the conventions of language to communicate ideas effectively. **Also 3.4.B.2, 3.4.B.3, 3.4.E.2, 3.4.E.4, 3.16.A.1, 3.16.B.1, 3.29.A.1.**

Let's **Learn** It!

READING STREET ONLINE
ONLINE STUDENT EDITION
www.TexasReadingStreet.com

Vocabulary

Multiple-Meaning Words

Context Clues Multiple-meaning words are spelled the same but have different meanings. Homographs are spelled the same but have different meanings and pronunciations. Use context clues to figure out what meaning or pronunciation to use.

Practice It! Write sentences for two multiple-meaning words and two homographs. Switch sentences with a partner. Write down the different meanings and pronunciations for each word using the context of the sentence. Use a dictionary if necessary.

Fluency

Appropriate Phrasing

Notice the different lengths of sentences when you read. Paying attention to the rhythm of sentences makes the story flow more smoothly.

Practice It! With your partner, practice reading page 130. Remember to pause at commas and other punctuation. Read with rhythm to give meaning to the events in the story.

148

Listening and Speaking

When giving a presentation, speak loudly and clearly.

Sportscast

A sports announcer describes the action of a sports event in a sportscast. Expression is important when reporting.

Practice It! Prepare and deliver a three-minute TV sportscast that includes news about Gertrude Ederle's swim. Choose two additional sports events to describe in your sportscast. Discuss how using video would change the descriptions.

Tips

Listening ...

- Draw conclusions about how design influences the message.

Speaking ...

- Determine your purpose for speaking.
- Use visual and sound aids.

Teamwork ...

- Ask and answer questions about how using sound and video changes communication in a sportscast.

149

TEKS

3.30.A.2 Speak coherently, employing eye contact, speaking rate, volume, enunciation, and the conventions of language to communicate ideas effectively. **3.31.A.1** Participate in teacher-led discussions by posing questions with appropriate detail.

Oral Vocabulary

Let's Talk About

Unique Animal Behaviors

- Describe unique animals.

- Pose and answer questions about why animals exhibit unique behaviors.

- Discuss what behaviors are unique to specific animals.

READING STREET ONLINE
CONCEPT TALK VIDEO
www.TexasReadingStreet.com

Phonics

🎯 Syllable Pattern VCCCV

Words I Can Blend

hundreds
children
complete
explain
instead

Sentences I Can Read

1. Hundreds of children go to school in my town.

2. Did you complete the test?

3. Explain why we are going tomorrow instead of today.

I Can Read!

Children in my apartment complex have a concrete area where we play. Sometimes we complain that there simply is not enough room there, but we get constant use out of it anyway.

A man came to inspect the area last week. He explained they are going to destroy the old playground and improve the area. That's what Mom said, anyway.

I can't wait until it is complete and we have an outstanding new place to play.

You've learned

⊙ Syllable Pattern VCCCV

TEKS

3.2.B.4 Seek clarification about other texts. **3.13.C.1** Identify explicit cause and effect relationships among ideas in texts. **RC-3.C.1** Monitor comprehension. **RC-3.C.2** Adjust comprehension. **Also 3.2.C.2, 3.2.C.3.**

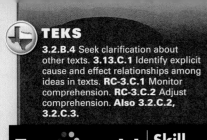

Envision It! | Skill Strategy

Skill

Strategy

READING STREET ONLINE
ENVISION IT! ANIMATIONS
www.TexasReadingStreet.com

Comprehension Skill

Cause and Effect

- A cause tells why something happened.

- An effect is what happened.

- *Because* and *so* are clue words that show a cause-and-effect relationship.

- Use what you learned about cause and effect and a graphic organizer like the one below to read "Birds of Prey." Then use your graphic organizer to write a paragraph that explains the cause-and-effect relationship.

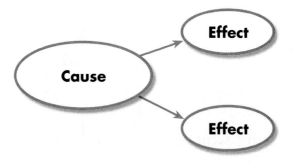

Comprehension Strategy

Monitor and Clarify

Good readers think about what they are reading. They stop reading when they are confused and try to figure out what's wrong. When you are confused, go back and reread to help clarify your understanding.

Birds of Prey

Eagles are large birds of prey that are members of the falcon family. Like all birds of prey, eagles have very large hooked beaks, strong legs, and powerful talons or claws. Another advantage that eagles have is their keen eyesight. Eagles can spot their prey from very long distances because they have large pupils.

Eagles are different from many other birds of prey. They are larger, have a more powerful build, and have heavier heads and bills. Most eagles are larger than any other birds of prey apart from vultures.

Eagles build their nests in tall trees or on high cliffs so that their young chicks are protected from other animals. In recent years, eagles have fallen prey to their environment. Many eagles have moved away from the heavily populated areas in the United States or disappeared entirely because of human expansion.

Skill What clue word is in this paragraph? What cause and effect does it show?

Strategy Are you having trouble understanding how eagles are different from other birds of prey? Go back and reread this paragraph aloud.

Your Turn!

❙❙ Need a Review? See *Envision It! Handbook* for help with cause and effect and monitoring and clarifying.

▶ Ready to Try It? As you read *Fly, Eagle, Fly!*, use what you've learned about cause and effect and monitoring and clarifying to understand the text.

155

TEKS

3.4.E.2 Use a dictionary or glossary to determine meanings of unknown words. **3.4.E.3** Use a dictionary or glossary to determine syllabication of unknown words. **3.4.E.4** Use a dictionary or glossary to determine pronunciation of unknown words.

Envision It! | Words to Know

gully

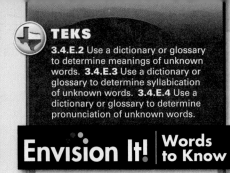

reeds

valley

clutched

echoed

scrambled

thatch

Vocabulary Strategy for

🎯 Unknown Words

Dictionary/Glossary You can use a dictionary or glossary to find the meaning, syllable division, and pronunciation of an unknown word.

1. Find the entry word and pronunciation in the dictionary or glossary.

2. Look at the pronunciation key and each syllable to pronounce the word correctly.

3. Read all of the definitions. Which meaning best fits the sentence?

4. Try that meaning in the sentence. If it doesn't make sense, try another meaning of the word.

Read "Eagle Watching" on page 157. Use a dictionary or glossary to find the meanings, syllable divisions, and pronunciations of the Words to Know.

Words to Write Reread "Eagle Watching." What kind of animals are you interested in studying? Write about your interest. Use words from the Words to Know list in your answer.

Eagle Watching

José and his father scrambled up the side of the gully. Near the top of the gully was their favorite eagle-watching spot. José and his father looked for the bald eagles that lived in the area. First, they used their binoculars to scan the tops of the trees. Eagles usually perch in high places so that they can look for food. Next, José and his father listened for the eagles. Loud eagle cries often echoed across the valley.

In the valley below where José and his father hid was a large lake. The eagles swooped over the reeds and thatch along the lake's edge, skimmed over the surface, and dipped down and snatched fish out of the water. Then the eagles flew away with the fish clutched in their sharp talons, or claws. They carried the fish back to their nests, high in the tall trees or on the cliffs. It was an amazing sight, and José never got tired of watching it.

Your Turn!

⏸ **Need a Review?** For help with using a dictionary or glossary to find the meanings of unknown words, see *Words!*

▶ **Ready to Try It?** Read *Fly, Eagle, Fly!* on pp. 158–171.

Genre **Folk tales** are stories or legends from other lands and are handed down from one generation to the next. Where is this story from?

Fly, Eagle, Fly!

An African Tale

retold by
Christopher Gregorowski
illustrated by Niki Daly

Question of the Week
**What behaviors are unique
to different animals?**

A farmer went out one day to search for a lost calf. The little herd boys had come back without it the evening before. And that night there had been a terrible storm.

He went to the valley and searched. He searched by the riverbed. He searched among the reeds, behind the rocks, and in the rushing water.

He wandered over the hillside and through the dark and tangled forests where everything began, then out again along the muddy cattle tracks.

He searched in the long thatch grass, taller than his own head. He climbed the slopes of the high mountain with its rocky cliffs rising to the sky. He called out all the time, hoping that the calf might hear, but also because he felt so alone. His shouts echoed off the cliffs. The river roared in the valley below.

He climbed up a gully in case the calf had huddled there to escape the storm. And that was where he stopped. For there, on a ledge of rock, close enough to touch, he saw the most unusual sight—an eagle chick, very young, hatched from its egg a day or two before and then blown from its nest by the terrible storm.

He reached out and cradled it in both hands. He would take it home and care for it. And home he went, still calling, calling in case the calf might hear.

He was almost home when the children ran out to meet him. "The calf came back by itself!" they shouted. He was very pleased. He showed the eagle chick to his wife and children, then placed it carefully in the warm kitchen among the hens and chicks and under the watchful eye of the roosters.

"The eagle is the king of the birds," he said, "but we shall train it to be a chicken."

So the eagle lived among the chickens, learning their ways. His children called their friends to see the strange bird. For as it grew, living on the bits and pieces put out for the chickens, it began to look quite different from any chicken they had ever seen.

One day a friend dropped in for a visit. He and the farmer sat at the door of the kitchen hut. The friend saw the bird among the chickens. "Hey! That's not a chicken. It's an eagle!"

The farmer smiled at him and said, "Of course it's a chicken. Look—it walks like a chicken, it talks like a chicken, it eats like a chicken. It *thinks* like a chicken. Of course it's a chicken."

But the friend was not convinced. "I will show you that it is an eagle," he said.

"Go ahead," said the farmer.

The farmer's children helped his friend catch the bird. It was fairly heavy but he lifted it above his head and said: "You are not a chicken but an eagle. You belong not to the earth but to the sky. Fly, Eagle, fly!"

The bird stretched out its wings as the farmer and his family had seen it do before. But it looked about, saw the chickens feeding, and jumped down to scratch with them for food.

"I told you it was a chicken," the farmer said, and roared with laughter.

Next day the friend was back. "Farmer," he said, "I will prove to you that this is no chicken but an eagle. Bring me a ladder." With the large bird under one arm, he struggled up the slippery thatch of the tallest hut.

The farmer doubled over with laughter. "It eats chicken food. It thinks like a chicken. It *is* a chicken."

The friend, swaying on top of the hut, took the eagle's head, pointed it to the sky, and said: "You are not a chicken but an eagle. You belong not to the earth but to the sky. Fly, Eagle, fly!"

Again the great bird stretched out its wings. It trembled and the claws that clasped his hand opened. "Fly, Eagle, fly!" the man cried.

But the bird scrambled out of his hands, slid down the thatch, and sailed in among the chickens.

There was much laughter.

Very early next morning, on the third day, the farmer's dogs began to bark. A voice was calling outside in the darkness. The farmer ran to the door. It was his friend again. "Give me one more chance with the bird," he begged.

"Do you know the time? It's long before dawn. Are you crazy?"

"Come with me. Fetch the bird."

Reluctantly the farmer went into the kitchen, stepping over his sleeping children, and picked up the bird, which was fast asleep among the chickens. The two men set off, disappearing into the darkness.

"Where are we going?" asked the farmer sleepily.

"To the mountains where you found the bird."

"And why at this ridiculous time of the night?"

"So that our eagle may see the sun rise over the mountain and follow it into the sky where it belongs."

They went into the valley and crossed the river, the friend leading the way. The bird was very heavy and too large to carry comfortably, but the friend insisted on taking it himself.

"Hurry," he said, "or the dawn will arrive before we do!"

The first light crept into the sky as they began to climb the mountain. Below them they could see the river snaking like a long, thin ribbon through the golden grasslands, the forest, and the veld, stretching down toward the sea. The wispy clouds in the sky were pink at first and then began to shimmer with a golden brilliance.

Sometimes their path was dangerous as it clung to the side of the mountain, crossing narrow shelves of rock and taking them into dark crevices and out again. They were both panting, especially the friend who was carrying the bird.

At last he said, "This will do." He looked down the cliff and saw the ground thousands of feet below. They were very near the top.

Carefully the friend carried the bird onto a ledge of rock. He set it down so that it looked toward the east, and began talking to it.

The farmer chuckled. "It talks only chickens' talk."

But the friend talked on, telling the bird about the sun, how it gives life to the world, how it reigns in the heavens, giving light to each new day.

"Look at the sun, Eagle. And when it rises, rise with it. You belong to the sky, not to the earth."

At that moment the sun's first rays shot out over the mountain, and suddenly the world was ablaze with light.

The golden sun rose majestically, dazzling them. The great bird stretched out its wings to greet the sun and feel the life-giving warmth on its feathers. The farmer was quiet. The friend said, "You belong not to the earth, but to the sky. Fly, Eagle, fly!"

He clambered back to the farmer.

All was silent. Nothing moved. The eagle's head stretched up; its wings stretched outwards; its legs leaned forward as its claws clutched the rock.

And then, without really moving, feeling the updraft of a wind more powerful than any man or bird, the great eagle leaned forward and was swept upward, higher and higher, lost to sight in the brightness of the rising sun, never again to live among the chickens.

TEKS

3.2.B.3 Seek clarification about stories. **3.5.B.1** Compare settings in myths and traditional folktales. **3.8.A.3** Explain the plot's main events' influence on future events. **Also** 3.2.C.2, 3.2.C.3, 3.5.B.2, RC-3.C.1, RC-3.C.2, 3.10.A.1.

Envision It! Retell

Think Critically

1. The author writes this folk tale about the journey of returning the eagle to the mountain. Have you ever read another folk tale about a journey? What was the setting? Compare and contrast both folk tales. **Text to Text**

2. *Fly, Eagle, Fly!* is a folk tale and has a lesson to teach. What lesson do you think the author is trying to teach?

   Think Like an Author

3. Why do you think the eagle acted like a chicken? **Cause and Effect**

4. Look back through the selection. What parts did you reread to help you understand? What parts did you visualize? What background knowledge did you use? What questions did you ask yourself? **Monitor and Clarify**

5. **Look Back and Write** Look back at pages 162–165. Write about why everyone thought the eagle was a chicken. Provide evidence to support your answer.

    **TEST PRACTICE** **Extended Response**

**READING STREET ONLINE
STORY SORT**
www.TexasReadingStreet.com

Meet the Illustrator

Niki Daly

Niki Daly was born in Cape Town, South Africa, and he lives there today. His picture books have won awards all over the world.

Mr. Daly uses watercolors with pen or pencil to create his lively pictures. For his books, Mr. Daly says he first watches people. Then he draws his characters many times, "until they become as real as the people around me."

As a child, Mr. Daly read a lot of comic books. They taught him to tell stories through pictures. In his books, Mr. Daly tries to show children of all races in South Africa. Mr. Daly also likes to write songs. He has even recorded two albums.

Read more books by Niki Daly.

Jamela's Dress

Old Bob's Brown Bear

Use the Reader's and Writer's Notebook to record your independent reading.

TEKS

3.20.C.2 Write responses to literary texts that demonstrate understanding. **3.22.A.1.v.1** Use and understand prepositions in the context of reading, writing, and speaking. **Also: 3.22.A.1.v.2.**

Let's Write It!

Key Features of a Summary

- retells a piece of writing
- includes only the most important information
- shorter than the original

READING STREET ONLINE
GRAMMAR JAMMER
www.TexasReadingStreet.com

Summary

A **summary** is a short retelling of a piece of writing, such as an article or a story. A summary contains only the main points, not the details. The student model on the next page is an example of a summary.

Writing Prompt *Fly, Eagle, Fly!* is an African tale. Think about a tale that you know well. Now write a summary of the plot, telling the events in time order.

Writer's Checklist

Remember, you should . . .

☑ write about a tale you know well.

☑ include only the main points.

☑ leave out unimportant details.

☑ use prepositions and prepositional phrases correctly.

Summary of Paul Bunyan and the 10,000 Lakes of Minnesota

The mighty lumberjack Paul Bunyan had a pet, a giant blue ox named Babe. One day Babe was acting up something awful, so Paul put a rope around Babe's neck and tied the rope **to** a tree. Then Paul went to work, and Babe pulled the rope loose and ran **off.** After work, Paul came back and started chasing Babe. They ran all **over** the state of Minnesota. Everywhere they ran, they left huge footprints. Later, the rains came and filled **up** the footprints. And that's how Minnesota got 10,000 lakes.

Genre A **summary** tells the most important parts of a story or article.

Writing Trait Word Choice Time-order transition words help explain the order of events.

Prepositions are used correctly.

Conventions

Prepositions

Remember A **preposition** is a word that shows how a noun or pronoun is related to other words in the same sentence. *We sing* in *the car.*

TEKS

3.5.B.1 Compare settings in myths and traditional folktales. **3.5.B.2** Contrast settings in myths and traditional folktales. **3.8.C.2** Identify whether the narrator of a story is third person. **Also** 3.5.A.1, 3.5.A.2, 3.8.B.1, 3.8.B.2.

Social Studies in Reading

Genre
Trickster Tale

- A Trickster tale is a folk tale that has one clever character who tricks another character. Characters are often animals that act like people.

- Trickster and other folk tales often involve fantastic, or unbelievable, situations that are set in other lands to add excitement to the plot.

- The themes of folk tales usually teach lessons about human behavior.

- Read the trickster tale "Purple Coyote." How does this setting compare and contrast to the settings of other folk tales?

Purple Coyote

by Cornette
illustrated by Rochette

176

In the middle of a flat and arid desert stood a hill of sand and rock.

Near this hill was a small house.

Jim played alone in the garden with his old truck, which was missing one wheel.

One day, a coyote appeared on the hill. A coyote unlike any other. A purple coyote.

Jim watched him.

The coyote did a little dance. Then he balanced himself on his right front paw and let out a strange howl:

"WULULI WULA WULILA WUWU WA!"

He sat down, letting the evening wind slowly untangle his purple fur.

Night fell and the moon rose. Jim watched the purple coyote until his mother called him for dinner.

Let's Think About...

Is this written in first or third person? How do you know?

Trickster Tale

The next day, Jim didn't play with his truck, which had lost a second wheel.

He went to wait for the coyote at the bottom of the hill.

The purple coyote appeared. He did his little dance, balanced himself on his right front paw, and let out his "WULULI WULA WULILA WUWU WA!"

Jim climbed up the hill.

It wasn't very hard, as the hill was neither high nor steep.

He went up to the animal, greeted him and asked, "Why are you purple? That's not normal for a coyote!"

"I won't tell you!" answered the coyote.

"Why not?"

"Because it's a secret! But you can ask me questions if you want."

Let's  About...

What details in the plot make it a fantastic situation?
Trickster Tale

178

Jim thought hard. He looked the purple coyote straight in the eyes and asked, "Did you eat too many blueberries?"

"I never eat blueberries," the coyote replied.

Every afternoon, the purple coyote returned to the hill, did his little dance, balanced himself on his right front paw, and howled:

"WULULI WULA WULILA WUWU WA!"

Every afternoon, Jim joined the coyote, greeted him, and asked him a question. "Did you put purple dye on your fur?"

"No," answered the coyote.

"Were you born purple?"

"No."

"Did you catch purple-itis?"

"No."

"Did you catch purple fever?"

"No."

The days went by. Jim began to lose patience.

"I don't care if I never find out why you're purple!" he shouted at the coyote.

Let's Think About...

Who do you think is the clever character? Who will be tricked? Why? **Trickster Tale**

In his anger, he thought about not coming up the hill anymore, but his curiosity was too strong.

"Tell me instead why you do that dance and why you howl in that funny way," he asked.

The coyote smiled. "That's my second secret," he said.

Jim tried very hard to keep calm. He acted as though he didn't care. "That's a stupid secret," he said. "Anyone can dance and howl like that! Look!"

Jim did a little dance, then leaned over on his right arm and howled a piercing "WULULI WULA WULILA WUWU WA!"

All at once, Jim turned purple.

Let's Think About...

How is this Coyote similar to the Coyote in the myth "Catch It and Run"? **Trickster Tale**

As for the coyote, he got his color back. He was once again the color of desert and sand.

"Well done!" said the coyote. "You've discovered my two secrets in one try! You've given me back my natural color. Now I can leave. Goodbye, Jim!"

He disappeared into the vast desert.

Jim was now all purple and all by himself.

Night had fallen on the hill when a little raccoon came up to him.

"Hello," the raccoon said.

"Hello!" replied the purple kid.

"Did you see?" said Jim. "I'm purple all over."

"Yes," said the small animal.

"It's my secret," Jim went on.

"Do you want to find out why?"

"No."

Let's **Think** About...

Explain the interaction between Jim and the coyote. What changes did they undergo?
Trickster Tale

Let's **Think** About...

Summarize the theme and supporting details from the story in your own words. What does this show about human behavior?
Trickster Tale

Let's **Think** About...

Reading Across Texts Compare and contrast the settings in the two folk tales, *Fly, Eagle, Fly!* and "Purple Coyote." How are they alike and different?

Writing Across Texts Make a Venn diagram that compares and contrasts the settings in each of these folk tales.

TEKS

3.29.A.1 Listen attentively to speakers. **3.31.A.4** Participate in student-led discussions by posing questions with appropriate detail. **3.31.A.5** Participate in student-led discussions by answering questions with appropriate detail. **3.31.A.6** Participate in student-led discussions by providing suggestions that build upon the ideas of others. **Also 3.3.A.1, 3.3.A.2, 3.4.E.2, 3.4.E.3, 3.4.E.4, 3.22.A.1.v.1, 3.22.A.1.v.2, 3.29.B.1, 3.30.A.2.**

READING STREET ONLINE
ONLINE STUDENT EDITION
www.TexasReadingStreet.com

Vocabulary

Unknown Words

Dictionary/Glossary Use a dictionary or glossary to find the meanings of unknown words. The words are listed in alphabetical order and shown with their syllable divisions, pronunciations, and meanings. Choose the meaning that fits the context of the text you are reading.

Practice It! Use a dictionary to look up *shimmer*, *brilliance*, and *majestically* from *Fly, Eagle, Fly!* Write down the definitions and pronunciations of the words as they are used in the story.

Fluency

Rate

The rate at which you read can depend on your interest or familiarity with the topic. You can improve your rate by reading a selection more than once. You can also speed up or slow down when you read aloud to match the mood of the story.

Practice It! With a partner, practice reading aloud *Fly, Eagle, Fly!* pages 160–161. Read the pages a second time. Did your rate improve? Does reading faster or slower help make your reading more interesting?

Listening and Speaking

Make contributions and keep the discussion going.

Book Review

A book review tells your opinion about a book. It should focus on themes, the author's purpose for writing, and what effect the book might have on readers.

Practice It! Follow directions for presenting a book review in a group. Discuss your reactions to the story, and decide if you would recommend it to friends. Present your review to the class.

Tips

Listening ...

• Face the speakers.

• Draw conclusions about what the speakers say.

Speaking ...

• Use appropriate persuasive techniques.

• Use appropriate emotional clues.

• Use prepositions and prepositional phrases correctly.

Teamwork ...

• Ask and answer questions with detailed information.

• Give suggestions for why others may or may not like the book.

TEKS

3.6.A.1 Describe characteristics of various forms of poetry. **3.6.A.2** Describe how the characteristics of various forms of poetry create imagery. **3.10.A.1** Identify language that appeals to the senses. **RC-3.D.1** Make inferences about text.

Poetry

- **Limericks** are humorous, often silly, poems told in five lines. The first, second, and fifth lines rhyme and have matching beats. The third and fourth lines are shorter, rhyme, and have matching beats.

- **Free verse poems** express powerful emotions and images using comparisons and sensory language, and don't use **rhyme patterns** or a regular **rhythm,** or **cadence.**

- **Rhyming poems** have rhyming words at the ends of their lines and sometimes within lines. They may use vivid **imagery** too.

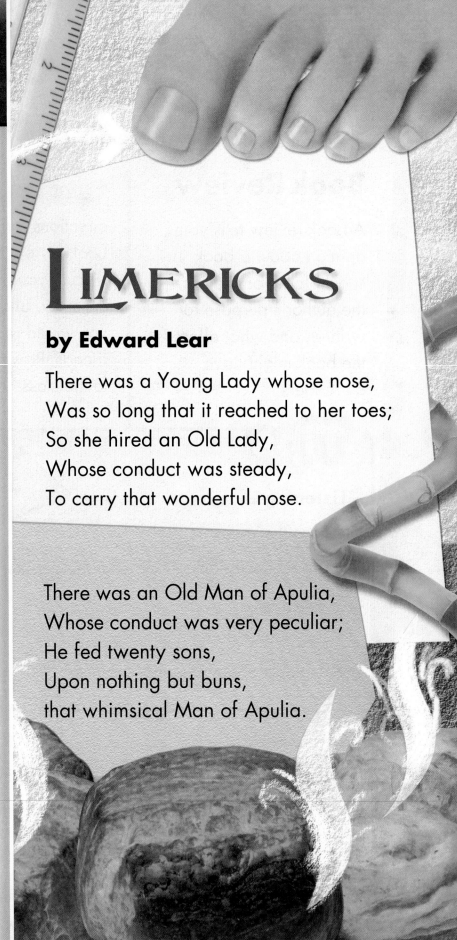

LIMERICKS

by Edward Lear

There was a Young Lady whose nose,
Was so long that it reached to her toes;
So she hired an Old Lady,
Whose conduct was steady,
To carry that wonderful nose.

There was an Old Man of Apulia,
Whose conduct was very peculiar;
He fed twenty sons,
Upon nothing but buns,
that whimsical Man of Apulia.

Written at the Po-Shan Monastery

by Hsin Ch'i-chi
translated by Irving Y. Lo

I would rather be myself:
Why pretend being someone else?
Having traveled everywhere, I've returned
   to farming.
One pine, one bamboo, is a real friend;
Mountain birds, mountain flowers are my
   brothers.

Let's Think About...

What are the characteristics of the **limericks,** and how do they create **imagery**?

Let's Think About...

What are the characteristics of the **free verse** poem, and how do they create **imagery**?

185

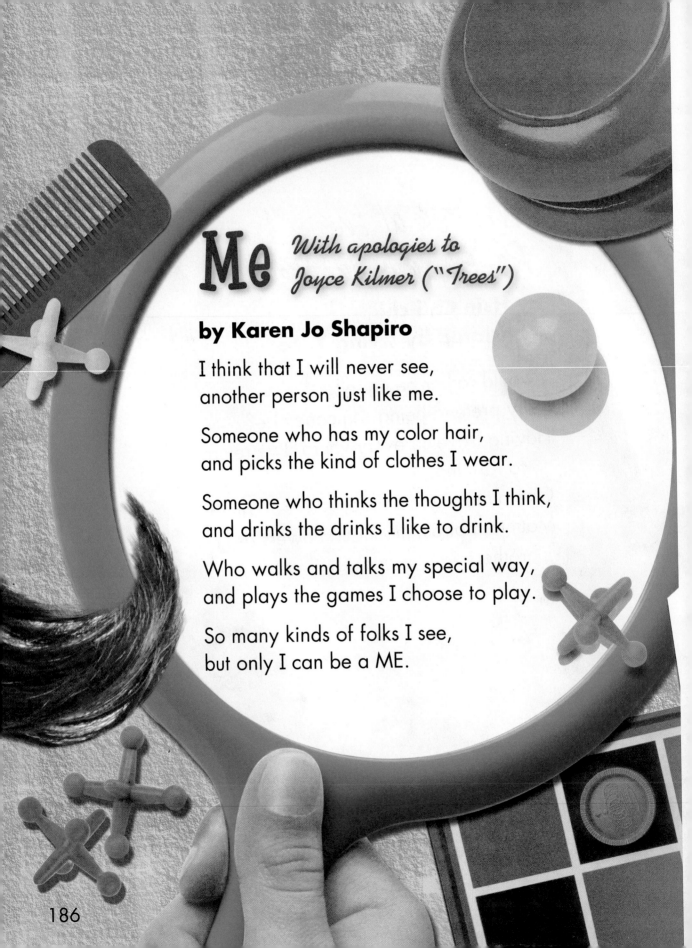

Me

With apologies to Joyce Kilmer ("Trees")

by Karen Jo Shapiro

I think that I will never see,
another person just like me.

Someone who has my color hair,
and picks the kind of clothes I wear.

Someone who thinks the thoughts I think,
and drinks the drinks I like to drink.

Who walks and talks my special way,
and plays the games I choose to play.

So many kinds of folks I see,
but only I can be a ME.

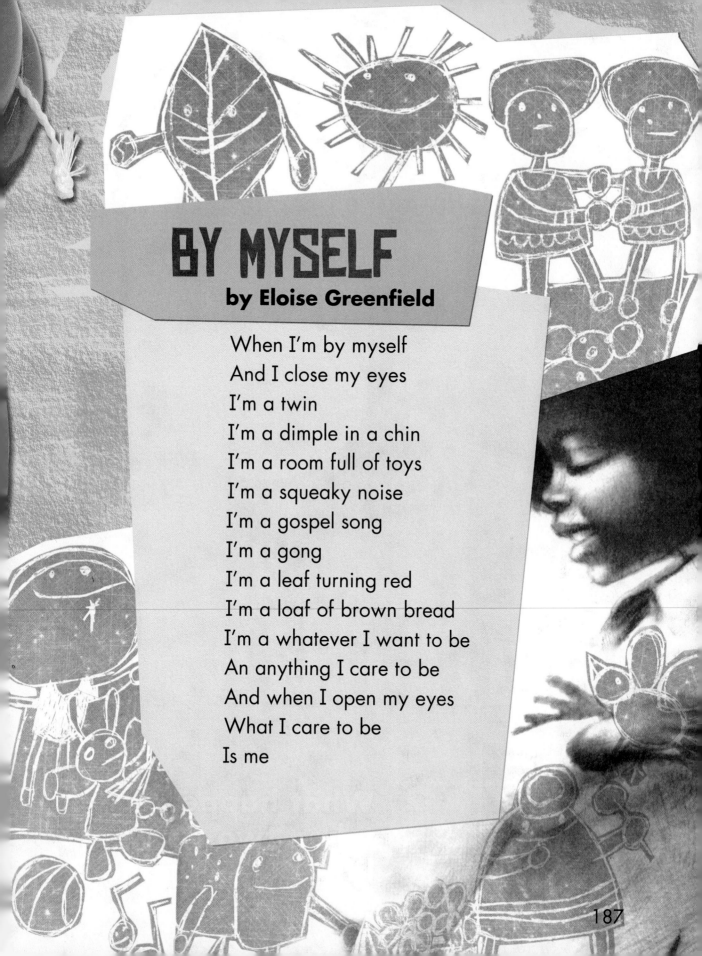

BY MYSELF

by Eloise Greenfield

When I'm by myself
And I close my eyes
I'm a twin
I'm a dimple in a chin
I'm a room full of toys
I'm a squeaky noise
I'm a gospel song
I'm a gong
I'm a leaf turning red
I'm a loaf of brown bread
I'm a whatever I want to be
An anything I care to be
And when I open my eyes
What I care to be
Is me

CULTURES

THE BIG
?

What happens when two ways of life come together?

218

Let's Talk About

Cultures and Clothing

- Ask relevant questions about how culture influences clothing.

- Work together to summarize ideas about wearing traditional clothing.

- Pose and answer questions about special clothes for holidays and traditions.

READING STREET ONLINE
CONCEPT TALK VIDEO
www.TexasReadingStreet.com

TEKS

3.1.B.1.ii Use common syllabication patterns to decode words including open syllable (CV).

Envision It! | Sounds to Know

piano

CV/VC

READING STREET ONLINE
INTERACTIVE VOCABULARY
www.TexasReadingStreet.com

Phonics

Syllable Pattern CV/VC

Words I Can Blend

ideas

violets

piano

neon

create

Sentences I Can Read

1. Yesterday I had three great ideas.

2. Ginny placed a small vase of violets on the piano.

3. Some crafters use neon to create signs.

I Can Read!

Dear Diary,

This morning I was listening to the radio on our stereo as I ate my cereal. The announcer was reporting the news as usual, when suddenly there was a message about an annual geography contest in our area.

My friend Luis and I love to study geography. I think we might be able to cooperate to create an unusual project.

I phoned Luis immediately, and we got together to discuss a variety of ideas. I'll have more on this tomorrow, Diary.

You've learned

 Syllable Pattern CV/VC

Envision It! | Skill Strategy

Skill

Strategy

Comprehension Skill

Compare and Contrast

- When you compare and contrast two or more things, you tell how they are alike and different.

- Clue words such as *like, both, also, but, however,* and *instead of* show comparisons and contrasts.

- Use what you learned about compare and contrast and the graphic organizer below as you read "The Boxed Lunch." Then write a short paragraph comparing the two lunches.

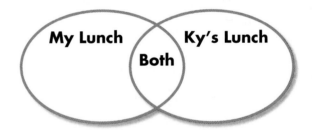

Comprehension Strategy

Visualize

While reading, look for words that help you form pictures in your mind. Forming pictures about what is happening in the story can help you enjoy and remember a story. Forming pictures in your mind can help you monitor and adjust or correct your comprehension as you read.

THE BOXED LUNCH

Ky was nervous about his first day in his new school. In Japan, Ky always brought his lunch in a bento box, which was carefully packed with eye-catching foods. Ky loved the sausage that looked like a tiny octopus. Instead of carrot sticks, he had hard-boiled eggs that looked like baby chicks just hatching. And instead of tortilla chips, he had a rice ball covered with pieces of dried seaweed so that it looked like a soccer ball.

At lunchtime, Ky's classmates began eating their lunches. Ky opened his box slowly, not sure of what his new friends would think. But they were very interested. He explained each item and showed them how to eat with chopsticks. Some boys asked to try the chopsticks. Ky promised to bring some for everyone the next day. One friend said, "I wonder how they'll work with peanut butter and jelly sandwiches."

Skill Note the clue words—*instead of*. What things are being compared? How are they the same or different?

Strategy Form a picture in your mind of a friend trying to eat a peanut butter and jelly sandwich with chopsticks. What do you see?

Your Turn!

Need a Review? See *Envision It! Handbook* for help with comparing and contrasting and visualizing.

Let's Think About..

Ready to Try It? As you read *Suki's Kimono*, use what you've learned about comparing and contrasting and visualizing to understand the text.

TEKS

3.4.B.1 Use context to determine the relevant meaning of unfamiliar words. **3.4.C.2** Identify synonyms. **3.4.C.6** Use synonyms.

Envision It! | **Words to Know**

festival

handkerchief

snug

cotton
graceful
paces
pale
rhythm

Vocabulary Strategy for

🎯 Synonyms

Context Clues Sometimes, you might read a word you don't know. The author may have used a synonym that gives you a clue to the meaning of the unknown word. A synonym is a word that has the same or almost the same meaning as another word. For example, *difficult* is a synonym for *hard*.

1. Look at the words and sentences near the unknown word. The author may have used a synonym.

2. Do you recognize a word that might be a synonym?

3. Use the synonym in place of the unknown word. Does it make sense?

Read "Pass It Down" on page 197. Use synonyms to help you understand the meanings of unknown words.

Words to Write Reread "Pass It Down." Recall a story about someone in your family. Write it down or make one up. Use words from the Words to Know list and synonyms in your story.

Pass It Down

Emily Douglas is named after her grandmother, Emily Kelly. Every summer Emily Kelly's village in Ireland held a dance festival and contest. Emily K. was eight the first time she entered the contest. She had practiced for weeks, but she was very nervous and started to worry. One shoe felt comfortably snug while the other felt too tight. When the fiddles began playing, her heart was thumping so loudly that she couldn't hear the rhythm. So she started a few paces, or steps, behind the beat. That's the way she did the entire dance!

When she finished, everyone applauded and cheered. The judges told her how graceful she was and how original her dance was! She won first prize—a pale blue cotton handkerchief embroidered with white flowers. When Emily K. came to the United States, the handkerchief was one of the few things she brought with her. Later she gave it to her granddaughter, Emily. Emily has kept the handkerchief. It makes her think about another girl named Emily.

Your Turn!

⏸ **Need a Review?** For additional help with synonyms, see *Words!*

▶ **Ready to Try It?** Read *Suki's Kimono* on pp. 198–211.

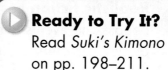

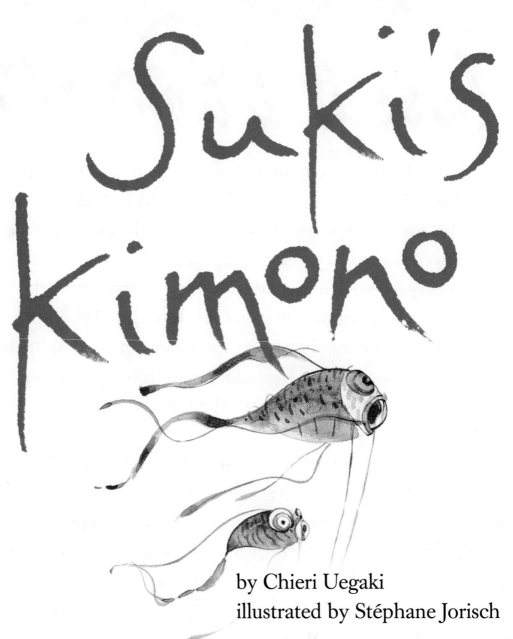

Suki's Kimono

by Chieri Uegaki
illustrated by Stéphane Jorisch

Realistic fiction has characters and events that are like
people and events in real life. As you read, decide if any
of the characters remind you of someone you know. How
does this help you to better understand the story?

Question of the Week
How does culture influence the clothes we wear?

Let's
Think
About
Reading!

On the first day of school, Suki wanted to wear her kimono. Her sisters did not approve.

"You can't wear that," said Mari. "People will think you're weird."

"You can't wear that," said Yumi. "Everyone will laugh, and no one will play with you."

"You need something new, Suki."

"You need something cool."

But Suki shook her head. She didn't care for new. She didn't care for cool. She wanted to wear her favorite thing. And her favorite thing was her kimono.

Let's Think About...

How does the art help you form a picture in your mind of Suki in her kimono?

Visualize

200

Suki's obāchan had given her the kimono. The first time Suki wore it, her obāchan took her to a street festival where they slurped bowls of slippery, cold sōmen noodles and shared a cone of crunchy, shaved ice topped with a sweet red bean sauce.

Under strings of paper lanterns, Suki joined her obāchan in a circle dance. She followed her and copied her movements, trying to be as light and as graceful. She watched the other women and children who danced, especially those who were dressed in cotton kimonos like her.

Let's Think About...

The words in this description are meant to help you visualize. What can you do if you don't understand them?
⦿ Monitor and Clarify

201

Let's **Think** About...

What words help you visualize the stage and the souvenir stand?

Visualize

Later, Suki sat so close to the stage that when the taiko drummers performed, *bom-bom-bom-bom,* she felt like she'd swallowed a ball of thunder, and her whole insides quaked and quivered.

Before they left the festival, Suki and her obāchan stopped at a souvenir stand. There were many things to choose from, but her obāchan found the prettiest thing of all—a handkerchief of pale pink linen, decorated with tiny maple leaves and cherry blossoms. When she gave it to Suki, she said, "This will help you remember our day."

Now, it was time for school. Mother checked Suki's obi one last time and took a picture of Mari, Yumi, and Suki together by the front steps.

Then, as she watched, the three sisters made their way down the block to their school. Mari and Yumi stayed several paces ahead of Suki and pretended they didn't know her.

But Suki didn't mind.

She turned and waved to her mother before she clip-clopped along in her shiny red geta, feeling very pleased in her fan-patterned blue kimono.

Let's **Think** About...

What do you know about older brothers and sisters that helps you understand Mari and Yumi?
Background Knowledge

Once in a while, Suki would lift her arms and let the butterfly sleeves flutter in the breeze. It made her feel like she'd grown her own set of wings.

When they reached the school, Mari and Yumi hurried across the yard to a group of their friends. Suki stopped and looked around. Some of the children turned and stared at her, and others giggled and pointed at her kimono.

But Suki ignored them.

Let's **Think** About...

How do you feel when others tease you? How might Suki feel?

Background Knowledge

She took a seat on a swing to wait for the bell. A girl dressed in overalls just like a pair Suki had at home sat on the swing beside her.

"Hi, Suki," said the girl.

"Hi, Penny," said Suki.

"How come you're dressed so funny?" Penny asked. "Where did you get those shoes?"

Suki lifted her feet off the sand and wiggled her toes. "I'm not dressed funny," she said. "My grandma gave me these shoes."

Suki started pumping her legs. After a moment, Penny did the same, and soon they were both swinging as fast and as high as they could. *Swoosh, swoosh,* up and up.

Let's **Think** About...

What do you think might happen next for Suki and Penny? **Predict**

Let's **Think** About...

Can you visualize why the boys say that Suki is a bat?

Visualize

When the bell rang, Suki and Penny jumped off their swings and ran to the gym for the first day assembly. Once they were finally taken to their new classroom, Suki chose a desk near the window. Penny chose a desk next to Suki.

As they waited for everyone to find a seat, two boys in front of Suki turned and snickered behind their hands. One of the boys reached over and snatched at Suki's sleeve. "Look at this," he said. "She's a bat!"

Suki felt her cheeks burn, but she did not respond. Instead, she concentrated on sitting up straight and tall, the way her obāchan always did. It was easy to do with an obi wrapped snug around her middle. Her obi was golden yellow, and in its folds Suki had tucked away her pale pink handkerchief.

"Welcome to the first grade," said the teacher. "My name is Mrs. Paggio." She smiled. "Let's introduce ourselves and tell everyone what we did this summer."

When it was her turn to speak, Suki stood up and told the teacher her name.

"Hello, Suki," said Mrs. Paggio. "What did you do this summer?"

"My grandma visited us," she said, straightening her sleeves. "She brought me my kimono and my geta." Suki raised her foot to show the teacher her wooden clog.

Let's **Think** About...

As you visualize being Suki, are you sitting straight and tall? Do you feel the obi around you? What words help you by appealing to your senses?

⊙ **Visualize**

Let's **Think** About...

Can you visualize Suki being so caught up in the dancing that she doesn't hear her classmates?

⊙ Visualize

Somewhere in the classroom, someone laughed, but Suki took a deep breath and continued. "The best thing was that she took me to a festival. And there were dancing girls, dressed like me, and they danced like this." She took a few steps and swayed her arms sideways.

"Look, now she's *dancing,*" someone said. But Suki didn't hear.

She hummed the music she remembered hearing at the festival.

She remembered how it felt to dance barefoot in the open air, on fresh-cut grass that tickled her toes.

She tried to picture the other dancers. How they moved forward in the circle with the rhythm of the music. How they stamped their feet, first right, then left, swung their arms, first up, then down. How they stepped back, and back, and back, then clapped.

When Suki couldn't remember the next step, she made it up, just to keep dancing. *One-two, one-two, one-two, stop.*

When she finished, the room seemed very quiet. Everyone was watching her.

Suki sat down, wondering if she was in trouble.

Let's **Think** About...

What words help you know how Suki dances? How did the other dancers look and act?
Visualize

Let's **Think** About...

How do the sounds and sights help you visualize what happens after Suki dances?

⊙ **Visualize**

But Mrs. Paggio said, "That was wonderful, Suki." And she started to clap.

Then, so did Penny.

And after a moment, so did the entire class.

After school, as the three sisters walked home together, Mari and Yumi grumbled about their first day.

"No one even noticed my new sweater," said Mari.

"No one even noticed my cool shoes," said Yumi.

But Suki just smiled.

As she clip-clopped along behind them, Suki pulled out the pale pink handkerchief from her obi and held it up over her head to catch the wind. And in her blue cotton kimono and in her shiny red geta, Suki danced all the way home.

Let's Think About...

What happens when Suki wears a kimono on the first day of school? Use evidence from the story to support your answer.
Summarize

TEKS

3.10.A.1 Identify language that creates a graphic visual experience. **RC-3.C.1** Monitor comprehension. **RC-3.C.2** Adjust comprehension. **Also 3.2.B.1, 3.2.B.3, 3.2.B.5, 3.2.B.7, 3.2.B.9, 3.10.A.2, 3.11.A.1, 3.11.A.2, 3.11.A.3.**

Envision It! | Retell

READING STREET ONLINE
STORY SORT
www.TexasReadingStreet.com

Think Critically

1. In "The Boxed Lunch," Ky is nervous about his first day at a new school. In what ways is Suki different from Ky? What evidence from *Suki's Kimono* tells you this? **Text to Text**

2. As you read the story, you get to know Suki. How does the author help you do that? **Think Like an Author**

3. At school, Suki meets her friend, Penny. How are Penny's clothes different from Suki's? **Compare and Contrast**

4. Imagine seeing Suki dancing in the classroom. How does she look? How do the other students look? How does the author's language help you clarify the image in your mind? What would you ask Suki if you were there? **Visualize**

5. **Look Back and Write** Look back at the question on page 199. Think about the day Suki wore her kimono to the street festival. Now write a response to the question. Provide evidence to support your answer.

TEST PRACTICE Extended Response

Chieri Uegaki

Chieri Uegaki began writing at the age of 7 when she published a family newspaper called *The Pender Street Times.* At the time, she lived on Pender Street in Vancouver, British Columbia.

Ms. Uegaki says this about her writing: "It makes me very happy to think that something I've written could touch someone and perhaps even become someone's favorite." Ms. Uegaki based *Suki's Kimono* on her relationship with her Japanese grandmother.

Ms. Uegaki offers this advice to young writers: "Listen more than you speak. Read everything and take notes."

Read more books about children like Suki.

First Day, Hooray!
by Nancy Poydar

It's Back to School We Go!
First Day Stories from Around
the World by Ellen Jackson

Use the Reader's and Writer's Notebook to record your independent reading.

213

TEKS

3.20.B.1 Write letters whose language is tailored to the audience. **3.20.B.2** Write letters whose language is tailored to the purpose. **Also: 3.20.B.3, 3.21.A.1, 3.21.A.2, 3.22.A.1.iii.1, 3.22.A.1.iii.2, 3.22.A.1.iii.3.**

Persuasive

Let's Write It!

Key Features of a Letter to the Editor

- includes the features of a letter: date, salutation, body, closing, and signature

- written to bring attention to an issue or problem

- often tries to be persuasive

**READING STREET ONLINE
GRAMMAR JAMMER**
www.TexasReadingStreet.com

Letter to the Editor

A **letter to the editor** is a letter sent to a newspaper or magazine that tries to bring attention to an issue. The student model on the next page is an example of a letter to the editor.

Writing Prompt Write a letter to the editor about an issue occurring in your community or school.

Writer's Checklist

Remember, you should . . .

☑ share your opinion or position on an issue.

☑ support your ideas with details.

☑ ask readers to take action.

☑ use a tone that fits your audience and purpose.

☑ use descriptive and limiting adjectives and articles correctly.

214

March 12, 20___

Dear Editor,

My parents told me that **the** city council is thinking about closing Trager Park. They said the city wants to sell the land so that houses can be built there. This is **a** very **bad** idea.

Trager Park is very **important** to me and the other people in my neighborhood. My friends and I play in the park almost every day, even in the winter. It's one of the **few** places in our neighborhood where we can get exercise and have a **safe** place to play. Adults also use the park to relax, visit with neighbors, have picnics, and play sports too. Without it, we'd have nowhere else nearby to do these things.

There are already lots of places for people to live in this neighborhood. We don't need any more. We need to tell the city council to save Trager Park!

Sincerely,

Gina Marchetti

Adjectives and articles are used correctly.

Writing Trait Organization Supporting details follow the main idea.

Genre A letter to the editor takes a position on an issue.

Conventions

Adjectives and Articles

Remember An **adjective** is a word that can describe a person, place, or thing. Adjectives tell more about nouns. *A, an,* and *the* are special adjectives called **articles.**

TEKS

3.13.D.1 Use text features to locate information. **3.13.D.2** Make predictions about contents of text. **3.13.D.3** Verify predictions about contents of text. **Also** 3.2.A.1, 3.2.A.2, 3.2.B.6, 3.2.B.8, 3.2.B.9, 3.12.A.1, 3.13.A.1, 3.13.B.1, 3.13.B.2, RC-3.F.1, RC-3.F.2.

Social Studies in Reading

Genre
Expository Text

- Expository texts are nonfiction. They give details and facts that support the main idea about a topic.

- Expository texts use graphic sources and text features to help the reader predict, locate, and verify information.

- Use the title, the illustration on this page, and the keywords *moccasins, berets,* and *ponchos* to predict what this selection will be about. Locate information about what the key words have in common to verify your predictions as you read.

Clothes
Bringing Cultures Together

by Elizabeth Massie

Next time you walk through town, look at the clothes people are wearing. You might see ponchos, blue jeans, and sneakers. You might see moccasins (MOK-uh-sunz), t-shirts, and berets (bur-AYZ). Many of the clothes we wear today are new designs. However, some were first made in other countries or by other cultures long ago. They have become part of modern American fashion.

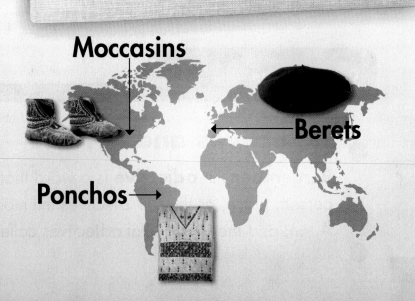

Moccasins

Berets

Ponchos →

216

South American Ponchos

Thousands of years ago, people of South America made and wore ponchos. A poncho is a square cloak. It has a hole in the middle for the wearer's head.

South American ponchos were woven out of wool. The wool came from llamas and other pack animals. The ponchos were often decorated with flowers, birds, and people. Ponchos kept the wearers warm in cold weather.

Ponchos are still part of everyday wear in many South American countries. The style is much the same as it was long ago.

During the 20th century, people in the United States began to wear ponchos. Americans liked their style and warmth. Ponchos were also adapted into rain gear. Rain ponchos are made of waterproof material. They often have hoods.

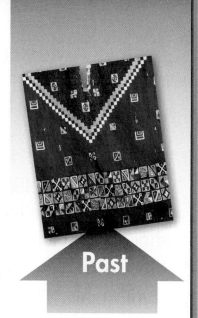

Past

The poncho above was made in South America more than two thousand years ago. You might see the ponchos below on our streets today.

Present

Let's **Think** About...

What does the title tell you about the topic and main idea? What facts and details can you find to support the main idea?
Expository Text

217

Native American Moccasins

Long ago, native people of North America made shoes out of animal hides. These shoes were called moccasins. Moccasins were tough and comfortable. They kept the wearer's feet warm. They also protected feet from cold, rough ground.

Past

Moccasin styles were different from tribe to tribe. You could tell what tribe people belonged to by looking at their shoes. For example, the Blackfeet tribe was called that because they dyed their moccasins black.

Members of the Blackfeet tribe (top) wore moccasins that were dyed black. These colorful moccasins (above) were made years ago by Native Americans. The moccasins below are similar to those worn today.

Native Americans taught European settlers how to make moccasins. Trappers and explorers wore these shoes in the wilderness. Even Lewis and Clark made and wore moccasins on their trip west.

Present

Today, Americans of many backgrounds wear moccasins. They like the soft comfort of the shoe.

Let's **Think** About...

How do the illustrations and captions verify the information from the text?
Expository Text

Let's **Think** About...

How did moccasins connect Native American cultures? How do moccasins bring together Native American cultures and ours today?
Expository Text

Basque Berets

A beret is a soft, round hat. Hundreds of years ago, the Basque (BASK) people made these hats out of wool. Basque shepherds tended their flocks in the cold mountains between France and Spain. These hats kept their heads warm.

In the 1920s, British tank soldiers started wearing black berets. The hats were comfortable. They didn't show grease stains. During World War II, some British soldiers gave American soldiers berets to wear. The hats were seen as special. Today, some units of the United States military wear berets.

Berets became popular with American women in the 1930s. Berets are still worn by men, women, and children as part of everyday outfits.

Past

British General Bernard Law Montgomery, above, popularized the use of berets during World War II. Even today, traditional clothes for Basque men, below, often include berets.

Present

Let's **Think** About...

What text feature separates the topic of this page from the topic on the previous page? What are the different topics?
Expository Text

Let's **Think** About...

Reading Across Texts Elizabeth Massie describes ponchos, moccasins, and berets in "Clothes: Bringing Cultures Together." How might she describe Suki's kimono?

Writing Across Texts Write what you think the author's description of Suki's kimono would be.

219

TEKS

3.4.D.1 Identify playful uses of language. **3.4.D.2** Apply playful uses of language. **3.29.B.1** Follow oral instructions that involve a series of related sequences of action. **3.29.B.2** Restate oral instructions that involve a series of related sequences of action. **Also 3.3.A.1, 3.3.A.2, 3.4.C.2, 3.4.C.6, 3.22.A.1.iii.1, 3.22.A.1.iii.2, 3.22.A.1.iii.3, 3.29.B.3, 3.30.A.1, 3.30.A.2, 3.31.A.1, 3.31.A.2, 3.31.A.3, 3.31.A.4, 3.31.A.5, 3.31.A.6.**

**READING STREET ONLINE
ONLINE STUDENT EDITION**
www.TexasReadingStreet.com

Vocabulary

Synonyms

Context Clues An analogy is a way to show relationships between words. Read the analogy: *take* is to *snatch* as *sway* is to *move*. *Take* and *snatch* are synonyms just like *sway* and *move* are synonyms. The relationship between words before and after *as* is the same in an analogy.

 Finish the analogy by writing a synonym from *Suki's Kimono.* Then write your own analogies. *Look* is to *stare* as *laugh* is to _____. *Shoes* is to *geta* as *outfit* is to _____. *Laugh* is to *giggle* as *copy* is to _____.

Fluency

Rate

When reading, sometimes you come to a part of a story that has more difficult words. Your rate of reading might slow down. Reviewing the difficult words and practicing reading them will help you read at an appropriate rate.

 With your partner, practice reading *Suki's Kimono*, page 201. Before you begin, practice the difficult words, such as *Suki's, obāchan, kimono,* and *sōmen noodles.* Then practice reading the entire paragraph until you can read it at an appropriate rate.

Listening and Speaking

Follow the etiquette, or rules, for conversation, including making eye contact.

Introduction

Introductions are conversations that follow rules for polite ways of meeting people in a culture.

Practice It! Think about how we make introductions in our culture. Follow oral directions for making introductions in groups. Role play other people, such as a teacher or coach, as you practice introductions.

Tips

Listening ...

- Execute multi-step directions.

Speaking ...

- Speak clearly and distinctly.

- Use adjectives and articles correctly.

Teamwork ...

- Restate the directions to the group to make sure you understand them.

- Give clear directions to your group before role playing other people.

3.29.A.1 Listen attentively to speakers. **3.29.A.2** Ask relevant questions. **3.30.A.2** Speak coherently, employing eye contact, speaking rate, volume, enunciation, and the conventions of language to communicate ideas effectively.

Let's Talk About

Comparing Cultures

- Ask questions about how cultures are alike and different.

- Express and listen to comments about cultural values.

- Pose and answer questions about cultural ties to different countries.

READING STREET ONLINE
CONCEPT TALK VIDEO
www.TexasReadingStreet.com

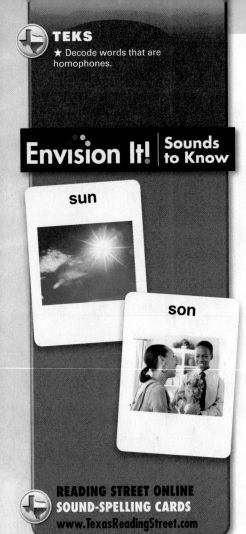

Phonics

🎯 Homophones

Words I Can Blend

stare	**stair**
rays	**raise**
chili	**chilly**

Sentences I Can Read

1. Did you see him stare at me from under the stair?

2. The golden rays of the sun helped raise my spirits.

3. Chili is my favorite food on a chilly day.

I Can Read!

My aunt would never allow an ant on a picnic. I picnicked with her and eight others last week, and the picnic was ant-free.

We were all seated on Auntie's red picnic blanket. The menu couldn't be beat: beet salad, rose hip tea, and rows of delicious tarts, and it suited me to a tee.

After we ate, I read them the tale of "How the Bear Got a Stumpy Tail." It was like a scene one might have seen in a movie.

You've learned

 Homophones

TEKS

3.2.B.5 Locate facts about stories.
3.12.A.1 Identify the topic of the text.
3.13.A.1 Identify details or facts that support the main idea. **RC-3.D.1** Make inferences about text.
RC-3.D.2 Use textual evidence to support understanding. **Also 3.14.A.1.**

Envision It! | Skill Strategy

Skill

Main Idea and Details

What is the selection all about? What details support the main idea?

Strategy

Envision It! Visual Strategies Handbook

Inferring

When we **infer** we use background knowledge with clues in the text to come up with our own ideas about what the author is trying to present.

To infer
• identify what you already know
• combine what you know with text clues to come up with your own ideas

Bicycle Safety Test

Let's **think** About Reading!

When I infer, I ask myself
• What do I already know?
• Which text clues are important?
• What is the author trying to present?

EI•20

Comprehension Skill

Main Idea and Details

• The topic is what a piece of writing is about. The main idea is the most important idea about the topic.

• Details are pieces of information that tell more about the main idea.

• Use what you learned about main idea and details and a graphic organizer like the one below as you read "The Best Game." Then use the organizer to help you write a summary of the text.

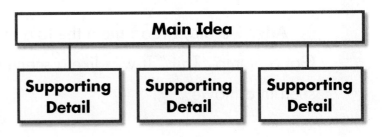

Main Idea		
Supporting Detail	**Supporting Detail**	**Supporting Detail**

Comprehension Strategy

Inferring

When you infer, you combine your background knowledge with evidence in the text to come up with your own ideas or conclusions about what the author is saying. Active readers infer the ideas, morals, lessons, and themes of a written work.

The Best Game

I think board games are the best family activity. Playing a board game with family or friends is my favorite thing to do on a rainy day. However, my sister doesn't agree. She likes playing charades with a group. To her, board games are boring.

Board games include everything you need right in the box. There is nothing to think up or to make. The rules are printed out. That's the best part! There shouldn't be any arguments among players. Thousands of board games are sold every year. The people who buy them can't all be wrong.

On the other hand, my sister says charades is a creative game. Players must think of books, movies, or songs that will stump the other team. Players have a great time using their imagination and acting.

Here you have two kinds of games, two people, and two ideas. Which game is best? You decide.

Strategy What do you think the author is trying to persuade you to think or do?

Skill What details does this paragraph include about board games?

Strategy Who do you think is better at charades—the narrator or the sister? Why do you think so?

Your Turn!

⏸ Need a Review? See the *Envision It! Handbook* for information about main ideas and details and inferring.

▶ Ready to Try It? As you read *I Love Saturdays y domingos*, use what you've learned about main ideas and details and inferring to understand the text.

227

TEKS

3.4.B.1 Use context to determine the relevant meaning of unfamiliar words.
3.4.C.4 Identify homophones.
3.4.C.8 Use homophones.

Envision It! | Words to Know

bouquet

circus

pier

difficult

nibbling

soars

swallow

READING STREET ONLINE
VOCABULARY ACTIVITIES
www.TexasReadingStreet.com

Vocabulary Strategy for

ⓢ Homophones

Context Clues You may read or hear a word you know, but the meaning doesn't make sense in the sentence. The word might be a homophone. Homophones are words that are pronounced the same but have different meanings and spellings. For example, the words *bear* and *bare* are homophones. A *bear* is "a large mammal" and *bare* means "not covered."

1. If the word you know doesn't make sense in the sentence, it might be a homophone.

2. Look at the words around it. Can you figure out another meaning?

3. Try the new meaning in the sentence. Does it make sense?

Read "Island Vacation" on page 229. Use context clues to determine the meanings of homophones.

Words to Write Reread "Island Vacation." What kind of places are you interested in traveling to? Write about your interest. Use homophones and words from the Words to Know list.

Island Vacation

Every summer my family goes to Cherry Island for a vacation. It is my favorite place in the whole world. Cherry Island is a small island with just a few cabins and houses. You can't drive to Cherry Island because there is no bridge. You have to take a boat.

My sisters and I play all over the island. We like to pick wildflowers and make a bouquet for our mother. We also like to pack a picnic lunch and eat it down by the water. We sit on the pier, nibbling on sandwiches. Sometimes a gull soars over us while we eat. Once my sister, Jane, threw some pieces of bread in the water. A huge crowd of gulls came and tried to eat the bread. It was like a circus, so crowded and noisy! Now I am always careful not to leave my sandwich on the pier because I know a gull might grab it and swallow it in one big bite.

At the end of our vacation, it is always difficult to say good-bye to Cherry Island. As the boat pulls away, I start counting the days until I can come back again.

Your Turn!

❚❚ Need a Review? For additional help with homophones, see *Words!*

▶ Ready to Try It? Read *I Love Saturdays y domingos* on pp. 230–245.

I Love Saturdays y domingos

by Alma Flor Ada
illustrated by Claudia Degliuomini

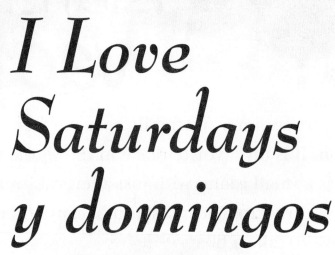

Question of the Week
**How are cultures
alike and different?**

231

Saturdays and Sundays are my special days.
I call Sundays *domingos,* and you'll soon see why.

On Saturdays, I go visit Grandpa and Grandma.
Grandpa and Grandma are my father's parents.
They are always happy to see me.
I say, "Hi, Grandpa! Hi, Grandma!" as I walk in.
And they say, "Hello, sweetheart! How are you?
Hello, darling!"

I spend *los domingos* with *Abuelito y Abuelita.*
Abuelito y Abuelita are my mother's parents.
They are always happy to see me.

I say: —*¡Hola, Abuelito! ¡Hola, Abuelita!*— as I get
out of the car.

And they say: —*¡Hola, hijita! ¿Cómo estás?*
¡Hola, mi corazón!

On Saturdays, Grandma serves me
breakfast: milk, scrambled eggs, and pancakes.

The pancakes are spongy. I like to put
a lot of honey on my pancakes.

Grandma asks me, "Do you like them sweetheart?"
And I answer, "Oh, yes, Grandma, I love them!"

Los domingos,
Abuelita serves me
a large glass of papaya
juice and a plate of eggs
called *huevos rancheros.*
The *huevos rancheros* are wonderful.
No one makes them better than *Abuelita.*

Abuelita asks me if I like them: —¿*Te gustan, hijita?*

First I need to swallow, and then I answer: —*Sí,*
Abuelita, ¡me encantan!

Grandma has a tabby cat. Her name is Taffy. I roll on the carpet and call, "Come, Taffy, let's play."

Abuelita has a dog. His name is *Canelo.* When I go out to the garden, *Canelo* follows me. I call out to him: —*Ven, Canelo. ¡Vamos a jugar!*

Grandma collects owls. Every time that she and Grandpa go on a trip she brings back an owl for her collection.

Each one is different. I count them: One, two, three, four, five, six, seven, eight, nine, ten, eleven, twelve…to see how her collection is growing.

Abuelita loves animals. When she was little she lived on a farm. She is glad that now they have a large backyard so she can keep chickens.

One of her hens has been sitting on her eggs for many days. Now the chicks have hatched. I count them: — ***Uno, dos, tres, cuatro, cinco, seis, siete, ocho, nueve, diez, once, doce…***

236

One Saturday, Grandpa and Grandma play a movie about the circus for me on their VCR.

"I like the circus, especially the lions and tigers," says Grandpa.

"And the giraffes," says Grandma.

When Grandma and Grandpa ask me what part I like best, I answer:

"I like the mother elephant and her little elephant best."

Un domingo, Abuelito y Abuelita take me to a real circus.

—Me encanta el circo, Abuelito—I say.

—Mira los leones y los tigres—says Abuelita.

—¡Y las jirafas!—Abuelito adds.

When they ask me what I like best, I say:

—La mamá elefanta y su elefantito.

Grandpa has a beautiful aquarium. He keeps it very clean.

"Look at that big fish!" Grandpa says, and points to a big yellow fish.

"I like the little ones," I answer.

It's fun to watch the big and little fish. I watch, my nose pressed against the glass, for a long time.

Abuelito takes me to the seashore. He loves to walk by the ocean. We sit on the pier and look down at the water.

—*Mira el pez grande*— *Abuelito* says. He points to a big fish.

—*Me gustan los chiquitos*— I answer, and show him some little silver fish that are nibbling by a rock.

We stay at the pier *un buen rato,* for a long time.

Grandpa knows I love surprises.

One Saturday, when I arrive, he has blown up a bunch of balloons for me. The balloons look like a big bouquet of flowers: yellow, red, orange, blue, and green.

"What fun, Grandpa" I say, and run with my balloons up and down the yard.

Un domingo, Abuelito also has a special surprise for me. He has made me a kite. The kite is made of colored paper and looks like a giant butterfly: *amarillo, rojo, anaranjado, azul, y verde.*

—¡*Qué divertido, Abuelito!*— I say. And I hold on to the string of my kite as it soars high in the air.

239

Grandpa likes to tell stories. He tells me about how his mother, his father, and his older brother came to America in a big ship from Europe.

He also tells me about growing up in New York City. When he was a young boy, he delivered papers early in the morning, before school, to help his family.

Abuelito also likes to tell stories. He tells me about the times when he was growing up on a *rancho* in Mexico. He worked in the fields when he was very young.

He also tells me how his father went to Texas, looking for work, and *Abuelito* was left in charge of his family. And he was only twelve!

Grandma loves to tell me about her grandmother whose parents came to California in a covered wagon. It was a long and difficult trip.

Grandma's grandmother was born on the trail. Later she became a teacher.

Grandma is very proud of her grandmother. I feel proud too.

Abuelita loves to tell me about her *abuelita* and her *mamá*. Her *abuelita*'s family are Native Americans.

Abuelita is very proud of her Indian blood because the Indians really know how to love the land.

Abuelita feels *orgullo,* and I feel *orgullo,* too.

It's my birthday. This time, Grandpa and Grandma come to our house. They have brought me a new doll.

Grandma has made her a dress in my favorite color.

"What a beautiful doll, Grandpa!" I tell him, and I give him a big kiss.

"What a pretty blue dress! Thank you, Grandma, I love you very much!" I say.

242

Abuelito y Abuelita also come.

Abuelito has made me a dollhouse.

Abuelita has made me a dress for my birthday party. The dress is exactly like my doll's dress.

Abuelita and Grandma must have planned this surprise together!

—*¡Qué linda casa de muñecas, Abuelito! ¡Gracias!*— I say, and give Abuelito a big hug.

—*¡Y qué bonito vestido azul, Abuelita! El azul es mi color favorito*— I tell her. —*Gracias, Abuelita. Te quiero mucho.*

All my cousins and friends come to the party. We gather together to break the *piñata* that my Mom has filled with gifts.

   Abuelito is holding the rope to make the *piñata* go up and down.

   We all line up. The younger kids in front.

   Abuelita covers our eyes with a folded scarf so that we can't see the *piñata*.

Some say, "Happy
birthday!" and some say
—¡*Feliz cumpleaños!*
For me it's a wonderful
day, *un día maravilloso*.

245

Envision It! Retell

READING STREET ONLINE
STORY SORT
www.TexasReadingStreet.com

Think Critically

1. In the story, the author writes about a girl visiting her grandparents on the weekends. Do you ever visit with your grandparents or other relatives? What you do during your visits? What would you like to do if you had a chance?

   Text to Self

2. The author of *I Love Saturdays y domingos* has a purpose. What do you think the author's purpose is for writing this story? What would you ask the author if you had a chance?

   Think Like an Author

3. Look back at the story. What do you think is the main idea? Find details that support your choice. **Main Idea and Details**

4. What do you think the author feels about different cultures and families? Explain your answer using details from the story. **Inferring**

5. **Look Back and Write** Look back at the question on page 231. How are the girl's two sets of grandparents alike? How are they different? Use information from the selection to write about how they each celebrate their culture. Provide evidence to support your answer.

    TEST PRACTICE **Extended Response**

Meet the Author

Alma Flor Ada

Alma Flor Ada was born in Cuba and has lived in Spain and Peru. She currently lives in California and teaches at the University of San Francisco. Ms. Ada writes most of her books, such as *Jordi's Star* and *Gathering the Sun*, in both English and Spanish and her daughter does a lot of her translations!

Use the *Reader's and Writer's Notebook* to record your independent reading.

TEKS

3.19.A.1 Write about important personal experiences. **3.22.A.1.iii.1** Use and understand descriptive adjectives in the context of reading, writing, and speaking.

Let's Write It!

Key Features of a Personal Narrative

- tells about a personal experience
- written in first person
- usually written in the order in which the events happened

READING STREET ONLINE GRAMMAR JAMMER
www.TexasReadingStreet.com

Personal Narrative

A **personal narrative** is a true story about a personal memory or other experience. The student model on the next page is an example of a personal narrative.

Writing Prompt *I Love Saturdays y Domingos* is a personal narrative about the cultures in a girl's family. Think about the things that are important to you, such as happy memories. Now write a personal narrative about one of your happy memories.

Writer's Checklist

Remember, you should . . .

✓ choose a real personal memory.

✓ explain your thoughts and feelings using descriptive adjectives.

✓ add details that will appeal to your audience.

✓ make sure your writing is clear and well-organized.

The Camping Trip

Last year, my **older** brother Darrell and I went on a camping trip for four days with our aunt and uncle. It was exciting because we live in a big city, so we don't get a chance to spend a lot of time in the woods.

Our parents put us on a train from Chicago to Grand Rapids, Michigan. I was nervous about riding a train without my parents, but I didn't tell Darrell. When the train pulled into the station, my aunt and uncle were waiting for us. They had all the camping equipment stuffed in the car.

For the next four days I did lots of really cool things. I made a big campfire with Darrell and my uncle. Everyone went on hikes, but I went on **longer** hikes than Darrell. Compared to Darrell, my aunt, and my uncle, I took the **longest** swim in the lake.

Being in the woods is a lot different than being in the city. It's quiet. Even though I wasn't nervous on the train ride home, Chicago seemed a little more crowded when we got back.

Genre A **personal narrative** tells about a true personal memory.

Writing Trait Conventions Consistent verb tense helps make meaning clear.

Comparative and superlative adjectives are used correctly.

Conventions

Comparatives and Superlatives

Remember Comparative adjectives compare two people, places, things, or ideas. **Superlative adjectives** compare three or more people, places, things, or ideas.

249

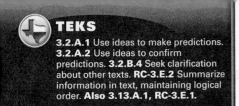

TEKS

3.2.A.1 Use ideas to make predictions. **3.2.A.2** Use ideas to confirm predictions. **3.2.B.4** Seek clarification about other texts. **RC-3.E.2** Summarize information in text, maintaining logical order. **Also 3.13.A.1, RC-3.E.1.**

Social Studies in Reading

Genre
Textbook

- Textbooks provide information about a specific subject in a logical order.

- Textbooks include facts and details that describe important ideas about the specific subject.

- Textbooks have text features to help readers predict, locate, and verify information. Graphic sources show information visually.

- Use the text features as you read "Communities Celebrate Cultures" to predict the topic and the summarize the important ideas.

Communities Celebrate Cultures

Many communities have celebrations that started in other countries. The celebrations honor the ethnic groups who helped build the community. These celebrations are sometimes called ethnic celebrations.

Cinco de Mayo (SIN ko day MY oh) means the fifth of May. It is a Mexican holiday that celebrates the victory of the Mexican people over the French who invaded their country. After a battle on May 5, 1862, the French left Mexico.

For many people, the holiday is a symbol. It shows that the people of Mexico could become free of rulers from other countries.

Today, many people in Mexico and other countries celebrate Cinco de Mayo. In the United States people dance in colorful clothes. They play music on guitars and eat traditional Mexican food. They show that they are proud to be Mexican Americans.

St. Patrick's Day is celebrated in many communities around the United States and the world. The holiday started as a religious holiday in Ireland, a country in Europe.

On St. Patrick's Day both Irish and non-Irish people celebrate Irish culture. Some people honor Irish culture by wearing green clothing, watching parades, and eating food that is dyed green.

REVIEW In what ways are Cinco de Mayo and St. Patrick's Day alike? How are they different?

Let's **Think** About...

How do the "Review" questions and the "Summarize the Lesson" box help you learn the important ideas on these pages? **Textbook**

Let's **Think** About...

Reading Across Texts The girl in *I Love Saturdays y domingos* tells about some family traditions that are different from those mentioned in this textbook article. Why do you think this is so?

Writing Across the Texts Make a list of the celebrations and traditions you have learned about.

Summarize the Lesson

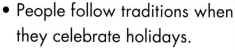

- People follow traditions when they celebrate holidays.
- Families celebrate religious and nonreligious holidays.
- Communities celebrate to honor ethnic groups who helped build their communities.

TEKS

3.4.C.4 Identify homophones.
3.4.C.8 Use homophones. **3.29.B.1**
Follow oral instructions that involve
a series of related sequences of
action. **3.29.B.2** Restate oral
instructions that involve a series of
related sequences of action. **3.29.B.3**
Give oral instructions that involve a
series of related sequences of action.
Also 3.3.A.1, 3.3.A.2, 3.29.A.1,
3.29.A.2, 3.30.A.1, 3.30.A.2,
3.31.A.1, 3.31.A.2, 3.31.A.3,
3.31.A.4, 3.31.A.5, 3.31.A.6.

Let's Learn It!

READING STREET ONLINE
ONLINE STUDENT EDITION
www.TexasReadingStreet.com

Vocabulary

Homophones

Context Clues Homophones are words that sound the same, but have different meanings and spellings, such as *pause* and *paws*. Context clues can help you determine the meanings of homophones.

 As you read *I Love Saturdays y domingos*, make a list of three or four words that have homophones. Write both the word and its homophone. Then write down the definition of each homophone.

Fluency

Accuracy

It is important to read with accuracy so you can understand the text. Reading each word as it is written on the page makes this possible. Listen to yourself as you read to make sure what you are reading makes sense.

Practice It! With a partner, practice reading aloud *I Love Saturdays y domingos*, page 238. Help each other pronounce difficult words correctly. How many words did you misread? Reread the section. Did your accuracy improve?

Listening and Speaking

Drama

In a dramatization, people act out scenes from a story or play. Actors can use clues in the dialogue to show the emotions of the characters.

Practice It! Work in groups to write a dramatization of *I Love Saturdays y domingos*. Choose one event in the story to create a script for a scene in the dramatization. Determine the character assignments, including a narrator. Perform your scene in front of the class.

Tips

Listening ...

• Determine their purpose for listening, such as for enjoyment.

• Listen to identify emotional clues.

Speaking ...

• Speak at an appropriate pace.

• Use expression and emotion.

Teamwork ...

• Make suggestions to help improve the performance.

• Give, follow, and restate directions for staging the dramatization.

253

TEKS
3.29.A.1 Listen attentively to speakers. **3.29.A.3** Make pertinent comments. **3.31.A.1** Participate in teacher-led discussions by posing questions with appropriate detail. **Also 3.31.A.2.**

Oral Vocabulary

Let's Talk About

Adapting to a New Culture

- Make and listen to comments about adapting to a new home or neighborhood.

- Ask about and describe new traditions.

- Pose and answer questions about what it might be like to adapt to a new culture.

READING STREET ONLINE
CONCEPT TALK VIDEO
www.TexasReadingStreet.com

Envision It! | Sounds to Know

thought
ough

daughter
augh

audience

ball
au

chalk
a

ball

hawk
al

aw

Phonics

Vowel Patterns *a, au, aw, al, augh, ough*

Words I Can Blend

ought

daughter

ball

fault

yawned

walking

Sentences I Can Read

1. The woman ought to buy her daughter a new dress.

2. He missed the ball, but it wasn't his fault.

3. Tracy yawned while walking home.

I Can Read!

One fall day at school I saw Paula draw a picture on the sidewalk with chalk. I talked to her about what she had drawn, and she said she did it because it brought her joy.

Paula calmly taught me how to crawl around on the pavement and launch my own art. I thought I ought to try it. My first drawing was awful, but I sought to improve.

Now I wouldn't call all my drawings works of art, but I have improved in small ways.

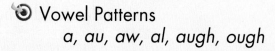

You've learned

🔵 Vowel Patterns
    a, au, aw, al, augh, ough

TEKS

3.2.B.3 Seek clarification about stories. **3.8.A.1** Sequence the plot's main events. **3.8.A.2** Summarize the plot's main events. **RC-3.C.1** Monitor comprehension. **RC-3.C.2** Adjust comprehension. **Also 3.2.C.2, 3.2.C.3, RC-3.E.1, RC-3.E.2.**

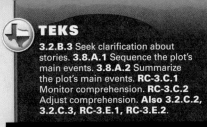

Skill

Strategy

READING STREET ONLINE
ENVISION IT! ANIMATIONS
www.TexasReadingStreet.com

Comprehension Skill

Sequence

- To sequence the events in a story, tell the order in which events happen.

- Transition words such as *first, next, then,* and *finally* are often used to sequence events in a story.

- Use what you learned about sequence and a graphic organizer like the one below as you read "Moving Day." Then write a paragraph to summarize the story in order, maintaining the meaning of the story.

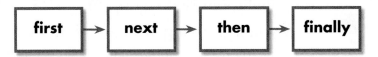

Comprehension Strategy

Monitor and Clarify

When reading, stop after a paragraph or two and ask, "What did I learn?" "What doesn't make sense?" and "How does this connect to what I already know?" Reread aloud to clarify or read on to look for answers. Monitoring and clarifying will help you understand what you read.

MOVING DAY

Tom's family was getting ready to move to Chicago. Tom's mom was starting a new job in two weeks. There was a lot to do to get ready for moving day!

Mom and Dad decided to pack things that they didn't need every day. Tom would help. First, he helped his dad pack tools in the garage. After that, Tom helped his mom carefully wrap special treasures from the attic. When they were done, the house seemed strange and there were boxes everywhere.

Skill Here are some clue words. In what sequence have events happened so far?

The day before moving day Tom got up early to pack his own clothes. After lunch, Tom packed all of his toys and other belongings. When Tom went to bed that night, his room was almost empty.

Moving day finally arrived. While the movers loaded all of their belongings into the truck, Tom helped his parents make sure nothing was forgotten. It had been a tremendous amount of work to get ready for moving day!

Strategy If you lost track of the events, what can you do to adjust or correct your comprehension?

Your Turn!

Need a Review?
See the *Envision It! Handbook* for help with sequence and monitoring and clarifying.

Ready to Try It?
As you read *Good-Bye, 382 Shin Dang Dong*, use what you've learned about sequence and monitoring and clarifying.

TEKS

3.4.B.1 Use context to determine the relevant meanings of unfamiliar words.

Envision It! | Words to Know

airport

delicious

raindrops

cellar
curious
described
farewell
homesick
memories

Vocabulary Strategy for

Compound Words

Word Structure You may come across a long word when you are reading. Look closely at it. Do you see two small words in it? Then it is a compound word. Use the two small words to figure out the meaning of the compound word. For example, a *classroom* is a room where a class is held.

1. Divide the compound word into its two small words.

2. Think of the meaning of each small word and then put the two meanings together. Does this help you understand the meaning of the compound word?

3. Try the new meaning in the context of the sentence. Does it make sense?

Read "How to Do a Move" on page 261. Use the two small words in each compound word to help you figure out its meaning.

Words to Write Reread "How to Do a Move." Write about what you think it would be like to move to a new place. Use words from the Words to Know list.

How to Do a Move

So you're moving. When you heard the news, did your stomach drop to the cellar? Did you become homesick before you had even left? Don't wait until you get to the airport to get ready for a move. Start planning now.

- Recognize that, just as raindrops are wet, you are going to be upset and unhappy. But that's OK. Just set a time limit. When the time is up, do something to make yourself feel better.

- Keep the memories. Take pictures of your old home, neighborhood, and friends. Make a scrapbook.

- Have a farewell party. Exchange addresses and telephone numbers with your friends.

- Be curious about your new town. Research the area at the library and on the Internet. It might be described in guidebooks. It might be known for a famous person or a delicious food. The more you know about the place, the more familiar it will feel when you get there.

Your Turn!

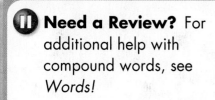 **Need a Review?** For additional help with compound words, see *Words!*

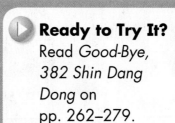 **Ready to Try It?** Read *Good-Bye, 382 Shin Dang Dong* on pp. 262–279.

Good-Bye,

382 Shin Dang Dong

by Frances Park and Ginger Park

illustrated by Yangsook Choi

Genre

Realistic fiction tells about events that could happen in real life. Does anything in this selection remind you of an event from your life?

Question of the Week
Why is it hard to adapt to a new culture?

My heart beats in two places: Here, where I live, and also in a place where I once lived. You see, I was born in Korea. One day my parents told me we were moving to America. I was eight years old, old enough to keep many lovely memories of my birthplace alive in my heart forever. But one very sad memory stays with me too. The day I cried, "Good-bye, 382 Shin Dang Dong!"

On that summer day I woke up to the sound of light rain tapping on my window. The monsoon season was coming. I didn't even need to open my eyes to know that. It was that time of year. It was also time to move.

In a few hours, I would be on an airplane.

When I opened my eyes, my heart sank. My bedroom was so bare! No hand-painted scrolls or colorful fans on my walls. No silk cushions or straw mats on my floor. All my possessions were packed away in a big brown box marked "Lovely Things."

I frowned and listened to the raindrops. One, two, three. . . . Soon the thick of the monsoon would arrive, and a thousand raindrops would hit our clay-tiled roof all at once. But I wouldn't be here to listen to them. I would be halfway around the world in a strange, foreign place called 112 Foster Terrace, Brighton, Massachusetts, U.S.A.

My parents were very excited.

"Jangmi, you will like America," Dad tried to assure me.

"Are the seasons the same?" I wondered.

"Oh, yes."

"With monsoon rains?"

"No, Jangmi, no monsoon rains."

"No friends either," I moaned.

"You will make many new friends in America," Mom promised me, "in your new home."

But I loved my home right here! I didn't want to go to America and make new friends. I didn't want to leave my best friend, Kisuni.

After breakfast, Kisuni and I ran out into the rain and to the open market. Monsoon season was also the season for sweet, yellow melons called *chummy*. Kisuni and I would often peel and eat chummy under the willow tree that stood outside my bedroom window. But today, the chummy were for guests who were coming over for a farewell lunch.

At the market we peered into endless baskets and took our time choosing the ripest, plumpest chummy we could find.

"Do they have chummy in America?" Kisuni wondered.

"No," I replied. "But my mom says they have melons called *honeydew*."

"Honeydew," Kisuni giggled. "What a funny name!"

Soon after we returned, family and friends began to arrive, carrying pots and plates of food. One by one they took off their shoes, then entered the house. Grandmother was dressed in her most special occasion *hanbok.* She set up the long *bap sang* and before I could even blink, on it were a big pot of dumpling soup and the prettiest pastel rice cakes I had ever seen. Kisuni and I peeled and sliced our chummy and carefully arranged the pieces on a plate.

Then everybody ate and sang traditional Korean songs and celebrated in a sad way. Love and laughter and tears rippled through our house. How I wanted to pack these moments into a big brown box and bring them with me to America.

Kisuni and I sneaked outside and sat beneath the willow tree. We watched the rain with glum faces.

"Kisuni, I wish we never had to move from this spot," I said.

"Me, too," she sighed. "Jangmi, how far away is America?"

"My mom says that it's halfway around the world. And my dad told me that when the moon is shining here, the sun is shining there. That's how far apart we'll be," I moaned.

"That's really far," Kisuni moaned back.

We watched the rain and grew more glum than ever. Then Kisuni perked up.

"So when you're awake, I'll be asleep. And when I'm awake, you'll be asleep," she declared. "At least we'll always know what the other one is doing."

That moment our faces brightened. But a moment later we had to say good-bye.

Kisuni held back her tears. "Promise you'll write to me, Jangmi."

"I promise, Kisuni."

It was time to go to the airport.

"Kimpo Airport," Dad instructed the taxi driver.

The taxi slowly pulled away. I looked at our beautiful home one last time. Like rain on the window, tears streaked down my face.

"Good-bye, 382 Shin Dang Dong!" I cried.

On the long ride to the airport, Dad asked me, "Do you want to know what your new home looks like?"

"Okay," I shrugged.

"Let's see," Dad began, "it's a row house."

"A house that's attached to other houses," Mom explained.

"And inside the house are wooden floors," Dad added.

"No *ondal* floors?" I asked him. "How will we keep warm in the winter without ondal floors?"

"There are radiators in every room!" Mom said with an enthusiastic clap. "And a fireplace in the living room! Imagine!"

No, I could not imagine that. In our home we had a fire in the cellar called the *ondal.* It stayed lit all the time. The heat from the ondal traveled through underground pipes and kept our wax-covered floors warm and cozy. A fireplace in the living room sounded peculiar to me.

"And the rooms are separated by wooden doors," Mom added.

"No rice-paper doors?" I wondered.

My parents shook their heads. "No, Jangmi."

My eyes closed with disappointment. I had a hard time picturing this house. Would it ever feel like home?

On the airplane, I sat by the window. We flew over rice fields and clay-tiled roofs. Already I felt homesick.

The next thing I knew, we were flying over the ocean. At first I could see fishing boats rocking in the waters. As we climbed higher into the clouds, the boats grew smaller and smaller. Suddenly, the world looked very big to me.

"Good-bye, 382 Shin Dang Dong," I cried again.

Dad sat back in his seat and began to read an American newspaper. The words were all foreign.

"Dad," I asked, "how will I ever learn to understand English?"

"It's not so hard," he said. "Would you like to learn an English word?"

"Okay," I sighed.

After a pause, Dad came up with—

"Rose."

"Rose?" I repeated. "What does that mean?"

"That's the English translation of your Korean name," Mom said.

"Rose means Jangmi?" I asked.

"Yes," my parents nodded.

"Rose," I said over and over.

"Would you like to adopt Rose as your American name?" Mom asked me.

"No, I like *my* name," I insisted.

On a foggy morning four days later, we arrived in Massachusetts. After we gathered our luggage, we climbed into an airport taxi.

Even through the fog, I could see that things were very different in America. There were big, wide roads called *highways*. The rooftops were shingled instead of clay-tiled. People shopped in glass-enclosed stores instead of open markets. No rice fields, no monsoon rains. So many foreign faces.

Slowly, the taxi pulled up to a row house on a quiet street. Red brick steps led up to a wooden door.

"Here we are, Jangmi," Dad said, "112 Foster Terrace, Brighton, Massachusetts, U.S.A."

The house was just as my parents had described. I took off my shoes and walked on wooden floors. They felt very cold. I opened wooden doors. They felt very heavy. Outside, the fog had lifted. But inside, everything felt dark and strange.

"Look," Dad pointed out the window, "there's a tree just like the one at home."

"No, it's not, Dad. It's not a willow tree," I said.

"No," he agreed. "It's a maple tree. But isn't it beautiful?"

382 Shin Dang Dong, 382 Shin Dang Dong. I wanted to go home to 382 Shin Dang Dong right now. Only a knock at the door saved me from tears.

Mom announced, "The movers are here!"

The house quickly filled up with furniture and big brown boxes. The box marked "Lovely Things" was the last to arrive.

I unpacked all my possessions. I hung my hand-painted scrolls and colorful fans on the walls. I placed my silk cushions and straw mats on the floor.

Then came another knock. To our surprise a parade of neighbors waltzed in carrying plates of curious food. There were pink-and-white iced cakes and warm pans containing something called *casseroles*.

A girl my age wandered up to me with a small glass bowl. Inside the bowl were colorful balls. They smelled fruity.

She pointed to a red ball and said, "Watermelon!" She pointed to an orange ball and said, "Cantaloupe!" Lastly she pointed to a green ball and said, "Honeydew!"

I took a green ball and tasted it. Mmm . . . it was as sweet and delicious as chummy.

The girl asked me a question. But I couldn't understand her.

"She wants to know what kind of fruit you eat in Korea," Dad stepped in.

"Chummy," I replied.

"Chummy," the girl repeated, then giggled—just like Kisuni!

She asked me another question.

"She wants to know your name," Dad said.

Maybe someday I would adopt Rose as my American name. But not today.

"Jangmi," I replied.

"Jangmi," the girl smiled. "My name is Mary."

"Mary," I smiled back.

I had made a new friend.

Later, when all the guests had gone, I went outside and sat under the maple tree. Dad was right, it *was* beautiful. Maybe someday Mary and I would sit beneath this tree and watch the rain fall. And maybe I would come to love it as much as our willow tree back home in Korea. But not today.

I began to write.

Dear Kisuni. . . .

My best friend was so far away from me. So very, very far. But at least I knew where Kisuni was and what she was doing. She was halfway around the world, sleeping to the sound of a thousand raindrops hitting her clay-tiled roof all at once.

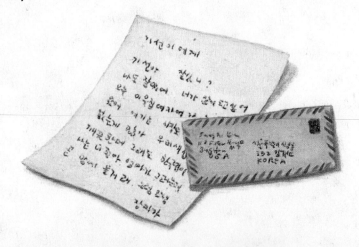

TEKS

3.8.A.1 Sequence the plot's main events. **3.2.B.3** Seek clarification about stories. **3.2.C.2** Monitor comprehension, making corrections when that understanding breaks down. **Also 3.2.B.1, 3.2.C.3, 3.8.A.2, RC-3.C.1, RC-3.C.2.**

Envision It! Retell

**READING STREET ONLINE
STORY SORT**
www.TexasReadingStreet.com

Think Critically

1. Think about moving. Tell how you or someone you know feels about moving. Explain why. **Text to Self**

2. Why do you think the authors wrote this story? Look at the Meet the Authors on page 281 for ideas. **Think Like an Author**

3. Make a time line showing the sequence of events during Jangmi's first day in her new home. **Sequence**

4. Was anything in this story confusing at first? How did you figure out the parts that were unclear? Did reading on, creating sensory images, using background knowledge, or asking questions help you? **Monitor and Clarify**

5. **Look Back and Write** Look back at the question on page 263. Think about Jangmi's life at 382 Shin Dang Dong. Now write a paragraph telling why she might have a hard time adapting to a new culture. Provide evidence to support your answer.

 **TEST PRACTICE** **Extended Response**

280

Frances and Ginger Park

Frances and Ginger Park are sisters. They often work as a team to create a book.

Ginger Park, the younger sister, loves to tell stories. Frances Park is more of a poet. She says, "I've always been in love with the beauty of language. For me, it's music—my way of playing an instrument." Together, they have written books for both children and adults.

Although their parents came from Korea, Frances and Ginger Park were born near Washington, D.C. The sisters own a chocolate shop in Washington, D.C., called Chocolate Chocolate. People often stop by to talk about their books. "We pack up their truffles, and then talk books," says Frances.

Read two more books by Frances Park and Ginger Park.

My Freedom Trip

Where on Earth Is My Bagel?

Use the Reader's and Writer's Notebook to record your independent reading.

281

TEKS

3.18.B Write poems that convey sensory details using the conventions of poetry **3.22.A.1.iv.1** Use and understand adverbs about time in the context of reading, writing, and speaking. **Also: 3.22.A.1.iv.2.**

Let's Write It!

Key Features of a Free Verse Poem

- words arranged in lines
- no fixed rhyme scheme
- may or may not have stanzas

READING STREET ONLINE
GRAMMAR JAMMER
www.TexasReadingStreet.com

Descriptive

Free Verse Poem

A **poem** is made up of words arranged in lines to create rhythm and express feelings. Most forms of poetry have a particular rhythm and rhyme scheme.

Free verse poetry is a form of poetry that does not have fixed patterns of rhyme or rhythm. The student model on the next page is an example of a free verse poem.

Writing Prompt Think about a time you were new to something or someplace. Write a free verse poem about the experience.

Writer's Checklist

Remember, you should . . .

☑ tell how you felt about the experience.

☑ rhyme lines only if you choose to.

☑ use strong describing words and figurative language.

☑ use adverbs about time and manner correctly.

282

Stir-Fry

I didn't want stir-fry,
But I ate it anyway,
Quickly, fast—
Because I was hungry.

The **next** time I ate stir-fry,
I was as hungry as a bear.
At first, I ate **fast.**
Then I ate **carefully,**
Looking at the rainbow of vegetables.
I didn't want stir-fry
Before I ate it.
Later on I liked it,
The thick sauce **beautifully**
Placed on my rice
Like a steaming crown.

**Genre
Free verse
poetry** uses no fixed rhyming pattern.

Adverbs, including those about time and manner, are used correctly.

**Writing Trait
Word Choice**
Figurative language compares unlike things.

Conventions

Adverbs

Remember An **adverb** is a word that can tell when, where, or how something happens. Adverbs can come before or after the verbs they describe.

TEKS

3.6.A.1 Describe characteristics of various forms of poetry. **3.6.A.2** Describe how the characteristics of various forms of poetry create imagery. **3.10.A.1** Identify language that creates a graphic visual experience. **Also 3.10.A.2.**

Poetry

Genre
Poetry

- Poetry is a creative expression of language, usually written to entertain or express feelings.

- Many poems have rhythm and rhyme, much like music.

- Poems use imagery, or sensory language that helps the reader picture the way something looks, sounds, feels, tastes, and smells.

- As you read "Sing a Song of People," try to picture what the poet is describing.

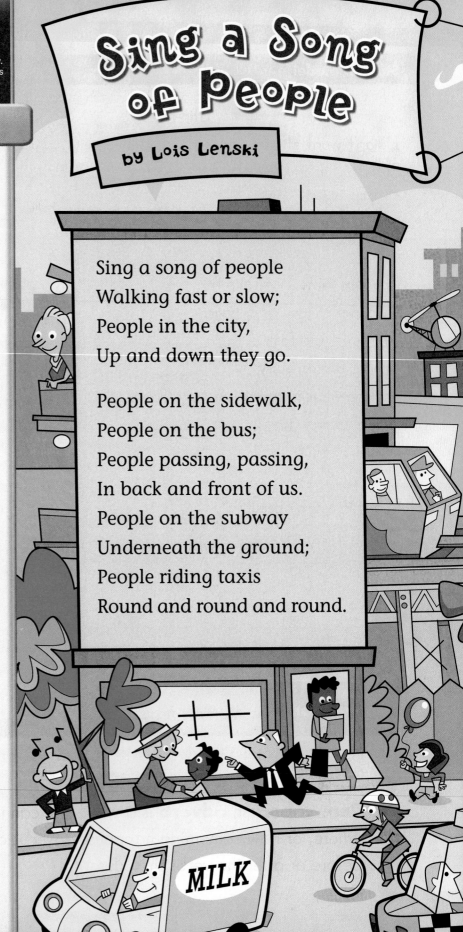

Sing a Song of People
by Lois Lenski

Sing a song of people
Walking fast or slow;
People in the city,
Up and down they go.

People on the sidewalk,
People on the bus;
People passing, passing,
In back and front of us.
People on the subway
Underneath the ground;
People riding taxis
Round and round and round.

People with their hats on,
Going in the doors;
People with umbrellas
When it rains and pours.
People in tall buildings
And in stores below;
Riding elevators
Up and down they go.

People walking singly,
People in a crowd;
People saying nothing,
People talking loud.
People laughing, smiling,
Grumpy people too;
People who just hurry
And never look at you!

Let's **Think** About...

How can I tell that "Sing a Song of People" is a poem and not a story?

Let's **Think** About...

How does the poet create an image of a crowded city street using words?

Let's **Think** About...

Reading Across Texts Which of Jangmi's homes is more like the place described in this poem, her old home in Korea or her new one in the United States?

Writing Across Texts Create a Venn diagram that compares Jangmi's home to the place described in "Sing a Song of People."

285

TEKS

3.29.A.3 Make pertinent comments.
3.30.A.2 Speak coherently, employing eye contact, speaking rate, volume, enunciation, and the conventions of language to communicate ideas effectively. **3.31.A.4** Participate in student-led discussions by posing questions with appropriate detail. **Also 3.3.A.1, 3.3.A.2, 3.6.A.1, 3.6.A.2, 3.4.D.1, 3.4.D.2, 3.22.A.1.iv.1, 3.22.A.1.iv.2, 3.22.A.1.iv.3, 3.22.A.1.viii.1, 3.22.A.1.viii.2, 3.30.A.1, 3.29.A.1, 3.29.A.2, 3.31.A.5.**

READING STREET ONLINE
ONLINE STUDENT EDITION
www.TexasReadingStreet.com

Vocabulary

Compound Words

Word Structure Remember that a compound word is one word made up of two smaller words, such as *airplane* or *halfway*. The two smaller words can help you figure out the meaning of the compound word.

Practice It! Read each riddle. Have a partner choose the compound word from *Good-Bye, 382 Shin Dang Dong* that answers the riddle. Then write your own riddles. Riddles: "room with a bed," "place for a fire," "place of your birth," "drops of rain," "sick for home," "papers full of news," and "watery melon."

Fluency

Expression

Show expression in your voice when reading aloud to make your reading lively. Note words in quotation marks and whether a sentence ends with a period or a question mark, and show these in your voice.

Practice It! Read aloud the first half of page 266 with a partner. Read the words of the characters as you think they might say them. Let your voice fall at the end of statements and rise at the end of questions.

286

Listening and Speaking

Make eye contact with your audience during a performance.

Song or Poem

The words, images, rhythm, and rhyme in a song or poem come alive when it is performed.

Practice It! Choose a song or poem you like and perform it from memory for the class. Your performance should last less than three minutes. Consider using props for your performance.

Tips

Listening ...

- Listen attentively.
- Ask relevant questions and make pertinent comments about the song or poem.

Speaking ...

- Create a mood using volume, rate, and expression.
- Use adverbs and time-order transition words correctly.

Teamwork ...

- Ask and answer questions about how you connect to the poem.

TEKS

3.29.A.2 Ask relevant questions.
3.30.A.1 Speak coherently about the topic under discussion.
3.31.A.2 Participate in teacher-led discussions by answering questions with appropriate detail.

Oral Vocabulary

Let's Talk About

Foods We Eat

- Share ideas about foods that come from different cultures.

- Ask relevant questions about foods unique to specific cultures.

- Pose and answer questions about the foods we eat.

READING STREET ONLINE
CONCEPT TALK VIDEO
www.TexasReadingStreet.com

288

289

TEKS

3.1.B.1.v.1 Use common syllabication patterns to read words including vowel digraphs. **3.1.C.1** Decode words applying knowledge of common spelling patterns.

Envision It! | Sounds to Know

ceiling

ei

neighbors

eigh

height

eigh

READING STREET ONLINE
SOUND-SPELLING CARDS
www.TexasReadingStreet.com

Phonics

Long *a, e, i* Spelled *ei* or *eigh*

Words I Can Blend

e i t h e r

e i g h t

w e i g h

n e i t h e r

h e i g h t

Sentences I Can Read

1. We can either ride or walk the eight blocks to the show.

2. Neither of us wanted to weigh the apples.

3. What is your height?

I Can Read!

Long ago, a tiny toad princess was given a choice. Either marry a frog king or spend the eight remaining years of her stepfather's reign in a dungeon. She wanted to do neither, but after weighing both choices, she decided to marry the frog.

On the day of the wedding, the princess wore a veil and set out for the frog's marsh in a sleigh. A huge weight lay on her shoulders. There was a difference in height, after all.

On arrival, the toad princess fell in love with the frog and his marsh. She reigned for eighteen joyful years.

You've learned

- Long *a, e, i,* Spelled *ei* or *eigh*

TEKS

3.13.B.1 Draw conclusions from facts presented in text. **3.13.B.2** Support assertions with textual evidence. **RC-3.E.1** Summarize information in text, maintaining meaning. **RC-3.E.2** Summarize information in text, maintaining logical order.

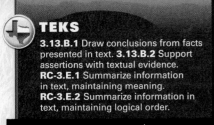

Envision It! | **Skill Strategy**

Skill

Strategy

READING STREET ONLINE
ENVISION IT! ANIMATIONS
www.TexasReadingStreet.com

Comprehension Skill

Draw Conclusions

- You draw conclusions when you use facts and details to make decisions about characters or events.

- Think about what you already know to help you draw conclusions.

- Use what you learned about drawing conclusions and a graphic organizer like the one below as you read "What Does a Baker Do?" Then use your conclusion as the topic sentence for a paragraph that tells what a baker does.

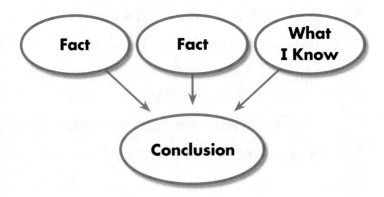

Comprehension Strategy

Summarize

Active readers summarize to help them understand. To summarize, tell the most important ideas or events in logical order, maintaining the meaning of what you read.

What Does a Baker Do?

Have you ever helped an adult bake something? A baker is a person who makes baked goods for a living. A baker makes bread, cakes, pies, and many other treats!

Skill What can you conclude about the other treats a baker makes?

Some bakers work in large stores, some work in small neighborhood bakeries, and some work in restaurants. Baked goods must be fresh, so bakers often get up early in the morning to make goods to be sold that day.

Bakers need to know what kinds of treats people in their neighborhood like. This helps them know what to make and how much.

Skill How do bakers find out what customers want?

Many bakers learn their job by working with experienced bakers. They watch, listen, and practice on the job. Some bakers go to special schools to learn how to bake.

Strategy Summarize the selection. Include why the author concludes that being a baker is an exciting career.

Some bakers like to experiment and create their own recipes for their customers' favorite baked goods. Working as a baker can be an exciting career!

Your Turn!

❚❚ Need a Review? See the *Envision It! Handbook* for more information about drawing conclusions and summarizing.

▶ Ready to Try It? As you read *Jalapeño Bagels*, use what you've learned about drawing conclusions and summarizing to understand the text.

293

TEKS

3.4.B.1 Use context to determine the relevant meaning of unfamiliar words.
3.15.A.1 Follow a set of written multi-step directions. **3.15.A.2** Explain a set of written multi-step directions.

Envision It! | Words to Know

bakery

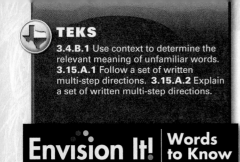

batch

dough

boils
braided
ingredients
mixture

Vocabulary Strategy for

🎯 Unfamiliar Words

Context Clues Sometimes you come across an unfamiliar word. How can you figure out what the word means? Look at the context, or the words and sentences around the word. You might find clues that can help you figure out the meaning of the word.

1. Read the words and sentences around the word you don't know. Sometimes the author tells you what the word means.

2. If not, use the words and sentences to predict a meaning for the word.

3. Try that meaning in the sentence. Does it make sense?

Read "Biscuits for Breakfast" on page 295. As you read, use context clues to help you understand the meanings of the Words to Know and other unfamiliar words.

Words to Write Reread "Biscuits for Breakfast." Write the directions explaining how to make your favorite breakfast food. Be sure to include the ingredients and the steps. Use words from the Words to Know list.

Biscuits for Breakfast

Would you like something for breakfast that you will not find in a bakery? Make biscuits! You'll need only a few ingredients to make one batch.

⅓ cup shortening

1 ¾ cups flour

2 ½ teaspoons baking powder

¾ teaspoon salt

¾ cup milk

Use a fork to add the shortening to the flour, baking powder, and salt. The mixture should look like fine crumbs. Add enough milk so that the dough rounds into a ball. Put the dough on a floured board. Knead it 10 times and only 10 times.

Roll the dough flat, about ½ inch thick. Cut out round circles using a biscuit cutter or an overturned glass. Place the circles on a baking sheet. Do not let the circles touch one another. Bake at 350° for 10 to 12 minutes or until the biscuits are light brown on top. Serve them with butter and honey.

Forget about braided coffee cakes. When the water boils for your morning tea and you are looking for something to go with it, grab a hot, fresh biscuit.

Your Turn!

Need a Review? For additional help with unfamiliar words, see *Words!*

Ready to Try It? Read *Jalapeño Bagels* on pp. 296–309.

Jalapeño Bagels

by Natasha Wing
illustrated by Antonio L. Castro

Genre **Realistic fiction** is a made-up story that can be set in a real place. What is the setting of this story?

"What should I bring to school on Monday for International Day?" I ask my mother. "My teacher told us to bring something from our culture."

"You can bring a treat from the *panaderia*," she suggests. Panaderia is what Mama calls our bakery. "Help us bake on Sunday—then you can pick out whatever you want."

"It's a deal," I tell her. I like helping at the bakery. It's warm there, and everything smells so good.

Early Sunday morning, when it is still dark, my mother wakes me up.

"Pablo, it's time to go to work," she says.

298

We walk down the street to the bakery. My father turns
on the lights. My mother turns on the ovens. She gets
out the pans and ingredients for *pan dulce*. Pan dulce is
Mexican sweet bread.

I help my mother mix and knead the dough. She shapes
rolls and loaves of bread and slides them into the oven.
People tell her she makes the best pan dulce in town.

"Maybe I'll bring pan dulce to school," I tell her.

Next we make *empanadas de calabaza*—pumpkin turnovers. I'm in charge of spooning the pumpkin filling. Mama folds the dough in half and presses the edges with a fork. She bakes them until they are flaky and golden brown. Some customers come to our bakery just for her turnovers.

"Maybe I'll bring empanadas de calabaza instead."
"You'll figure it out," she says. "Ready to make *chango* bars?" Chango means "monkey man."

301

Mama lets me pour in the chocolate chips and nuts.
When she's not looking, I pour in more chocolate chips.
"I could bring chango bars. They're my favorite dessert."
"Mine, too," says Mama. "This batch should be
especially good. I put in extra chips."

My father calls from the back room. "Pablo! Come
help me with the bagels!" Papa speaks English and
Yiddish. He learned Yiddish from his family in New
York City. I know some words too. *Bubbe* means
"grandmother." He uses my bubbe's recipe to make
the bagels.

First he makes the dough in a big metal bowl. Then
he rolls it out into a long rope shape. He cuts off pieces
and shows me how to connect the ends in a circle. We
put the circles on trays where they sit and rise.

While we are waiting my father makes *challah*, Jewish braided bread. He lets me practice braiding challah dough at my own counter. It's a lot like braiding hair. The customers say it is almost too beautiful to eat.

"Maybe I'll bring a loaf of challah to school," I tell Papa. He smiles.

When the bagel dough has risen, he boils the bagels in a huge pot of water and fishes them out with a long slotted spoon. I sprinkle on poppy seeds and sesame seeds, and then they go in the oven.

"Maybe I could bring sesame-seed bagels with cream cheese."

"No *lox?*" Lox is smoked salmon. My father's favorite bagel is pumpernickel with a smear of cream cheese and lox.

I crinkle my nose. "Lox tastes like fish. Jam is better."

305

My mother joins us and helps my father make another batch of bagels—*jalapeño* bagels. My parents use their own special recipe. While Papa kneads the dough, Mama chops the jalapeño *chiles*. She tosses them into the dough and adds dried red peppers. We roll, cut, make circles, and let them rise. I can't wait until they are done because I am getting hungry.

"Have you decided what you're going to bring to school?" asks Mama.

"It's hard to choose. Everything is so good," I tell her. I look at Papa. "Except for lox."

"You should decide before we open," warns Mama, "or else our customers will buy everything up."

307

I walk past all the sweet breads, chango bars, and bagels.

I think about my mother and my father and all the different things they make in the bakery. And suddenly I know exactly what I'm going to bring.

"Jalapeño bagels," I tell my parents. "And I'll spread them with cream cheese and jam."

"Why jalapeño bagels?" asks Papa.

"Because they are a mixture of both of you. Just like me!"

For this recipe you will need lots of time.
But these bagels are worth the wait!
Ask an adult to help you.

Jalapeño Bagels

1 3/4 cups lukewarm water

1/2 teaspoon dry yeast

2 teaspoons salt

1 1/2 tablespoons sugar

5 to 6 cups flour

1/3 cup jalapeños, chopped

1/4 cup dried red peppers

Mix water, yeast, salt, and sugar. Add flour and jalapeños and mix into a ball. Knead for 10 to 12 minutes, adding more flour if necessary, until dough is stiff. Add red peppers and knead for 3 minutes. Let dough rest 10 minutes, then cut into 12 pieces with a knife.

Roll each piece of dough on a table to form long, cigarlike shapes. Then, for each of the twelve pieces, connect the two ends by overlapping them about 3/4 of an inch and rolling the ends together to make a ring shape. Make sure each joint is secure, or it will come apart while boiling.

Cover with a damp towel and let rise 1 to 1 1/2 hours in a warm spot. In a large pot, bring 1 to 2 gallons of water to a rolling boil. Place bagels in boiling water and boil until they float (15 to 30 seconds). Remove with a slotted spoon and place on a lightly greased cookie sheet. Bake at 400 degrees for 10 to 15 minutes or until golden brown.

Note: A bakery uses dry malt instead of sugar, and high-gluten flour, which you may be able to get at a bakery or pizza parlor. For a milder bagel, reduce the quantities of the peppers.

TEKS

3.8.A.2 Summarize the plot's main events. 3.8.C.1 Identify whether the narrator of a story is first person. RC-3.E.1 Summarize information in text, maintaining meaning. **Also** 3.2.B.7, 3.2.B.9, 3.11.A.1, 3.11.A.2, 3.11.A.3, RC-3.E.2.

Envision It! Retell

READING STREET ONLINE
STORY SORT
www.TexasReadingStreet.com

Think Critically

1. In the story, Pablo takes jalapeño bagels to school for International Day because they combine his mother's and his father's cultures. What else can you think of that represents two different cultures? Explain your answer. **Text to World**

2. Is the narrator of this story first or third person? Why do you think the author chose to write the story from that point of view? What do you think the author's purpose is for writing this story? **Think Like an Author**

3. Is the family bakery successful? What details from the story support your answer? **Draw Conclusions**

4. Summarize the story in two to three sentences. Be sure to use logical order. **Summarize**

5. **Look Back and Write** Look back through the story. Think about the two cultures of Pablo's parents. Now write a paragraph telling why jalapeño bagels are special to Pablo. Be sure to include facts and details from the story in your paragraph.

TEST PRACTICE Extended Response

Meet the Author and the Illustrator

Natasha Wing

Natasha Wing lives in northern California, where she often buys jalapeño bagels at a bakery in town. The bakery, called Los Bagels Bakery and Cafe, gave Ms. Wing the idea for this story. Los Bagels offers many tasty snacks, like Mexican hot chocolate, pumpkin turnovers, and bagels topped with jalapeño jelly.

Ms. Wing is married and has two cats, Toonces and Jemima, and a dog named Sabaka.

Here are more books by Natasha Wing and Antonio L. Castro.

The Night Before Summer Vacation by Natasha Wing

Antonio L. Castro

Antonio L. Castro has illustrated many children's books. He is also an artist. He has displayed his art in museums in Texas, Mexico, Spain, and Italy.

Mr. Castro was born in Zacatecas, Mexico. He now lives in Juarez, Mexico, and is considered one of the best artists in the El Paso-Juarez area. He teaches art and local history classes to children in museums and libraries near his home.

Pájaro Verde/The Green Bird as told by Joe Hayes, illustrated by Antonio L. Castro

Reading Log

Use the Reader's and Writer's Notebook to record your independent reading.

311

TEKS

3.20 Write expository and procedural or work-related texts to communicate ideas and information to specific audiences for specific purposes. **Also: 3.22.A.1.iv.1, 3.22.A.1.iv.2, 3.23.A.1, 3.23.B.1.i.**

Let's Write It!

Key Features of an Invitation

- gives the reason for the invitation

- provides a date, time, and location

- includes contact information if a reply is needed

- may include creative pictures or drawings

READING STREET ONLINE
GRAMMAR JAMMER
www.TexasReadingStreet.com

Expository

Invitation

An **invitation** is a written offer asking someone to come to a party or other special event. The student model on the next page is an example of an invitation.

Writing Prompt Invite a friend to come over to your home for dinner, using specific details.

Writer's Checklist

Remember, you should . . .

✓ give a description of the event.

✓ note the date, time, and location.

✓ include contact information so people can reply.

✓ capitalize geographical names and places.

✓ write legibly in cursive with correct word spacing.

✓ use adverbs about time and manner correctly.

An Invitation for You!

What: Please join me for dinner and dessert to celebrate my birthday! After we eat dinner and cake, we'll sing our favorite karaoke songs. I will sing **loudest**! Someone else can sing **best**!

When: Thursday, April 8, at 6:00 PM

Where: Bethenny's house
21475 Richmond Ave.
Cedar Ridge, WA 98252

RSVP: Please call me at 206-555-9076, to let me know if you will be able to attend.

Writing Trait Focus The purpose of the invitation is clear.

Comparative and superlative adverbs are used correctly.

Genre An **invitation** gives the time and place of the event.

Conventions

Comparatives and Superlatives

Remember Comparative adverbs compare the actions of two people or things. **Superlative adverbs** compare the actions of three or more people or things.

TEKS

3.12.A.1 Identify the topic of the text.
RC-3.F1 Make connections between
literary and informational texts with
similar ideas. **Also 3.2.A.1, 3.2.A.2,
3.13.A.1, 3.13.D.1, 3.13.D.2,
3.13.D.3, 3.15.A.1, 3.15.A.2, RC-
3.D.1, RC-3.D.2, RC-3.F.2.**

Genre
Expository Text

- Expository text
  explains or describes
  the main idea about a
  topic, using facts and
  details.

- Graphic sources
  show the information
  visually.

- Text features, such as
  headings, italicized
  words, and captions
  help readers to
  predict, locate, and
  verify the information.

- As you read "Foods
  of Mexico," use
  the text features to
  predict, locate, and
  verify information
  about the topic.

Foods of Mexico
a Delicious Blend

From *Viva Mexico! The Foods*
by George Ancona

Panza llena, corazón contento is
an old Mexican proverb that means
"a full belly makes for a happy
heart." The foods of Mexico are a
treat to see, smell, taste, and eat.

Native Foods

The early people of Mexico developed maize (corn) from a small wild plant. They grew many varieties of maize: white, red, yellow, black, and other color combinations.

Between rows of corn they planted tomatoes, beans, chiles, pumpkins, sweet potatoes, and squash. They also raised avocados and amaranth, a nutritious grain that was ground into flour for tortillas and bread. Fields and forests supplied fruits, peanuts, cacao (cocoa) beans, honey, and mushrooms.

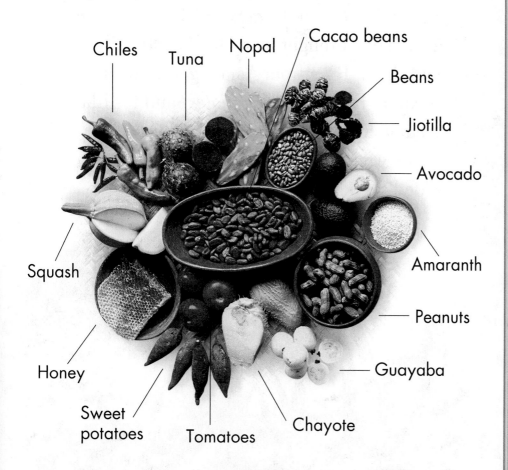

Chiles

Tuna

Nopal

Cacao beans

Beans

Jiotilla

Avocado

Amaranth

Squash

Peanuts

Honey

Guayaba

Sweet potatoes

Tomatoes

Chayote

Let's Think About...

According to the title, what is the topic going to be? How does the proverb help introduce the main idea about the topic?
Expository Text

Let's Think About...

What facts and details that support the main idea can you learn from the photos and captions?
Expository Text

The Spanish Flavor

The Spanish who came to the New World brought their traditions with them. Over the centuries Spain had had many influences. From the Greeks, who colonized Spain in the fifth century B.C., the Spanish learned to grow olives, grapes, and chickpeas. From the Moors, who ruled their country for eight hundred years, they learned to plant spinach, eggplants, artichokes, watermelons, sugarcane, and lime, lemon, and orange trees.

Spanish ships called galleons sailed across the Pacific Ocean from Spanish colonies in Asia. They brought many foods and spices with them. Rice from Asia together with Mexico's native beans *(frijoles)* and tortillas became the staple food of Mexico. African slaves who were brought to New Spain also added their ways of cooking.

Let's **Think** About...

How do the headings in this selection organize the text?
Expository Text

Let's **Think** About...

What do italicized words indicate? How do you know?
Expository Text

Beans *(frijoles)*

Rice

Tortillas or Bolillos?

The Spanish planted wheat because they preferred wheat bread to the native corn tortillas. They baked little rolls called *bolillos*. Serving *bolillos* was a status symbol among Europeans. But Mexicans never gave up their tortillas. Eventually the settlers began to eat them too.

Today it isn't necessary to choose between a *tamal* or a *bolillo*. Street-corner food vendors sell a breakfast snack that blends two cultures: a sliced *bolillo* with a hot tamale inside. This is called a *torta de tamal*, a tamale sandwich.

Tamales

Like seeds blown by the wind, people came to Mexico from distant lands, and they settled and flowered. The foods they brought with them blended with native cooking. The result is a Mexican cuisine that has traces of distant lands.

Bolillos

Let's **Think** About...

Reading Across Texts In this article, people from distant lands blended their foods with the foods of the Mexican people. How did Pablo's family in *Jalapeño Bagels* also do this?

Writing Across Texts Use the recipe at the end of *Jalapeño Bagels* to help you create a step-by-step recipe for a food you can make that combines two cultures.

TEKS

3.16.A.1 Understand how communication changes when moving from one genre of media to another. **3.16.B.1** Explain how various design techniques used in media influence the message. **3.30.A.2** Speak coherently, employing eye contact, speaking rate, volume, enunciation, and the conventions of language to communicate ideas effectively. **Also 3.3.A.1, 3.3.A.2, 3.29.A.1, 3.30.A.1, 3.31.A.4, 3.31.A.5, 3.31.A.6.**

Let's Learn It!

Vocabulary

Unfamiliar Words

Context Clues Use context clues to find the meanings of unfamiliar words while you are reading. The words or sentences around an unfamiliar word may provide clues to its meaning.

Practice It! Select three Words to Know words. Reread *Jalapeño Bagels*. Use context clues to determine the meaning of each word. Write the meaning of each word as it is used in the story. Record the words or phrases you used as context clues.

Fluency

Accuracy

When you read aloud it is important to pronounce words correctly. This will help everyone understand the meaning of the story you are reading.

Practice It! Read aloud pages 298–299 of *Jalapeño Bagels* with a partner. Take turns listening to each other to make sure you are both reading the words correctly.

Media Literacy

Advertisement

Ads inform people about and persuade them to buy a product or service or go to a place. An ad can be on the radio, on TV, in a newspaper, or on the Internet.

Practice It! Prepare a two-minute radio ad that persuades people to buy jalapeño bagels, and perform it for the class. Use sounds to influence them to buy the bagels. How would your ad change if you were creating a Web site for the bagels instead?

Tips

Listening ...

- Sit quietly, facing the speaker.
- Listen to identify persuasive techniques.

Speaking ...

- Use expression and persuasive techniques.

Teamwork ...

- Ask and answer questions about how communication changes when moving from the radio to the Internet.

TEKS

3.29.A.2 Ask relevant questions.
3.29.A.3 Make pertinent comments.
3.30.A.2 Speak coherently, employing eye contact, speaking rate, volume, enunciation, and the conventions of language to communicate ideas effectively.

Oral Vocabulary

Let's Talk About

City and Country Life

- Ask relevant questions about urban and rural life.

- Express opinions about life in the city versus life in the country.

- Describe life in the city or the country.

READING STREET ONLINE
CONCEPT TALK VIDEO
www.TexasReadingStreet.com

Envision It! | Sounds to Know

neighborhood

suffix -hood

greenish

suffix -ish

equipment

suffix -ment

sandy

suffix -y

Phonics

Suffixes -y, -ish, -hood, -ment

Words I Can Blend

bumpy

boyish

childhood

enjoyment

funny

Sentences I Can Read

1. It is difficult to ride on the bumpy street.

2. Nate has had a boyish grin since childhood.

3. I get a lot of enjoyment from funny stories.

I Can Read!

During childhood, my friends and I have gotten a lot of enjoyment out of acting in a clownish way. We try to be as funny and witty with each other as we can. Sometimes, though, we don't show the best judgment and get ourselves in tricky situations.

One day we were acting foolish and saying nutty things. I noticed a movement out of the corner of my eye. My coach was looking at us with a stormy expression on his face.

We felt pretty sheepish. I hope adulthood is easier than childhood sometimes is.

You've learned

 Suffixes -y, -ish, -hood, -ment

TEKS

3.12.A.2 Locate the author's stated purposes in writing the text. **3.14.A.1** Identify what the author is trying to persuade the reader to think or do. Also **3.2.C.2, 3.2.C.3, RC-3.C.1, RC-3.C.2.**

Envision It! | Skill Strategy

Skill

Strategy

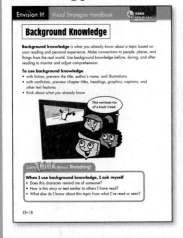

Comprehension Skill

Author's Purpose

- Sometimes authors tell you their purposes for writing. They write to inform, entertain, persuade, or express an opinion.

- An author can write to try to persuade you to think or do something by using "loaded words," or strong words.

- Use what you learned about author's purpose and a graphic organizer like the one below as you read "New York City." Then write a paragraph explaining the author's purpose.

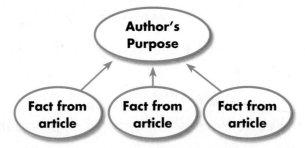

Comprehension Strategy

Background Knowledge

Good readers use what they already know to help them understand their reading. As you read, make connections to your own life. Have you ever seen or experienced what you are reading about? This will help you understand what you read.

NEW YORK CITY

I'm going to talk you into coming to New York City. It's a terrific place to visit. There are many things to see and do. New York City is the largest city in the United States.

In New York City you can visit the Empire State Building. This grand building opened in 1931. It is 102 stories tall! For many years, it was the tallest building in the world.

The Statue of Liberty is a breathtaking place! This statue stands on Bedloe's Island in New York Harbor. The Statue of Liberty rises to more than 300 feet. People come from all over the world to see this famous statue.

If you enjoy great plays and musical events, Broadway, a street in the center of New York City, has it all. It is the most famous theater district in the country. You will enjoy your visit and have a wonderful time when you come to New York!

Skill What is the author's stated purpose for writing?

Strategy What do you already know about New York City?

Strategy What do you already know about the Statue of Liberty?

Your Turn!

Need a Review? See the *Envision It! Handbook* for help with author's purpose and background knowledge.

Ready to Try It? As you read *Me and Uncle Romie*, use what you've learned about author's purpose and background knowledge to understand the text.

TEKS

3.4.B.1 Use context to determine the relevant meaning of unfamiliar words. **3.4.B.3** Use context to distinguish among homographs. **3.4.C.3** Identify homographs. **3.4.C.7** Use homographs.

cardboard

feast

treasure

fierce
flights
pitcher
ruined
stoops

Vocabulary Strategy for

Homonyms

Context Clues You may read a familiar word that doesn't make sense in the sentence. The word could be a homonym. Homonyms are words that are pronounced and spelled the same, but have different meanings. For example, *saw* means "looked at" and "a tool for cutting." Use the context—the words and sentences around the word—to figure out the correct meaning.

1. Reread the words and sentences around the word that doesn't make sense.

2. Draw a conclusion about another meaning for the word using context clues.

3. Try the meaning in the sentence. Does it make sense?

Read "A Different Treasure Hunt" on page 327. Use context clues to help you find the meanings of homonyms.

Words to Write Reread "A Different Treasure Hunt." Write your answer to the question at the end of the selection. Give reasons for your answer. Use homonyms and words from the Words to Know list in your answer.

A DIFFERENT TREASURE HUNT

The summer I turned eight, my family moved from New York City to North Carolina. In the city, we climbed four flights of stairs to our apartment. The building was ten stories high! People sat on their front stoops and listened to the noise. I was a pitcher on the neighborhood baseball team.

In North Carolina, we live in a house. All the houses have front porches and yards. At night it is very dark and quiet. At first, I thought my life was ruined.

My mother saw my fierce face. She suggested I have a treasure hunt, but instead of looking for gold, I should look for baseball players. She promised to help by preparing a feast with all my favorite food. I made signs on cardboard and posted them at the grocery store, the library, and the post office. The signs said:

I'm looking for baseball players.
Come to 124 Willow Street June 28 at 2:00 P.M.
FREE FOOD!

Do you think anyone showed up?

Your Turn!

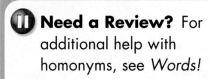 **Need a Review?** For additional help with homonyms, see *Words!*

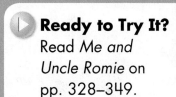 **Ready to Try It?** Read *Me and Uncle Romie* on pp. 328–349.

Genre

Historical fiction is set in the past. Some of the details are factual, but others are made up or loosely based on history. Look for the factual details as you read.

ME and UNCLE ROMIE

by Claire Hartfield

illustrated by Jerome Lagarrigue

Question of the Week

How does city life compare to life in the country?

It was the summer Mama had the twins that I first met my uncle Romie. The doctor had told Mama she had to stay off her feet till the babies got born. Daddy thought it was a good time for me to visit Uncle Romie and his wife, Aunt Nanette, up north in New York City. But I wasn't so sure. Mama had told me that Uncle Romie was some kind of artist, and he didn't have any kids. I'd seen his picture too. He looked scary—a bald-headed, fierce-eyed giant. No, I wasn't sure about this visit at all.

he day before I left home was a regular North Carolina summer day. "A good train-watching day," my friend B. J. said.

We waited quietly in the grass beside the tracks. B. J. heard it first. "It's a'coming," he said. Then I heard it too—a low rumbling, building to a roar. *WHOOO—OOO!*

"The *Piedmont!*" we shouted as the train blasted past.

"I'm the greatest train-watcher ever," B. J. boasted.

"Yeah," I answered, "but tomorrow I'll be *riding* a train. I'm the lucky one."

Lucky, I thought as we headed home. *Maybe.*

That evening I packed my suitcase. Voices drifted up from the porch below.

"Romie's got that big art show coming up," Mama said quietly. "I hope he's not too busy for James, especially on his birthday."

"Romie's a good man," Daddy replied. "And Nanette'll be there too."

The light faded. Mama called me into her bedroom. "Where's my good-night kiss?" she said.

I curled up next to her. "I'll miss the way you make my birthday special, Mama. Your lemon cake and the baseball game."

"Well," Mama sighed, "it won't be those things. But Uncle Romie and Aunt Nanette are family, and they love you too. It'll still be a good birthday, honey."

Mama pulled me close. Her voice sang soft and low. Later, in my own bed, I listened as crickets began their song and continued into the night.

The next morning I hugged Mama good-bye, and Daddy and I headed for the train. He got me seated, then stood waving at me from the outside. I held tight to the jar of pepper jelly Mama had given me for Uncle Romie.

"ALL A-BOARD!" The conductor's voice crackled over the loudspeaker.

The train pulled away. *Chug-a-chug-a-chug-a-chug.* I watched my town move past my window—bright-colored houses, chickens strutting across the yards, flowers everywhere.

After a while I felt hungry. Daddy had packed me a lunch and a dinner to eat one at a time. I ate almost everything at once. Then my belly felt tight and I was kind of sleepy. I closed my eyes and dreamed about Mama and Daddy getting ready for those babies. Would they even miss me?

Later, when I woke up, I ate the last bit of my dinner and thought about my birthday. Would they make my lemon cake and take me to a baseball game in New York?

The sky turned from dark blue to black. I was getting sleepy all over again.

"We're almost there, son," the man next to me said.

Then I saw it . . . New York City. Buildings stretching up to the sky. So close together. Not like North Carolina at all.

"Penn Station! Watch your step," the conductor said, helping me down to the platform. I did like Daddy said and found a spot for myself close to the train. Swarms of people rushed by. Soon I heard a silvery voice call my name. This had to be Aunt Nanette. I turned and saw her big smile reaching out to welcome me.

She took my hand and guided me through the rushing crowds onto an underground train called the subway. "This will take us right home," she explained.

Home was like nothing I'd ever seen before. No
regular houses anywhere. Just big buildings and stores
of all kinds—in the windows I saw paints, fabrics,
radios, and TVs.

We turned into the corner building and climbed the
stairs to the apartment—five whole flights up. *Whew!*
I tried to catch my breath while Aunt Nanette flicked
on the lights.

"Uncle Romie's out talking to some people about
his big art show that's coming up. He'll be home soon,"
Aunt Nanette said. She set some milk and a plate of
cookies for me on the table. "Your uncle's working
very hard, so we won't see much of him for a while.
His workroom—we call it his studio—is in the front of
our apartment. That's where he keeps all the things he
needs to make his art."

"Doesn't he just paint?" I asked.

"Uncle Romie is a collage artist," Aunt Nanette explained. "He uses paints, yes. But also photographs, newspapers, cloth. He cuts and pastes them onto a board to make his paintings."

"That sounds kinda easy," I said.

Aunt Nanette laughed.

"Well, there's a little more to it than that, James. When you see the paintings, you'll understand. Come, let's get you to bed."

Lying in the dark, I heard heavy footsteps in the hall. A giant stared at me from the doorway. "Hello there, James." Uncle Romie's voice was deep and loud, like thunder. "Thanks for the pepper jelly," he boomed. "You have a good sleep, now." Then he disappeared down the hall.

The next morning the door to Uncle Romie's studio was closed. But Aunt Nanette had plans for both of us. "Today we're going to a neighborhood called Harlem," she said. "It's where Uncle Romie lived as a boy."

Harlem was full of people walking, working, shopping, eating. Some were watching the goings-on from fire escapes. Others were sitting out on stoops greeting folks who passed by—just like the people back home calling out hellos from their front porches. Most everybody seemed to know Aunt Nanette. A lot of them asked after Uncle Romie too.

We bought peaches at the market, then stopped to visit awhile. I watched some kids playing stickball. "Go on, get in that game," Aunt Nanette said, gently pushing me over to join them. When I was all hot and sweaty, we cooled off with double chocolate scoops from the ice cream man. Later we shared some barbecue on a rooftop way up high. I felt like I was on top of the world.

As the days went by, Aunt Nanette took me all over the city—we rode a ferry boat to the Statue of Liberty . . . zoomed 102 floors up at the Empire State Building . . . window-shopped the fancy stores on Fifth Avenue . . . gobbled hot dogs in Central Park.

But it was Harlem that I liked best. I played stickball with the kids again . . . and on a really hot day a whole bunch of us ran through the icy cold water that sprayed out hard from the fire hydrant. In the evenings Aunt Nanette and I sat outside listening to the street musicians playing their saxophone songs.

On rainy days I wrote postcards and helped out around the apartment. I told Aunt Nanette about the things I liked to do back home—about baseball games, train-watching, my birthday. She told me about the special Caribbean lemon and mango cake she was going to make.

My uncle Romie stayed hidden away in his studio. But I wasn't worried anymore. Aunt Nanette would make my birthday special.

4 . . . 3 . . . 2 . . . 1 . . . My birthday was almost here!

And then Aunt Nanette got a phone call.

"An old aunt has died, James. I have to go away for her funeral. But don't you worry. Uncle Romie will spend your birthday with you. It'll be just fine."

That night Aunt Nanette kissed me good-bye. I knew it would not be fine at all. Uncle Romie didn't know about cakes or baseball games or anything except his dumb old paintings. My birthday was ruined.

When the sky turned black, I tucked myself into bed. I missed Mama and Daddy so much. I listened to the birds on the rooftop—their songs continued into the night.

The next morning everything was quiet. I crept out of bed and into the hall. For the first time the door to Uncle Romie's studio stood wide open. What a glorious mess! There were paints and scraps all over the floor, and around the edges were huge paintings with all sorts of pieces pasted together.

I saw saxophones, birds, fire escapes, and brown faces. *It's Harlem,* I thought. *The people, the music, the rooftops, and the stoops.* Looking at Uncle Romie's paintings, I could *feel* Harlem—its beat and bounce.

Then there was one that was different. Smaller houses, flowers, and trains. "That's home!" I shouted.

"Yep," Uncle Romie said, smiling, from the doorway. "That's the Carolina I remember."

"Mama says you visited your grandparents there most every summer when you were a kid," I said.

"I sure did, James. *Mmm.* Now that's the place for pepper jelly. Smeared thick on biscuits. And when Grandma wasn't looking . . . I'd sneak some on a spoon."

"Daddy and I do that too!" I told him.

We laughed together, then walked to the kitchen for a breakfast feast—eggs, bacon, grits, and biscuits.

"James, you've got me remembering the pepper jelly lady. People used to line up down the block to buy her preserves."

"Could you put someone like that in one of your paintings?" I asked.

"I guess I could." Uncle Romie nodded. "Yes, that's a memory just right for sharing. What a good idea, James. Now let's get this birthday going!"

He brought out two presents from home. I tore into the packages while he got down the pepper jelly and two huge spoons. Mama and Daddy had picked out just what I wanted—a special case for my baseball cards, and a model train for me to build.

"Pretty cool," said Uncle Romie. "I used to watch the trains down in North Carolina, you know."

How funny to picture big Uncle Romie lying on his belly!

"B. J. and me, we have contests to see who can hear the trains first."

"Hey, I did that too. You know, it's a funny thing, James. People live in all sorts of different places and families. But the things we care about are pretty much the same. Like favorite foods, special songs, games, stories . . . and like birthdays." Uncle Romie held up two tickets to a baseball game!

It turns out Uncle Romie knows all about baseball— he was even a star pitcher in college. We got our mitts and set off for the game.

Way up in the bleachers, we shared a bag of peanuts, cracking the shells with our teeth and keeping our mitts ready in case a home run ball came our way. That didn't happen—but we sure had fun.

Aunt Nanette came home that night. She lit the
candles, and we all shared my Caribbean birthday cake.

After that, Uncle Romie had to work a lot again. But at
the end of each day he let me sit with him in his studio and
talk. Daddy was right. Uncle Romie is a good man.

The day of the big art show finally came. I watched
the people laughing and talking, walking slowly around
the room from painting to painting. I walked around
myself, listening to their conversations.

"Remember our first train ride from Chicago to New York?" one lady asked her husband.

"That guitar-playing man reminds me of my Uncle Joe," said another.

All these strangers talking to each other about their families and friends and special times, and all because of how my uncle Romie's paintings reminded them of these things.

Later that night Daddy called. I had a brand-new brother and sister. Daddy said they were both bald and made a lot of noise. But he sounded happy and said how they all missed me.

This time Aunt Nanette and Uncle Romie took me to the train station.

"Here's a late birthday present for you, James," Uncle Romie said, holding out a package. "Open it on the train, why don't you. It'll help pass the time on the long ride home."

I waved out the window to Uncle Romie and Aunt Nanette until I couldn't see them anymore. Then I ripped off the wrappings!

And there was my summer in New York. Bright sky in one corner, city lights at night in another. Tall buildings. Baseball ticket stubs. The label from the pepper-jelly jar. And trains. One going toward the skyscrapers. Another going away.

Back home, I lay in the soft North Carolina grass. It was the first of September, almost Uncle Romie's birthday. I watched the birds streak across the sky.

Rooftop birds, I thought. *Back home from their summer in New York, just like me.* Watching them, I could still feel the city's beat inside my head.

A feather drifted down from the sky. In the garden tiger lilies bent in the wind. *Uncle Romie's favorite flowers.* I yanked off a few blossoms. And then I was off on a treasure hunt, collecting things that reminded me of Uncle Romie.

I painted and pasted them together on a big piece of cardboard. Right in the middle I put the train schedule. And at the top I wrote:

TEKS

3.8.C.1 Identify whether the narrator of a story is first person. **RC-3.F.1** Make connections between literary and informational texts with similar ideas. **RC-3.F.2** Provide textual evidence. **Also 3.2.C.2, 3.2.C.3, 3.11.A.1, 3.11.A.2, 3.11.A.3, RC-3.C.1, RC-3.C.2.**

Envision It! | Retell

Think Critically

1. Compare and contrast North Carolina and New York City back in the 1920s. How are these places alike and different from where you live now? **Text to World**

2. Is this story written in first or third person? Why do you think the author wrote from this point of view?

   Think Like an Author

3. Read "Meet the Author" on page 351. Why did the author write this story? Why do you think the author chose to write this selection as historical fiction and not as a biography like *Rocks in His Head*? Explain your answer with evidence from the text.

   Author's Purpose

4. What did you know about New York City or Harlem before you read the story? How did your knowledge help you as you read? **Background Knowledge**

5. **Look Back and Write** Look back at the adventures James had in New York City. Now write about why you would or would not like to visit Uncle Romie in Harlem. Provide evidence to support your answer.

    **TEST PRACTICE** Extended Response

Meet the Author and the Illustrator

Claire Hartfield and Jerome Lagarrigue

Claire Hartfield began taking dance lessons when she was five. Dance is her way of telling stories. In *Me and Uncle Romie,* she wanted to show how an artist can use art to tell stories. Although *Me and Uncle Romie* is fiction, it is based on the life of collage artist Romare Bearden.

Today, Ms. Hartfield is a lawyer in Chicago.

Jerome Lagarrigue grew up in Paris, France, in a family of artists. His art has appeared in magazines, and he has illustrated several picture books. Mr. Lagarrigue teaches drawing and painting in New York City. For *Me and Uncle Romie,* he used some elements of collage in his paintings—like Romare Bearden.

Read some books about great art projects.

Loo-Loo, Boo, and Art You Can Do by Denis Roche

Recycled Crafts Box by Laura C. Martin

Use the Reader's and Writer's Notebook to record your independent reading.

351

TEKS

3.20.C Write responses to literary or expository texts that demonstrate an understanding of the text. **3.22.A.1.vii** Use and understand coordinating conjunctions in the context of reading, writing, and speaking. **Also: 3.23.D.1.**

Let's Write It!

Key Features of a Book Review

- tells what a book is about

- gives an opinion about the story

- often urges others to read, or avoid, the book

READING STREET ONLINE
GRAMMAR JAMMER
www.TexasReadingStreet.com

Narrative

Book Review

A **book review** is a kind of written report that provides an opinion about a book. The student model on the next page is an example of a book review.

Writing Prompt Think about this story or another story or book you have read recently. Write a book review of it, explaining to readers whether they should read it.

Writer's Checklist

Remember, you should . . .

✓ give the name of the book in the first paragraph.

✓ explain what the book is about.

✓ tell readers if you think they might want to read it.

✓ use conjunctions to combine sentences.

✓ indent paragraphs correctly.

Name: Marta Moran

Book Review: <u>Moving to the Country</u>

    If you like horses, then you'll love reading the exciting fiction story, <u>Moving to the Country</u>. The story is about a girl named Lucie who has to move from the city to the country. She really doesn't want to leave her friends behind. She likes riding her bike, **and** she doesn't want to live out in the middle of nowhere with nothing to do.

    When Lucie finally gets to the country, she finds herself living on a ranch with horses. Lucie is glad she moved, because she loves the horses.

    Read this book, **or** you'll never find out what happens on the ranch. You'll be glad you did. It's a really exciting book with a great ending!

Writing Trait Conventions
Good writers check their work for correct use of conventions.

Conjunctions are used in compound sentences.

Genre A **book review** explains what a book is about.

Conventions

Conjunctions

Remember Conjunctions are words used to join words or groups of words together. The words *and, or,* and *but* are conjunctions.

Country to City

TEKS

3.16.A.1 Understand how communication changes when moving from one genre of media to another. **3.16.C.1** Compare various written conventions used for digital media. **Also 3.16.B.1.**

21st Century Skills
INTERNET GUY

Online Reference Sources What is the first thing to do at a new Web site? Find out who wrote the information. Use the "About this site" button. Can you believe them? How else can you evaluate information?

- You can find reference sources, such as atlases, dictionaries, and encyclopedias, on Internet Web sites. Some Web sites give you different sources in one place. These reference sources use similar conventions as printed sources, and they're organized the same way.

- Design features of reference sources help guide the user.

- Read "Country to City" and notice how it communicates facts. Where would you find opinions about similar topics?

Denise learned a little about Romare Bearden from reading *Me and Uncle Romie*. She was curious to learn more about his life in the country and in the city. She wondered how the cultures were different.

Denise knew that she could look up information about Romare Bearden in an encyclopedia, but she didn't have one handy.

She remembered seeing a link to online reference sources when she was on the Internet. It had links to an atlas, almanac, dictionary, and encyclopedia.

File   Edit   View   Favorites   Tools   Help

http://www.url.here

ENCYCLOPEDIA

Romare Bearden   GO

File   Edit   View   Favorites   Tools

After finding an article on Romare Bearden, she learned these facts.

Romare Bearden

- He was born in Charlotte, North Carolina.

- He lived in Harlem, which is in New York City.

- He is best known for his collages, but he created paintings as well.

- He was part of the Harlem Renaissance, a period of time when African American art flourished.

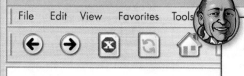

Now that Denise knew where Romare Bearden lived, she wanted to know more about those places.

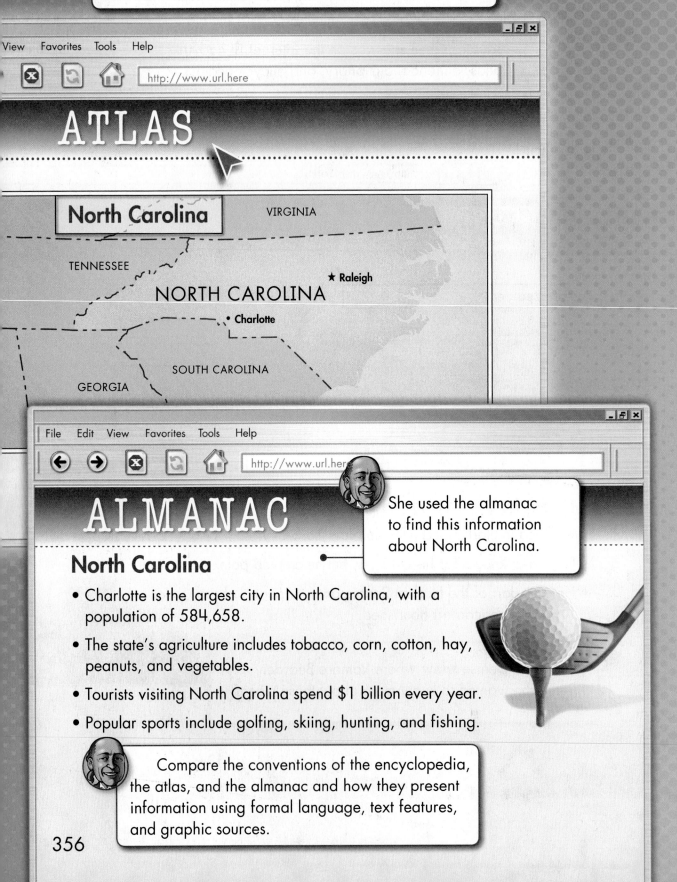

Denise used the atlas to find a map of North Carolina.

View   Favorites   Tools   Help

http://www.url.here

ATLAS

North Carolina

VIRGINIA

TENNESSEE

NORTH CAROLINA   ★ **Raleigh**

• **Charlotte**

SOUTH CAROLINA

GEORGIA

File   Edit   View   Favorites   Tools   Help

http://www.url.here

ALMANAC

She used the almanac to find this information about North Carolina.

North Carolina

- Charlotte is the largest city in North Carolina, with a population of 584,658.

- The state's agriculture includes tobacco, corn, cotton, hay, peanuts, and vegetables.

- Tourists visiting North Carolina spend $1 billion every year.

- Popular sports include golfing, skiing, hunting, and fishing.

Compare the conventions of the encyclopedia, the atlas, and the almanac and how they present information using formal language, text features, and graphic sources.

356

Then Denise used the atlas to find a map of New York.

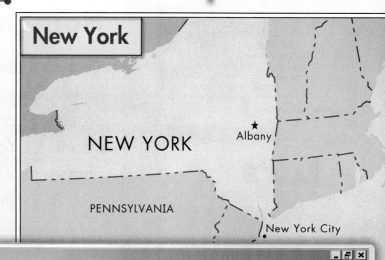

New York

NEW YORK

★ Albany

PENNSYLVANIA

New York City

The almanac gave her some facts about the state of New York. Denise looked at the information she had gathered and saw some differences between the two places Romare Bearden had lived in.

Help

http://www.url.here

ALMANAC

New York

- The largest city in the state is New York City, which has a population of 8,085,742.

- New York City is a leader in manufacturing, banking, and book publishing.

- New York City is a popular travel destination in the state of New York.

- The state produces grapes, strawberries, cherries, pears, onions, potatoes, and dairy products.

If Denise wanted to travel to New York, she could read online accounts or tourist Web sites that communicate recommendations, or opinions based on experiences, for what to do and see during her visit.

for more practice

Get
Online!
www.TexasReadingStreet.com
Use online reference sources to find out more about Romare Bearden.

**21st Century Skills
Online Activity**
Log on and follow the step-by-step directions for using online reference sources to find out more about the places where Romare Bearden lived.

TEKS

3.29.A.1 Listen attentively to speakers. **3.29.A.2** Ask relevant questions. **3.30.A.1** Speak coherently about the topic under discussion. **3.30.A.2** Speak coherently, employing eye contact, speaking rate, volume, enunciation, and the conventions of language to communicate ideas effectively. **3.4.C.3** Identify homographs. **3.4.C.7** Use homographs. **Also** 3.3.A.1, 3.3.A.2, 3.4.B.1, 3.4.B.3, 3.22.A.1.viii.2, 3.29.A.3, 3.31.A.4, 3.31.A.5, 3.31.A.6.

READING STREET ONLINE
ONLINE STUDENT EDITION
www.TexasReadingStreet.com

Vocabulary

Homonyms

Context Clues Remember that homonyms are words that have the same pronunciations and spellings, but different meanings. You can use nearby words and phrases to tell which meaning is being used in a sentence.

Practice It! Write two definitions for the homonym *pupil*. Then read the following sentence: *The pupil sat in the middle of the classroom.* Now circle the definition that is used in this sentence. Write down the other words or phrases in the sentence that tell you which definition is being used.

Fluency

Appropriate Phrasing

When you group together words and phrases according to the punctuation and meaning of a sentence, the story flows more smoothly.

Practice It! Read aloud page 340 of *Me and Uncle Romie* with a partner. Do you and your partner group certain words and phrases differently? Which way helps you better understand the story?

Listening and Speaking

Speak clearly and with expression, and then evaluate your performance.

Retelling

Retelling a story means to tell what happened in the story in your own words. Retellings include the most important events.

Practice It! Work in groups of three to retell *Me and Uncle Romie*. Listen for cues to know when your part begins. Each group member should talk the same amount of time.

Tips

Listening . . .

- Listen attentively.

- Respond to the literature, taking turns to ask questions and make comments.

Speaking . . .

- Determine your purpose for speaking.

- Speak clearly, with expression.

- Use transition words correctly.

Teamwork . . .

- Answer questions with detail.

TEKS

3.6.A.1 Describe characteristics of various forms of poetry. **3.6.A.2** Describe how the characteristics of various forms of poetry create imagery. **3.10.A.1** Identify language that creates a visual experience.

Poetry

- **Narrative poems** tell a story. Their stories can be simple, dramatic, humorous, or even a little sad.

- A narrative poem can be told in **free verse.** This means that it doesn't have **rhyme** patterns or a regular **rhythm,** or **cadence.** The words may appear in unusual ways, sometimes even without punctuation.

- A free verse poem may use the words and rhythms of everyday speech.

- A poet may use **alliteration,** or the repeated sounds of consonants, or **assonance,** the repeated sounds of vowels, to create more vivid images.

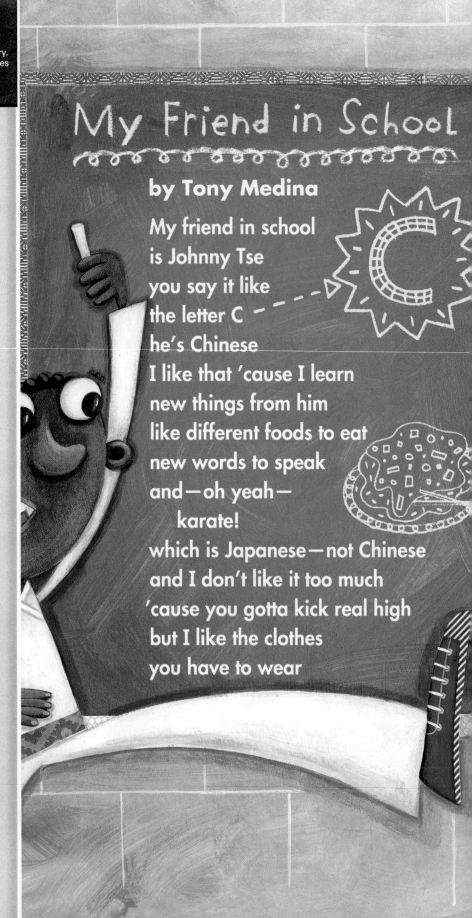

My Friend in School

by Tony Medina

My friend in school
is Johnny Tse
you say it like
the letter C
he's Chinese
I like that 'cause I learn
new things from him
like different foods to eat
new words to speak
and—oh yeah—
karate!
which is Japanese—not Chinese
and I don't like it too much
'cause you gotta kick real high
but I like the clothes
you have to wear

I go over to his house
to play video games
he comes over to my house
to eat and to watch cartoons

My friend in school
is Johnny Tse
which sounds like C
or see or sea
or sí (that's Spanish
if you didn't know)

My friend in school
is Johnny Tse
he's Chinese
and likes to sneeze
and when he does that
in school or outside
we laugh and laugh
and people wonder what
and wonder why and
what's so funny all the time

Let's **Think** About...

Can you find the **assonance,** or repetition, of the long *e* sound in this poem? Can you find the **alliteration** of the *w* sound at the end?

Let's **Think** About...

What makes "My Friend in School" a free verse poem? What pictures does this poem create in your mind?

Lunch Survey

by Kristine O'Connell George

We open our paper bags:

> Peanut butter plain
> Peanut butter tortilla
> Peanut butter pita
> P B & J
> P B & mayo
> P B & banana
> P B & pickles

Zach lifts the lid of his
insulated aluminum lunch box:
> sushi.

SAYING YES

By Diana Chang

"Are you Chinese?"
"Yes."

"American?"
"Yes."

"*Really* Chinese?"
"No . . . not quite."

"*Really* American?"
"Well, actually, you see. . ."

But I would rather say
yes

Not neither-nor
not maybe,
but both, and not only

The homes I've had,
the ways I am

I'd rather say it
twice,
yes

Unit 6

FREEDOM

THE BIG What does freedom mean?

TEKS

3.31.A.1 Participate in teacher-led discussions by posing questions with appropriate detail. **3.31.A.3** Participate in teacher-led discussions by providing suggestions that build upon the ideas of others. **Also 3.31.A.2**

Oral Vocabulary

Let's Talk About

Symbols of Freedom

- Comment about symbols of freedom.

- Pose and answer questions about symbols of freedom and unity.

- Offer suggestions for what it means to be free.

**READING STREET ONLINE
CONCEPT TALK VIDEO**
www.TexasReadingStreet.com

You've learned
2 4 6
Amazing Words
so far this year!

Envision It! | Sounds to Know

moon
oo

book
oo

push
u

newt
ew

glue
ue

fruit
ui

Phonics

Vowel Sounds in *moon* and *foot*

Words I Can Blend

raccoon

suit

threw

tissue

understood

input

Sentences I Can Read

1. A raccoon looks like a little bandit in its brown and black suit.

2. Megan threw the tissue in the wastebasket.

3. Has Tom understood how to input his address?

I Can Read!

We took our new pooch Moochie from an animal rescue shelter. The folks there understood we were looking for a dog that would suit our whole family.

The minute we set foot in there, we could see the place was full of cool pets. And we knew Moochie was the pet for us when he pushed past the others and shook my hand.

Moochie does drool a little, and sometimes he chews up tissues, but when he snoozes on my bed, he suits me just fine.

You've learned

🔵 Vowel Sounds in *moon* and *foot: oo, ew, ue, ui,* and *oo, u*

TEKS

3.2.B.2 Ask relevant questions about other texts. **3.2.B.6** Locate facts about other texts. **Also 3.2.B.4, 3.2.B.8, 3.2.B.9, 3.2.C.2, 3.2.C.3, 3.13.B.1, 3.13.B.2, RC-3.C.1, RC-3.C.2, RC-3.B.1, RC-3.B.2, RC-3.B.3.**

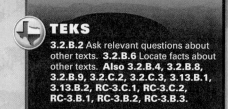

Envision It! | Skill Strategy

Skill

Strategy

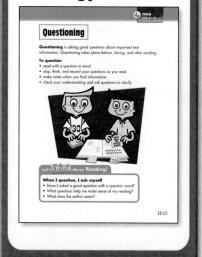

READING STREET ONLINE
ENVISION IT! ANIMATIONS
www.TexasReadingStreet.com

Comprehension Skill

🔄 Fact and Opinion

- A statement of fact tells something that can be proven true or false. You can prove it by reading a reference source.

- A statement of opinion tells someone's ideas or feelings. Words that tell feelings, such as *should* or *best*, are clue words.

- Use what you learned about fact and opinion and a chart like the one below as you read "Coming to America." Then use the facts to draw a conclusion about immigrants in America.

Fact	How to Prove

Opinion	Clue Words

Comprehension Strategy

🔄 Questioning

Active readers use questions to help them understand what they read. While you read, ask literal questions to make sure you understand. You can also ask yourself questions using what you already know or have read to interpret, connect to, or evaluate what you are reading.

Coming to America

The country where you were born is called your *homeland*. People who leave their homeland and come to another country—such as America—are called *immigrants*. America has been called a "nation of immigrants." Why?

Skill What are the facts in the paragraph? How could you prove whether they are true or false?

Everyone who lives in America now (except for Native Americans) once came from somewhere else. This may have happened a very long time ago in your family. Or maybe you and your family arrived here recently.

Immigrants leave their homeland for different reasons. Some came to America looking for religious freedom. Others came to escape war or hunger. But mostly, people came looking for a better life.

Strategy Ask questions to make sure you understand the text, such as *What are the different reasons people immigrate?*

People came to America from all over the world, but together we are one nation!

Your Turn!

⏸ **Need a Review?** See the *Envision It! Handbook* for more information about fact and opinion and questioning.

Let's **Think** About..

▶ **Ready to Try It?** As you read *The Story of the Statue of Liberty*, use what you've learned about fact and opinion and asking questions to understand the text.

371

TEKS

3.4.A.1 Identify the meaning of common prefixes. 3.4.A.2 Know how prefixes change the meaning of roots.

Envision It! | Words to Know

crown

liberty

torch

models

symbol

tablet

unforgettable

unveiled

Vocabulary Strategy for

Prefix *un-*

Word Structure Prefixes can give you clues to the meanings of unfamiliar words. The prefix *un-* at the beginning of a word means "not ____." For example, *un*pleasant means "not pleasant." When *un-* is added to a verb, it usually means the reverse of the verb. For instance, *un*cover means "to remove a cover."

1. When you see an unfamiliar word with a prefix, cover up the prefix.

2. What does the base word mean without the prefix?

3. Add "not" in front of the word. Does this meaning make sense in the sentence?

Read "Emma and Liberty" on page 373. Look for words that have prefixes. Use your knowledge of prefixes to find the meanings of these words.

Words to Write Reread "Emma and Liberty." What symbols of freedom have you seen or heard about? Write about symbols of freedom. Use as many words from the Words to Know list as you can.

Emma and Liberty

Emma is visiting New York City. What she wants to see more than anything else is the remarkable Statue of Liberty. Emma knows everything about Liberty. She knows why the statue was made, who made it, and when it was unveiled. She knows how tall it is from its base to its crown, what its torch is made of, and what is written on the tablet. Emma has collected pictures of the statue and reproduced models of it. However, she has never seen the real Liberty.

From Battery Park in Lower Manhattan, Emma has a breathless view of the Statue of Liberty in the distance. She waits in line for the boat that will safely take her to the island. As the boat gets nearer, Emma imagines what it was like for the immigrants who sailed past Liberty as they arrived in America.

At last Emma is standing at Liberty's feet. She tilts her head back to look up at this symbol of freedom. It is an unforgettable moment.

Your Turn!

⏸ **Need a Review?** For additional help with prefixes, see *Words!*

▶ **Ready to Try It?** Read *The Story of the Statue of Liberty* on pp. 374–385.

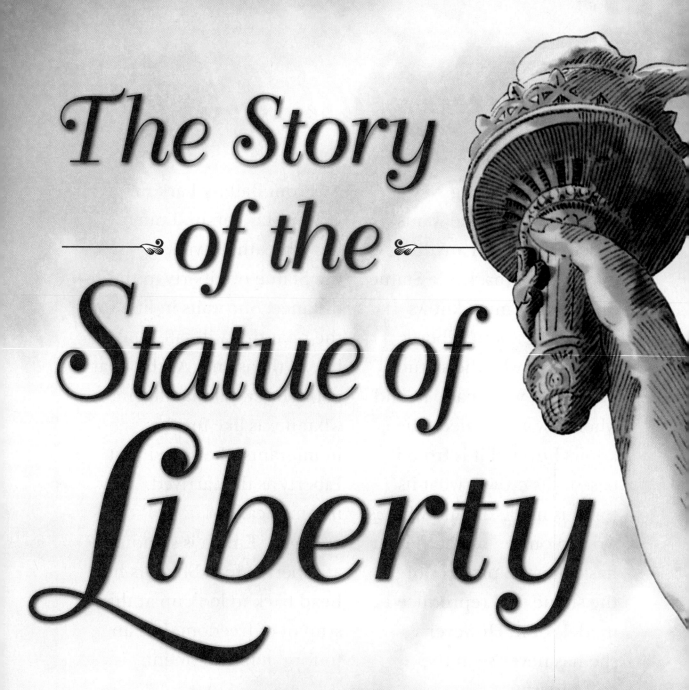

The Story of the Statue of Liberty

by Betsy & Giulio Maestro

Narrative nonfiction gives information about real people and events in the form of a story. What special event does this selection tell about?

Question of the Week

Why do we have symbols that represent freedom?

Let's Think About Reading!

The Statue of Liberty stands on an island in New York Harbor. She is a beautiful sight to all who pass by her. Each year, millions of visitors ride the ferry out to the island. They climb to the top of the statue and enjoy the lovely view.

A young French sculptor named Frédéric Auguste Bartholdi visited America in 1871. When he saw Bedloe's Island in New York Harbor, he knew it was just the right place for a statue he wanted to build.

Bartholdi had created many other statues and monuments, but this one was to be very special. It was to be a present from the people of France to the people of America, as a remembrance of the old friendship between the two countries.

When Bartholdi got back to Paris, he made sketches and some small models. The statue would be a woman whom he would call Liberty. She would be a symbol of the freedom in the New World. She would hold a lamp in her raised hand to welcome people who came to America. She would be *Liberty Enlightening the World.*

Let's **Think** About...

Ask yourself, "Who, what, where, why, how?"

▶ **Questioning**

The statue would be very large and very strong. Bartholdi wanted people to be able to climb up inside the statue and look out over the harbor from the crown and torch.

Many well-known artists, engineers, and craftsmen gave him ideas about how to build the statue. First, a huge skeleton was constructed from strong steel.

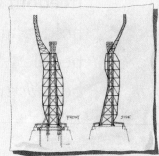

Many people worked together in a large workshop. Some worked on Liberty's head and crown. Others worked on her right hand, which would hold the torch.

In her left hand she would hold a tablet with the date July 4, 1776, written on it. This is when the Declaration of Independence was signed.

Let's Think About...

Why was the date July 4, 1776, included on the statue? Why is that important?
Important Ideas

The arm holding the torch was sent to Philadelphia for America's 100th birthday celebration in 1876. Afterward, it stood in Madison Square in New York City for a number of years.

Liberty's head was shown at the World's Fair in Paris during this time. Visitors were able to climb inside and look around. In this way, money was raised to pay for the statue.

Let's **Think** About...

Why might the makers of the Statue of Liberty exhibit it in different parts and places for a few years?
Inferring

Then, skin of gleaming copper was put onto the skeleton and held in place with iron straps. As the huge statue grew, all of Paris watched with great fascination.

Finally, in 1884, Liberty was completed. There was a big celebration in Paris. Many famous people came to see her. Only a few had the energy to climb all the way to the crown—168 steps!

Then began the hard work of taking Liberty apart for the long voyage across the Atlantic Ocean. Each piece was marked and packed into a crate. There were 214 crates in all. They were carried by train and then put on a ship to America.

Let's **Think** About...

Why did they take the statue apart after it was finally finished?
Inferring

381

Let's **Think** About...

What big structure have you seen being built, and how does that help you understand how Liberty was built?

Background Knowledge

But in America people had lost interest in the Statue of Liberty. Money had run out and work on Bedloe's Island had stopped. The base for the statue was not finished. With the help of a large New York newspaper, the money was raised. People all over the country, including children, sent in whatever they could. By the time the ship reached New York in 1885, it was greeted with new excitement.

The work on the island went on, and soon the pedestal was completed. Piece by piece, the skeleton was raised. Then the copper skin was riveted in place. Liberty was put back together like a giant puzzle. The statue had been built not once, but twice!

At last, in 1886, Liberty was standing where she belonged. A wonderful celebration was held. Boats and ships filled the harbor. Speeches were read, songs were sung. Bartholdi himself unveiled Liberty's face and she stood, gleaming in all her glory, for everyone to see. There was a great cheer from the crowd. Then President Grover Cleveland gave a speech.

Let's **Think** About...

Do you understand what you've read? Can you summarize the text using information from the selection to support your answer?
Summarize

Over the years, immigrants have arrived to begin new lives in America. To them, the Statue of Liberty is a symbol of all their hopes and dreams. She has welcomed millions of people arriving in New York by ship.

Every year, on the Fourth of July, the United States of America celebrates its independence. Fireworks light up the sky above New York Harbor. The Statue of Liberty is a truly unforgettable sight—a symbol of all that is America.

"Give me your tired, your poor,
Your huddled masses yearning to breathe free,
The wretched refuse of your teeming shore.
Send these, the homeless, tempest-tost to me,
I lift my lamp beside the golden door!"

–from "The New Colossus" by Emma Lazarus, 1883, placed on
a tablet on the pedestal of the Statue of Liberty in 1903

Let's **Think** About...

In the poem at the base of the Statue of Liberty, who are the people the Statue of Liberty invites? Why does she invite them?

⊙ **Questioning**

385

TEKS
3.12.A.1 Identify the topic of the text.
3.12.A.2 Locate the author's stated
purposes in writing the text. **Also**
3.2.B.2, 3.2.B.4, 3.2.B.6, 3.2.B.8,
3.2.B.9, 3.2.C.2, 3.2.C.3, 3.13.A.1,
RC-3.B.1, RC-3.B.2, RC-3.B.3, RC-
3.C.1, RC-3.C.2.

Envision It! Retell

READING STREET ONLINE
STORY SORT
www.TexasReadingStreet.com

Think Critically

1. In the story, the author writes about celebrating the Fourth of July. What do you do with your family, friends, and community to show your feelings about freedom? **Text to Self**

2. Read "Meet the Authors" on page 387. What is the topic in this selection? Why did the author write this story? What questions would you ask the authors about why they write? **Think Like an Author**

3. Look back at the story. Find some statements of opinion. Do you agree or disagree with any of the opinions? Tell why or why not using evidence from the text to support your answer. **Fact and Opinion**

4. What questions does the story bring up for you? Ask a literal, an interpretive, and an evaluative question and see if you or your classmates can answer them. **Questioning**

5. Look Back and Write Look back through the story to find what is interesting or important about the Statue of Liberty. Write a paragraph using facts and details to support this idea.

TEST PRACTICE Extended Response

Betsy and Giulio Maestro

Betsy and Giulio Maestro are husband and wife. They have published more than 100 books together! "We work on so many interesting books about so many different topics that we're always learning new things," Ms. Maestro says.

Ms. Maestro wrote this story because she feels a special connection to the Statue of Liberty. Her grandmother saw the statue for the first time as she arrived at Ellis Island from Russia in 1918. Because Ms. Maestro grew up in New York City, she visited the Statue of Liberty many times. On a class field trip, she even climbed to the crown. Ms. Maestro feels the statue is "a symbol of human freedom and human rights throughout the world."

Read more books by Betsy and Giulio Maestro.

The New Americans: Colonial Times: 1620–1689

The Story of Money

Use the Reader's and Writer's Notebook to record your independent reading.

TEKS

3.23.B.1.i Use capitalization for geographical names and places. **3.26.C.1** Take simple notes.

Expository

Notes

Taking **notes** helps you keep track of the most important information from an article or story. When you take notes, you write down in your own words the information that you want to make sure to remember. The student model on the next page is an example of note taking.

Writing Prompt Think about the most important ideas in *The Story of the Statue of Liberty*. Now write notes about one part of the selection.

Key Features of Notes

- capture important ideas from a story or article

- often help with a future writing task

- may include abbreviations, short sentences, and sentence fragments

**READING STREET ONLINE
GRAMMAR JAMMER**
www.TexasReadingStreet.com

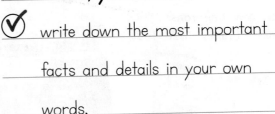

Writer's Checklist

Remember, you should . . .

☑ write down the most important facts and details in your own words.

☑ use short sentences, sentence fragments, and abbreviations.

☑ capitalize proper nouns, including geographical names and places.

Notes on "The Story of the Statue of Liberty" (first three pages)

- the S. of L. was a gift from France to U.S., symbol of long friendship between the countries
- made by French sculptor—Frédéric Auguste Bartholdi
- built on Bedloe's Island, New York Harbor
- holds a lamp in one hand to light up the world with liberty
- holds tablet in other hand—July 4, 1776
- Bartholdi wanted statue big enough for people to climb up inside, look out over harbor
- got help from famous artists, engineers, craftsmen
- built huge skeleton out of steel
- started with statue's head and crown and her right hand

Use **capital letters** correctly to keep proper names and abbreviations clear.

Writing Trait Focus/Ideas Paraphrase the most important ideas.

Genre Notes help readers keep track of important information.

Conventions

Capital Letters

Capitalize days of the week, months of the year, countries, historical events, holidays, and other proper nouns.

TEKS

3.13.B.1 Draw conclusions from facts presented in text. **3.15.B.1** Locate specific information in graphic features of text. **3.15.B.2** Use specific information in graphic features of text. **Also 3.2.A.1, 3.2.A.2, 3.13.A.1, 3.13.B.2, 3.13.D.1, RC-3.D.1, RC-3.D.2.**

Social Studies in Reading

A Nation of Immigrants

Genre
Textbook

- A textbook is a source of information, usually written about a specific topic.

- Textbooks use text features to help readers locate and remember the information.

- Textbook authors often use graphic sources, such as charts, to organize information visually.

- As you read "A Nation of Immigrants," think about how the chart and photos relate to the text.

For decades, immigrants have come to the United States from almost every other country in the world. Some people wanted freedom or better opportunities. Some came because there was very little food in their home country. Some came to find jobs or to work on farms. Others came because they had no choice.

Ellis Island

Many ships that came from Europe arrived first at Ellis Island, in New York Harbor. Many immigrants from Asia arrived at Angel Island, in San Francisco Bay. Immigrants also entered through other cities, such as Boston, Massachusetts; Galveston, Texas; and New Orleans, Louisiana.

 ———————

REVIEW What were some reasons immigrants came to the United States?

Times When Many Immigrants Came

Time Period	Where Many Were From
Before 1820	United Kingdom, countries of Western Africa, such as those now known as Ghana, Togo, Benin, Nigeria, and Cameroon
1820–1860	Ireland, Germany, United Kingdom, France, Canada
1861–1890	Germany, United Kingdom, Ireland, Canada, Norway/Sweden
1891–1920	Italy, Austria/Hungary, Russia, United Kingdom, Germany
1961–1990	Mexico, Philippines, Canada, Korea, Cuba

Angel Island

Let's Think About...

How do the text features and graphic sources help you learn the important ideas? **Textbook**

Let's Think About...

Reading Across Texts Immigrants from which countries would have been the first to see the new Statue of Liberty on Bedloe's Island? How do you know?

Writing Across Texts Imagine that you are one of those immigrants. Write a journal entry telling your impression of the Statue of Liberty.

391

TEKS

3.4.A.1 Identify the meaning of common prefixes. **3.4.A.2** Know how prefixes change the meaning of roots. **3.16.A.1** Understand how communication changes when moving from one genre of media to another. **3.16.B.1** Explain how various design techniques used in media influence the message. **Also 3.3.A.1, 3.3.A.2, 3.29.A.1, 3.29.A.2, 3.29.A.3, 3.29.B.3, 3.30.A.1, 3.30.A.2, 3.31.A.4, 3.31.A.5, 3.31.A.6.**

READING STREET ONLINE
ONLINE STUDENT EDITION
www.TexasReadingStreet.com

Vocabulary

Prefix *un-*

Word Structure Use your knowledge of the structure of words to understand the meanings of words. You can figure out the meaning of a word with a prefix if you know what the base word and the prefix both mean. The prefix *un-* means "not" or "the opposite of."

 Using a sheet of paper, predict the meanings of the following words, based on your understanding of the prefix *un-*: *unhappy, unfamiliar, unkind, unlike, unfinished, unforgettable.*

Fluency

Rate

Rate is an important skill for comprehending what you read. You can improve the rate at which you read by reading a text more than once. Then you can use a rate that matches the mood of the text.

Practice It! With a classmate, practice reading aloud page 381 of *The Story of the Statue of Liberty*. Read the page a second time. Did your rate improve? How quickly should you read to match the mood of the text?

Listening and Speaking

When making an announcement, use formal language.

Announcement

In an announcement, give information about a certain topic to inform or persuade listeners.

Practice It! Prepare an announcement about a new sculpture that is being put up in your city or town. Your announcement should be two minutes long. Include all the information a listener would need to find the new sculpture and attend the unveiling.

Tips

Listening . . .

- Listen attentively.
- Ask relevant questions.

Speaking . . .

- Speak at an appropriate pace.
- Use verbal cues.

Teamwork . . .

- Ask and answer questions about the differences between radio and TV announcements.
- Give suggestions for ways to influence or enhance the message.

Oral Vocabulary

Let's Talk About

Granting Freedom

- Share ideas about how freedom is granted to people and animals.

- Ask questions about what it means to be granted freedom.

- Pose and answer questions about how freedom is granted through laws.

READING STREET ONLINE
CONCEPT TALK VIDEO
www.TexasReadingStreet.com

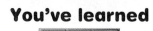

395

TEKS

3.1.B Use common syllabication patterns to decode words.

Phonics

Schwa

Words I Can Blend

ab**o**ut

b**e**n**e**fit

d**i**ff**i**cult

p**o**pul**a**r

an**o**nym**o**us

Sentences I Can Read

1. The fire chief told us about the benefits of having a working smoke detector.

2. Red is a popular color.

3. The gift was anonymous.

I Can Read!

My father is a chef in a restaurant. He often tries new dishes to interest the customers. Sometimes he brings home samples of his unusual creations for us to taste.

One of his specialties was called spaghetti surprise, and it was delicious. On analysis, the surprise contained meatballs stuffed with cheese, onions, and oregano.

My family enjoys being my father's official tasters. He is an excellent cook, and we are allowed to taste the first version.

You've learned

 Schwa spelled *a, e, i, o, u*

TEKS

3.13.C.1 Identify explicit cause-and-effect relationships among ideas in texts. **RC-3.D.1** Make inferences about a text. **RC-3.D.2** Use textual evidence to support understanding.

Envision It! | Skill Strategy

Skill

Strategy

READING STREET ONLINE
ENVISION IT! ANIMATIONS
www.TexasReadingStreet.com

Comprehension Skill

Cause and Effect

- An effect is something that happens.

- A cause is why that thing happens.

- An effect may have more than one cause.

- Use what you learned about cause and effect and a chart like the one below as you read "A New Life." Then write a short paragraph summarizing the cause-and-effect relationships.

Causes	Effects

Comprehension Strategy

Inferring

As you read a selection, you make inferences, or decisions that make sense after you combine the details or facts the author has included with what you already know. When you come up with your own ideas based on information in a text, you are inferring.

398

A New Life

An *immigrant* is a person who has moved from one country into another. According to the U.S. Census Bureau, in 1990, the foreign-born population in the United States was about 19.8 million. By the year 2000, that number had grown to 37.2 million! Immigrants make up about 12.5 percent of the United States population.

There are many reasons that people have immigrated to the United States. Many people view the United States as a place where people can achieve any goal if they put their minds to it and work hard. Some come here because of the opportunities to build better lives for themselves and their families. Some move here so they can experience the freedom that the United States offers.

Immigrants bring with them their cultural heritage, traditions, and new ideas. They have helped build the United States to make it what it is today.

Skill What has caused some people to move to the United States?

Strategy What are some of the benefits of people immigrating to the United States?

Your Turn!

⏸ Need a Review? See the *Envision It! Handbook* for help with cause and effect and inferring.

▶ Ready to Try It? As you read *Happy Birthday Mr. Kang,* use what you've learned about cause and effect and inferring to understand the text.

TEKS

3.4.B.1 Use context to determine the relevant meaning of unfamiliar words.
3.4.C.1 Identify antonyms.
3.4.C.5 Use antonyms.

Envision It! | Words to Know

foreign

narrow

recipe

bows

chilly

foolish

perches

Vocabulary Strategy for

🎯 Antonyms

Context Clues Sometimes you will read a word you don't know. The author may include an antonym for the word. An antonym is a word that means the opposite of another word. For example, *hot* is the opposite of *cold*. Look for an antonym to figure out the meaning of the word.

1. Look at the words around the unfamiliar word. The author may have used an antonym.

2. Do you recognize a word that seems to have the opposite meaning of the unfamiliar word?

3. Use the antonym to help you figure out the meaning of the unfamiliar word.

Read "Mr. Wang's Wonderful Noodles" on page 401. Look for antonyms to help you understand the meanings of unfamiliar words.

Words to Write Reread "Mr. Wang's Wonderful Noodles." Write about your favorite food. How does it taste? Why do you like it? Use words from the Words to Know list and antonyms in your story.

MR. WANG'S WONDERFUL Noodles

Mr. Wang is the best noodle maker in Shanghai, China. People who like wide, thick noodles may think people who like narrow, thin noodles are foolish. People who like narrow, thin noodles may think people who like wide, thick noodles are not very smart. But everyone agrees on one thing. Mr. Wang's noodles are the best.

One day, a stranger perches on a stool at the noodle shop. Mr. Wang bows his head in respect. The stranger says, "Mr. Wang, please bring your noodle recipe to the United States. Make noodles in my restaurant."

People stop slurping their noodles to listen to Mr. Wang's reply. The warm shop suddenly feels chilly.

Mr. Wang says, "Thank you. But I do not wish to go to a foreign land. I am happy making noodles in China."

Everyone heaves a sigh of relief. Everyone goes back to slurping Mr. Wang's wonderful noodles.

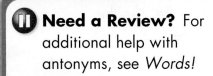

Your Turn!

Need a Review? For additional help with antonyms, see *Words!*

Ready to Try It? Read *Happy Birthday Mr. Kang*, pp. 402–419.

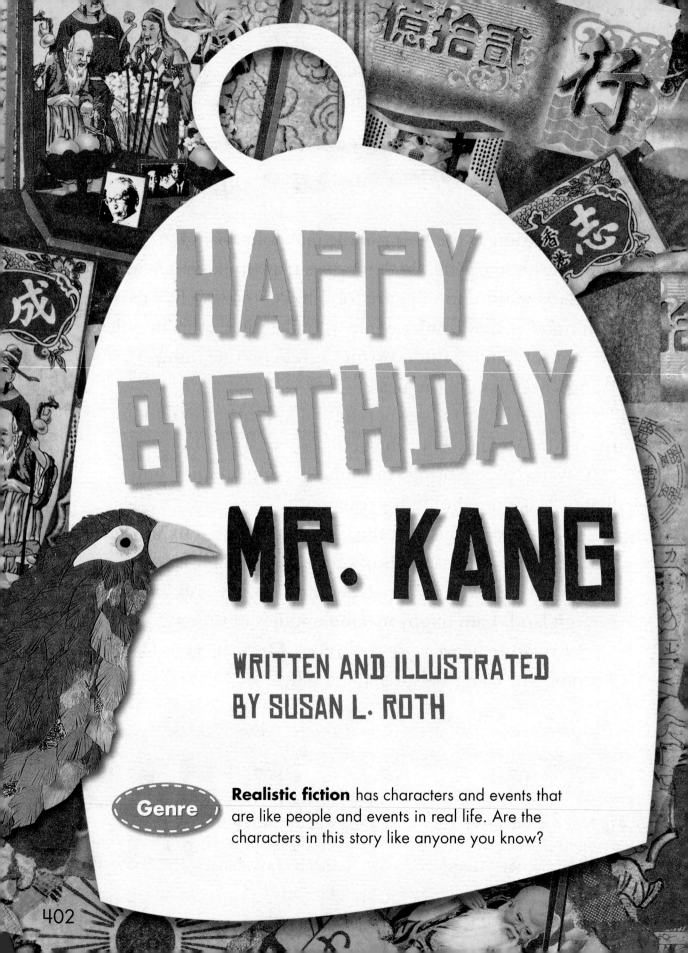

HAPPY BIRTHDAY MR. KANG

WRITTEN AND ILLUSTRATED BY SUSAN L. ROTH

Genre

Realistic fiction has characters and events that are like people and events in real life. Are the characters in this story like anyone you know?

Question of the Week
**What does it mean
to grant freedom?**

Forty-three years before his grandson, Sam, was born in the New World, Mr. Kang left China and came to America. Every day he chopped scallions, wrapped dumplings, and pulled noodle dough into long and perfect strands for the hungry people who ate at the Golden Dragon Restaurant in New York City.

When Mr. Kang turned seventy, Mrs. Kang had a birthday party for him.

"Make a wish!" said Sam as Mr. Kang shut his eyes, puffed his cheeks, and blew out all the candles on his cake. Everyone clapped and shouted hurray.

"What was your wish?" Sam asked.

"Three wishes," said Mr. Kang. "I want to read *The New York Times* every day. I want to paint poems every day. And I want a bird, a *hua mei*, of my own. I'll feed him every day, and on Sundays I'll take him to Sara Delano Roosevelt Park on Delancey Street. Enough cooking."

"Good idea," said Mrs. Kang. "I'll cook for you, and the Golden Dragon Restaurant can get a new cook."

"Grandpa, why do you want a bird in a cage? There are birds all over the place outside," said Sam.

"Sam," said Mr. Kang. "This is not just an American bird in a cage. This is a Chinese bird. My grandfather had a hua mei in a cage. Now I want a hua mei in a cage. And sometimes you and I will take him to Sara Delano Roosevelt Park on Delancey Street together."

And so it is that every morning Mr. Kang finds *The New York Times* on his doorstep. Every morning he reads it while he drinks his tea and eats his sweet and fragrant almond cakes, warm from the oven.

Mr. Kang sits at the kitchen table and thinks about the sun showing through the trees in the park or the moon peeking into his window. He listens to words in his head, then he picks up his brush and paints a poem. Sometimes he paints a poem twice to practice his brushwork. Mrs. Kang hangs the poems on the kitchen cabinets.

And then, after making sure that the door and the windows are shut, Mr. Kang opens his hua mei's cage. Speaking softly, he invites the bird to stand on the table.

Mr. Kang cleans the cage with a damp towel and dries it with a soft cloth. He takes out the hand-painted ceramic water bowl, rinses it, and puts it back in its stand, full of cool, clear water. He washes the hand-painted ceramic food bowl and puts it back, full of his own special recipe of millet coated with egg yolks and mixed with chopped meat. These days this is the only cooking Mr. Kang does.

Last, Mr. Kang takes a small piece of silk cloth, dampens it with water not too hot, not too cold, and gently wipes the sleek gray feathers of his bird. The hua mei walks right back into his cage. He prefers to give himself a bath.

"Never mind, Birdie," says Mr. Kang. "Instead of the bath, I'll read you my poem. I know you can understand. We both left our homeland. We still speak the old language."

Rushing to the Golden Dragon
against a chilly wind,
the icy tears on my cheeks melt
with memories of warm old days.

Those who never left their home
stay safe, wrapped
in the arms of their motherfather land.
When they look out
their narrow windows,
they see their own kitchen gardens.
They know every plum tree, every kumquat,
every blade of grass, each gray pebble.

We who long ago tossed on cold waters
looking only straight ahead
watch our city mountains
from wide windows, tall rooftops.
Yet our old hearts hold old places.
We save, in old, grown heads,
a full-blown rose in summer,
the sound of bamboo leaves when
the wind is gentle,
the taste of mooncakes.

The hua mei sings his own melody back
to Mr. Kang. Mr. Kang closes his eyes to listen.
"Beautiful, Birdie. You are a good poet
and a good friend to me," says Mr. Kang.

Sam usually comes to visit on Saturdays. If Mr. Kang is cleaning the cage, then the hua mei sings to Sam. Sam holds out his finger, and the hua mei holds on tightly. They stare at each other, each without blinking.

"Did he really fly from China?" Sam asks one time.

"In an airplane," says Mr. Kang. "China is so far, even for a bird."

"You should let him go. Maybe he wants to fly home."

"I don't think he could without an airplane. Anyway, he's like me. Home is here with you. If he went home now, I think he would miss his Sundays on Delancey Street." Mr. Kang puts his arm around Sam's shoulders and hugs him.

"I have a very smart grandson," he sighs. "Maybe one day we can visit China together."

And this is how Mr. Kang spends his days, except for Sundays.

On Sundays Mr. Kang gets up when it's dark. He washes his face and puts on his clothes. When he is ready, he picks up the cage by the ring on top. The freshly ironed cover is tied shut, and the bird is still sleeping. As he opens the door to leave the apartment, Mrs. Kang is padding quickly behind him.

"Wait for me!" she calls.

"Shhhh!" says Mr. Kang, but he waits as she closes the door and turns her key.

Mr. Kang and his bird lead the way. He walks gingerly, holding onto the banister to steady himself as he goes down the stairs. Out the door, down the block, across the street he glides, to Sara Delano Roosevelt Park on Delancey Street.

Mrs. Kang follows, three steps behind. She sees her friends and slips away to join them.

Mr. Kang hangs the cage on the fence, stretches his arms, and breathes in the morning.

Mr. Lum arrives with a cage in each hand. "How are you, my friend? How is the bird?"

"We are enjoying the morning," smiles Mr. Kang.

"Mr. Lum!
When I see your cages
resting on the green ivy floor
of Sara Delano Roosevelt Park in New York,

I remember my arm is lifted up to hold
Grandfather's big hand
and that ivy is green
from the Shanghai sun
and that ginkgo tree is blowing
in the soft Shanghai breeze
and that heat in my breast
is from my sweet and fragrant almond cake.
Grandmother slipped it into my pocket,
and it is still there,
warm from her oven."

"Even when you speak a greeting to your friend you are painting a poem," says Mr. Lum. Mr. Kang bows his head.

Today is a special Sunday morning because Sam and Mr. Kang are going to the park together. Sam slept at his grandparents' house last night. It is still dark, and he is rubbing his eyes as he jumps from his bed. Just like Grandpa, he washes his face and puts on his clothes. Together, at dawn's first light, they lift the cage. The cover is still tied, the bird is still sleeping. Sam opens the front door. Grandpa steps out, and Grandma is there right behind him, just as she is every Sunday morning.

"Wait for me!" she says.

"*Shhhh!*" say Mr. Kang and Sam, but they wait as she closes the door. Mrs. Kang takes one extra minute to slip two warm almond cakes into Sam's pocket. Then Sam and Mr. Kang lead the way down the stairs, out the front door, on to the corner, across the street, all the way to Sara Delano Roosevelt Park on Delancey Street.

As usual, Mrs. Kang follows until she sees her friends. Sam sets the bird cage gently on the ground. Mr. Lum's cages are already hanging.

"Look who's here!" says Mr. Lum. "How are you, Sam? You're getting so big. How old are you?"

"Seven," says Sam.

"Only seven?" says Mr. Lum. "You're handling that cage better than a twelve-year-old would!"

Sam smiles.

"An old grandfather does not mind growing old in a foreign land with such a grandson," says Mr. Kang.

"I am happy in this strange land:
I see my grandson planted
in the new, rich earth,
growing straight and smart and tall.
I water him.
The sun shines on his
firm young leaves
as I watch for his flowers
and for his fruit."

"More poems, Mr. Kang," says Mr. Lum. "I think you always speak in poems."

"Your ears are kind to my words, my friend," says Mr. Kang. Two more men with two more cages arrive, then another and yet another. Soon there are twenty-seven cages in the park.

Mr. Kang lets Sam untie the cover. A strand of light passes through the bamboo bars. As the sun climbs, the men and Sam open all the curtains, inch by inch.

A bird calls and is answered by another.

"They sing sad songs," says Sam.

"They sing of their strong young years," says Mr. Lum.

"They sing about their grandfathers," says Mr. Wu.

"Maybe they sing about their grandsons," says Sam.

"They sing about being in their cages," says Mr. Wu. "Probably they want to fly out."

"Like me in my cage," says Mr. Kang. "Like me, making noodles every day for fifty years."

"I would fly out if I were a bird," says Sam.

Mr. Kang stands away from the fence. "Maybe my smart grandson is right. Maybe this bird should be free."

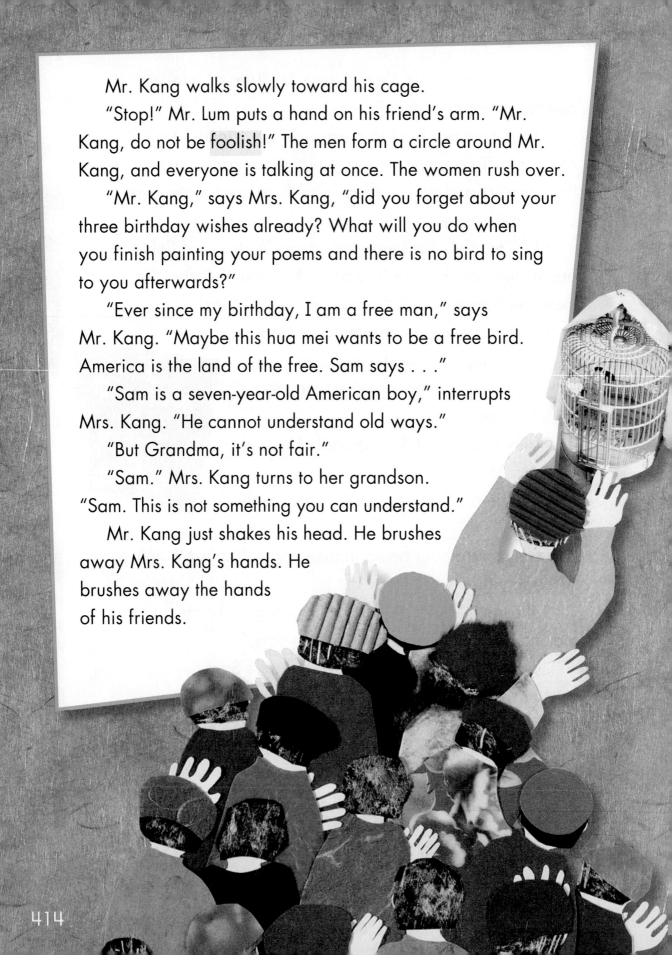

Mr. Kang walks slowly toward his cage.

"Stop!" Mr. Lum puts a hand on his friend's arm. "Mr. Kang, do not be foolish!" The men form a circle around Mr. Kang, and everyone is talking at once. The women rush over.

"Mr. Kang," says Mrs. Kang, "did you forget about your three birthday wishes already? What will you do when you finish painting your poems and there is no bird to sing to you afterwards?"

"Ever since my birthday, I am a free man," says Mr. Kang. "Maybe this hua mei wants to be a free bird. America is the land of the free. Sam says . . ."

"Sam is a seven-year-old American boy," interrupts Mrs. Kang. "He cannot understand old ways."

"But Grandma, it's not fair."

"Sam." Mrs. Kang turns to her grandson. "Sam. This is not something you can understand."

Mr. Kang just shakes his head. He brushes away Mrs. Kang's hands. He brushes away the hands of his friends.

Suddenly Sam is frightened. What if Grandma is right? What if Grandpa is sorry after the hua mei flies away? What if the hua mei gets lost? What if he starves? What if he dies?

"Grandpa, wait," says Sam. But Grandpa does not hear. Mr. Kang cannot hear any voice except the voice inside his own head, inside his own heart. He opens the bamboo door.

Mr. Kang's hua mei perches on the threshold of his cage. Perhaps he thinks it's cage-cleaning time. He slowly steps out. He stops to sing a long, sweet note, turns his head to the breeze, and flies into the sky.

Mr. Kang takes off his cap and covers his heart with his hand. For a moment there is silence. Mrs. Kang bends her head and hugs herself. Her mouth is a thin straight line. "Oh, Mr. Kang," she whispers in Chinese. "What can you be thinking?" Sam starts to cry.

"Sam and I are going home to paint poems," says Mr. Kang loudly, in English.

He lifts his empty cage, takes Sam's hand, and together they walk out of the park. Onto the sidewalk, over to the corner, across the street, up the block they walk.

NO DOGS

DOGS

SARA D.
ROOSEVELT
PARK

Just as they get to Mr. Kang's apartment, there, on the railing, sits the hua mei. Mr. Kang and Sam stop short. The bird flies onto Sam's head.

417

Then up the stairs and into the kitchen they run. They sit at the table, coats and caps still on. The hua mei hops onto Sam's paper. Mr. Kang paints his poem as Sam paints his picture. The bird helps.

After forty-three American years
I still speak my native tongue,
but any Chinese ear can hear
that I no longer speak
like a native. Sometimes

even I can hear
the familiar sounds bending
by themselves in my own throat,
coming out strangely,
sounding a little American. Yet

those same words in English suffer more.
I open up
my American mouth and
no one needs to see my face to know
my ship was never Mayflower. But

at home, with even you, my hua mei, peeping
a little like a sparrow,
I sit at my kitchen table, and I paint these words.
They sing out without accent:
We are Americans, by choice.

四十三個美國寒暑之後，
我仍說著自個兒的母語，
但是任何一個中國人都能聽出
我不再說得道地。有時候
甚至能聽見熟悉的聲調，
將異得帶些美國腔。然而
非常拗口地說出來。
受盡英語說出，更要
別人不需看我的面貌就能道
同樣的詞語用美語說出，只要一張口說美語
它們不帶一點口音地吟唱著，
我坐在釣魚餐桌旁畫眉
在家裏甚至和你一畫眉，
得像隻麻雀
吱吱喳喳
我們是美國人，全憑選擇。
是塔五月花船來的。
許許多多的字

HUA MEI

418

"This is your poem, Birdie," says Mr. Kang, "and Sam, it's your poem too."

Then Mr. Kang looks at Sam's painting. "My grandson is a great artist," he says. He hangs the paintings on the kitchen cabinet and sits back to admire them.

Mrs. Kang walks into the kitchen with her mouth still in that thin straight line, but there is the bird, and suddenly she is smiling.

"Today I'll cook for both of you, and for your hua mei," she says.

And she makes tea, and more sweet and fragrant almond cakes, warm from the oven.

419

TEKS

3.8.A.3 Explain the plot's main events' influence on future events. **RC-3.D.1** Make inferences about text. **RC-3.D.2** Use textual evidence to support understanding. Also **3.11.A.1, 3.11.A.2, 3.11.A.3.**

Envision It! | **Retell**

READING STREET ONLINE
STORY SORT
www.TexasReadingStreet.com

Think Critically

1. Compare this story to the historical fiction story *Me and Uncle Romie.* How are the two stories alike? How are they different? **Text to Text**

2. Find the most interesting illustration in the story. Pretend that you are the author. Explain why that illustration enhances your story. **Think Like an Author**

3. What caused Mr. Kang to change his mind about his *hua mei?* What was the effect? **Cause and Effect**

4. How do you know that Sam thinks the *hua mei* should be freed? Do you think Mr. Kang is happy he let the bird out of its cage? Use evidence from the story to explain your answer. **Inferring**

5. **Look Back and Write** What is special about Mr. Kang's birthday? Look back through the story and think about what Mr. Kang does during the days after his birthday. Write a response to the question, providing evidence to support your answer.

TEST PRACTICE | **Extended Response**

420

SUSAN L. ROTH

Susan L. Roth got the idea for *Happy Birthday Mr. Kang* from a story in the *New York Times.* She read about a group of Chinese men who brought their pet *hua mei* birds to the park each Sunday. Ms. Roth went to the park to check it out. "It was very noisy," she said. "They were clearly communicating with each other."

Happy Birthday Mr. Kang is dedicated to Ms. Roth's uncle, John Kang. "I used his real name, but he never worked in a Chinese restaurant or had a *hua mei*. But he did write poetry after he retired." Mr. Kang always wrote his poems in Chinese first. Then he translated them into English.

Ms. Roth says she hopes her books teach children to appreciate different people. "I live in Queens, New York, one of the most diverse places in the world. So I see different cultures every day." Ms. Roth says children who learn about different cultures are less likely to become prejudiced.

Read more books by Susan L. Roth.

The Biggest Frog in Australia

How Thunder and Lightning Came to Be

Use the Reader's and Writer's Notebook to record your independent reading.

421

TEKS

3.18.B.1 Write poems that convey sensory details using the conventions of poetry.

Key Features of a Limerick

- a form of poetry
- made up of five lines and a specific rhyme scheme
- sometimes humorous or witty

READING STREET ONLINE
GRAMMAR JAMMER
www.TexasReadingStreet.com

Limerick

A **limerick** is a form of poetry with five lines and its own special rhyme and rhythm structure. Limericks follow an a-a-b-b-a rhyming pattern. Each set of rhyming lines has a specific rhythm. The student models on the next page are examples of limericks.

Writing Prompt Write a limerick about the story *Happy Birthday Mr. Kang*.

Writer's Checklist

Remember, you should . . .

✓ write five lines of verse.

✓ follow the correct rhythm of two or three accents per line.

✓ make the first, second, and last lines rhyme.

✓ make the third and fourth lines rhyme.

✓ include sensory details in your poem.

Mr. Kang leaves the house so early
But then **Mrs.** Kang says, "Wait for me!"
They move across the floor,
and walk out the door.
Mrs. Kang locks the door with a key.

Mr. Kang has a bird called "hua mei,"
Which he takes outside with him one day.
The bird's freed at the park,
And it sings like a lark.
Does it come back or fly far away?

Abbreviations are used correctly.

Writing Trait Organization A limerick's first, second, and fifth lines rhyme and have three accents. The third and fourth lines rhyme and have 2 accents.

Genre A **limerick** is a form of poetry.

Conventions

Abbreviations

Remember An **abbreviation** is a shortened form of a word. Many abbreviations begin with a capital letter and end with a period.

TEKS

3.13.D.1 Use text features to locate information. **3.13.D.2** Make predictions about contents of text. **3.13.D.3** Verify predictions about contents of text. **Also 3.2.A.1, 3.2.A.2, 3.2.B.2, 3.2.B.6, 3.2.B.8, 3.2.B.9, 3.13.A.1, RC-3.D.2, RC-3.F.2.**

Social Studies in Reading

Genre
Expository Text

- In expository texts, the author presents facts and details to support the main idea about a topic.

- Expository texts are sometimes organized using questions and answers.

- Photographs, captions, and illustrations show information visually.

- As you read "Once Upon a Constitution," ask yourself, *What is the topic? What is the main idea about the topic? and What will I learn about the main idea as I keep reading?*

Once Upon a Constitution

BY RON FRIDELL

curlicues

quill pen

424

Once upon a time the United States of America was born. That was more than two centuries ago.

What did these new American citizens need most? A single set of laws and rules for everyone to live by. So some very wise men assembled in the year 1787 in Philadelphia, Pennsylvania, to write a document called the Constitution.

Let's **Think** About...

Look at the labels, captions, and illustrations on these two pages. What facts can you learn about the Constitution?
Expository Text

the Constitution

PHILADELPHIA

Back in those distant days, there were no typewriters or computers to work with. People wrote down everything by hand, using quill pens made from bird feathers, and their handwriting had all sorts of fancy loops and curlicues. The men who created the Constitution wrote on parchment made from animal skin. Parchment lasted longer than paper, and they wanted this document to last for centuries.

425

So, what did this Constitution say? It told who made the laws and how. Back then in most nations, a monarch or emperor held all the power. If those rulers made careless decisions regarding the government, they would end up harming people. What kind of rulers would America have?

There would be no monarchs or emperors in the United States. Instead, in America, many people would contribute to creating the laws because the Constitution said so. It made the United States a democracy, a nation where the power belongs to its citizens.

Let's **Think** About...

How do the questions in the text introduce important ideas and details?
Expository Text

Founding Fathers

Was this Constitution a perfect document? It was a good beginning, but would require some perfecting. It talked about freedoms and liberties, but it didn't actually name them. So in 1791, a new part was added: the Bill of Rights. These ten amendments granted Americans basic rights, or freedoms.

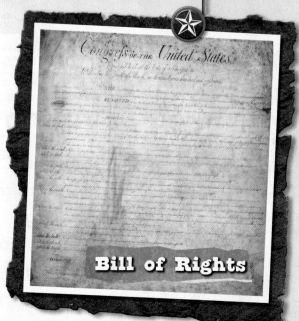

Bill of Rights

One of those basic rights is freedom of speech. It means that people can tell others what they think and feel. The government cannot stop people from saying or writing whatever they want.

Another right is freedom of religion. The Constitution grants people the right to attend any church and worship any way they wish.

In the centuries that followed, more amendments were added to grant more rights and freedoms. Today, the Constitution still keeps Americans free and safe, just as it did once upon a time, more than two hundred years ago.

Let's **Think** About...

Reading Across Texts Mr. Kang says, "America is the land of the free." Do you think the Constitution and the Bill of Rights are important to Mr. Kang?

Writing Across Texts List some reasons for your answer. Then write a paragraph summarizing what you have learned.

TEKS

3.4.B.1 Use context to determine the relevant meaning of unfamiliar words. **3.4.C.1** Identify antonyms. **3.4.C.5** Use antonyms. **3.30.A.1** Speak coherently about the topic under discussion. **3.30.A.2** Speak coherently, employing eye contact, speaking rate, volume, enunciation, and the conventions of language to communicate ideas effectively. **Also 3.3.A.1, 3.3.A.2, 3.4.D.1, 3.4.D.2, 3.29.A.1, 3.29.A.2, 3.29.A.3, 3.31.A.4, 3.31.A.5, 3.31.A.6.**

READING STREET ONLINE
ONLINE STUDENT EDITION
www.TexasReadingStreet.com

Vocabulary

Antonyms

Context Clues Remember that antonyms are words that have opposite meanings. Finding an antonym when reading is one way to figure out the meaning of an unfamiliar word.

 **Practice It!** Read this tongue twister. Then find and list three antonym pairs: *Ned will go for wide, thick noodles. Nellie needs narrow, thin noodles. Neither Ned nor Nellie will nibble chilly noodles. Nellie won't wait for warm noodles either.*

Fluency

Appropriate Phrasing

Pause when you come to a comma or a period when reading. When you read poetry, use punctuation, not line breaks, for grouping words together.

Practice It! Read aloud the poem on page 412, pausing at the end of lines. Then read the poem again, grouping together words using punctuation. Does this help you to better understand the poem?

Listening and Speaking

Use appropriate strategies—ask questions, make comments—to keep a discussion going.

Express an Opinion

When you express an opinion, use facts and explanations to support your opinion and prove your point.

Practice It! Deliver a speech that expresses your opinion about a topic that is important in your community. First, brainstorm a list of several topics being discussed in your community. Topics may include a new playground or swimming pool.

Tips

Listening ...

• Sit quietly and listen.

• Draw a conclusion about what the speaker says.

Speaking ...

• Use appropriate persuasive techniques.

• Speak clearly and distinctly.

• Make eye contact.

Teamwork ...

• Ask questions and give detailed answers about the topic.

TEKS

3.29.A.2 Ask relevant questions.
3.30.A.2 Speak coherently, employing eye contact, speaking rate, volume, enunciation, and the conventions of language to communicate ideas effectively.

Oral Vocabulary

Let's Talk About

Freedom of Expression

- Ask what people can gain from freedom of expression.

- Share ideas about how to express ideas or feelings constructively.

- Pose and answer questions about how to best convey a message.

READING STREET ONLINE
CONCEPT TALK VIDEO
www.TexasReadingStreet.com

430

You've learned
2 6 6
Amazing Words
so far this year!

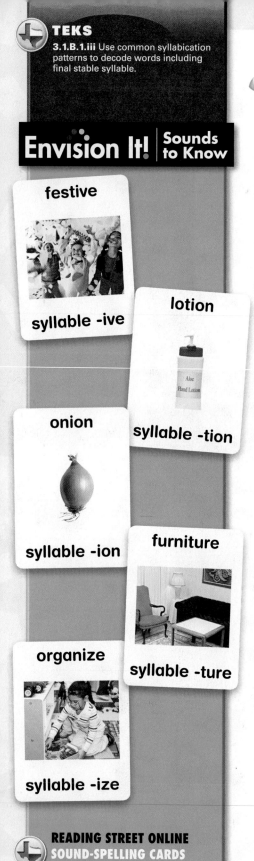

TEKS
3.1.B.1.iii Use common syllabication patterns to decode words including final stable syllable.

Envision It! | Sounds to Know

festive
syllable -ive

lotion
syllable -tion

onion
syllable -ion

furniture
syllable -ture

organize
syllable -ize

Phonics

Final Syllables *-tion, -ion, -ture, -ive, -ize*

Words I Can Blend

contraction

cushion

puncture

festive

specialize

Sentences I Can Read

1. The word *I'll* is a contraction.

2. The scissors created a puncture mark on the cushion.

3. Party planners specialize in festive occasions.

I Can Read!

Mary is a woman on a mission. She has a vision for building a creative arts center in her city. She visualizes a massive stage to dramatize stories, a room for painting, and a computer room for writing fiction. She will display art from her native land made by her relatives.

Her motive is to bring together a mixture of people from different cultures to create art and learn from each other's traditions—a union of people and ideas. Will others sympathize with her motive and donate money to help Mary to realize her goals? Your contribution will help Mary arrive at the finish line!

You've learned

🔘 Final Syllables -*tion*, -*ion*, -*ture*, -*ive*, -*ize*

TEKS

3.15.B.1 Locate specific information in graphic features of text. 3.15.A.2 Explain a set of written multi-step directions. 3.15.B.2 Use specific information in graphic features of text. **Also 3.2.B.4, 3.2.B.6, 3.2.B.8, 3.2.B.9, 3.13.D.1, 3.15.A.1.**

Envision It! | Skill Strategy

Skill

Strategy

Comprehension Skill

Graphic Sources

- Graphic sources are ways of showing information visually, or in a way you can see. They provide additional information to the text.

- Charts, photos, diagrams, and maps are all graphic sources.

- Use what you learned about graphic sources as you read "Ancient Cave Murals." Then, using the procedural text and the color wheel, write a paragraph explaining the steps to make purple paint.

Comprehension Strategy

Important Ideas

Active readers look for graphic sources and text features that often present important ideas. An author's most important ideas can be emphasized in graphic sources. Graphic sources help readers better understand the text.

434

Ancient Cave Murals

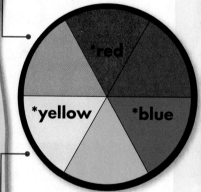

In 1940, four teenage boys discovered a cave covered with murals of animals. People had painted the murals about 17,000 years ago. Scientists studied the cave paintings and found that the ancient artists made their paint using pigment, which is a powder that gives paint its color. They were able to make very few colors of paint.

There are only three primary colors that, along with black and white, make all other colors. Today we can buy or make any color of paint we want!

Skill What colors do you see in the murals?

Strategy What important idea is shown by the color wheel?

*red

*yellow   *blue

*primary color

Skill What colors would you add together to make orange? Try it in art class!

How to Make Green Paint

1. Choose yellow and blue paint pigment.
2. Add water or oil and mix it together.
3. Add black or white pigment to make the green darker or lighter.
4. Add more blue or more yellow until you have a green you like!

Your Turn!

❚❚ Need a Review? See the *Envision It! Handbook* for information about graphic sources and important ideas.

▶ Ready to Try It? As you read *Talking Walls,* use what you've learned about graphic sources and important ideas to understand the text.

Talking Walls
Art for the People

435

TEKS

3.4.E.2 Use a dictionary or glossary to determine meanings of unknown words. **3.4.E.3** Use a dictionary or glossary to determine syllabication of unknown words. **3.4.E.4** Use a dictionary or glossary to determine pronunciation of unknown words.

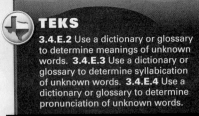

Envision It! | Words to Know

encourages

expression

native

local

settled

social

support

Vocabulary Strategy for

Unknown Words

Dictionary/Glossary When you read an unknown word, ask yourself if it's a noun, verb, or adjective. Knowing what part of speech a word is can help you find and understand its meaning. Then use a dictionary or glossary to find the correct meaning and how the word is pronounced.

1. Use the first letter in the word to find it in the dictionary or glossary.

2. Look at the pronunciation key and each syllable to pronounce the word correctly.

3. Read the definitions of the word. Choose a meaning for the correct part of speech.

4. Try your meaning in the sentence. Does it make sense? If not, try another meaning.

Read "Class Art" on page 437. Use a dictionary or glossary to find the meanings and pronunciations of the Words to Know.

Words to Write Reread "Class Art." Sort the Words to Know into three groups: nouns, adjectives, and verbs, according to how each is used in the selection.

Class Art

Ms. Ramsey's students are excited. They are planning to paint a mural on one wall in their classroom. Ms. Ramsey encourages the students to talk about what they will paint on the mural. Everyone has a different idea. Julio's family came to the United States from Mexico. He wants to paint something about his native country. Mary wants to paint something about the community's history. Her family settled here a long, long time ago. Gerrard thinks the mural should show the social life of the people who live in the community. Diana thinks the mural should be more about global, not local, issues. It should show how the community is part of the world. How can the students get all these ideas on one mural? Ms. Ramsey points out that the mural should be an expression of the group's interests and beliefs. She says that with a little planning, the students can paint a mural that will support everyone's ideas.

Your Turn!

❚❚ Need a Review? For additional help with unknown words, see *Words!*

▶ **Ready to Try It?** Read *Talking Walls: Art for the People*, on pp. 438–451.

Talking Walls
Art for the People

by Katacha Díaz

Question of the Week
**Why is freedom of
expression important?**

Immigrants travel to America from all over the world. They leave behind homes and villages in their native countries for the promise of a better life and for the freedom this country has to offer.

The people in America enjoy many different kinds of freedom, including the freedom of artistic expression. Writers, musicians, dancers, and artists are free to speak their minds through their art—in any way they choose. Do you know that some painters use walls as their canvas? These painted walls are called murals and are often painted in public places for all the people of the community to see.

Muralists are asked by a town, school, or business to create a work of art on a wall. Muralists paint many different kinds of murals. Some are inside, some are outside. Some tell the history of a town and everyday life of the people who settled there. Others show special celebrations and community festivals. Still others depict symbols of American freedom and democracy at work. All are great examples of artistic expression at its best.

"Community of Music," Long Beach, California ▶

440

Immigrant

On the walls of a meat market in Los Angeles is a mural about immigrants painted by Hector Ponce. It tells the history of the people who live in the Pico and Hoover neighborhood. This mural, titled "Immigrant," shows the Statue of Liberty just beyond reach and Latin American immigrants working hard to provide for their families. Do you see a woman with young children, a man selling bags of oranges, a seamstress, and a man looking for cans to recycle?

Hector Ponce, the artist, came from El Salvador more than 15 years ago. He says, "My mural shows what's in the hearts of many people who come to this country looking for a better life."

▲ "Immigrant," Los Angeles, California ▶

442

Reach High and You Will Go Far

Before artist Joshua Sarantitis creates a mural, he talks with the people of the community. He listens to their stories about the neighborhood. He interprets their stories by making sketches, and then he makes plans for the painting of the mural.

Over the years, Sarantitis has created many public murals across America, including "Reach High and You Will Go Far." This mural honors the hopes and dreams of the many children who live in a downtown neighborhood in Philadelphia. The painting is beautiful. It shows a young girl with her arms held high. Her hands and fingers become a tree rising over the building. The artist fashioned the top of the tree as a billboard extending above the roof to show how people can grow and change. The mural encourages children to reach for the future through education.

REACH HIGH AND YOU WILL GO FAR
© 2000 Joshua Sarantitis & PDRMAP
assisted by Veronica Hershberger and Jay Spivik
sponsored by CMS Companies

A Shared Hope

Paul Botello was 8 years old when he began helping his older brother, David, paint murals. Paul loved painting murals and was inspired to become an artist like his brother. When Paul graduated from high school, he went on to college to study art. Today he creates and paints murals, and he teaches art too!

Paul painted a special mural called "A Shared Hope" for an elementary school in Los Angeles, California. Most of the students at Esperanza School are immigrants from Central America. The mural speaks to the schoolchildren. It tells them that education is the key to success.

At the top of the mural, a teacher helps guide her students over the building blocks of life. Students are standing at the bottom of the painting holding objects that symbolize their future. Their parents stand behind to help guide and support them. Teachers, students, and parents from the school posed for the artist and his assistants as they created the mural.

"Education, hope, and immigration are my themes," says Paul Botello. "People immigrate to the United States because they hope for a better life. Through education, a better life can be accomplished."

"A Shared Hope," Los Angeles, California

447

Dreams of Flight

David Botello—the older brother of Paul—loved to paint and dreamed of becoming an artist. When he was in the third grade, he and his art partner, Wayne Healy, painted a mural of a dinosaur in art class. Little did David know that that dinosaur mural was the first of many murals he would paint with Wayne.

Years later, the childhood friends, now both artists, decided to go into business together painting murals. David and Wayne often create and paint murals together, but not always.

David painted a large mural called "Dreams of Flight" at Estrada Courts, a public housing project in Los Angeles. He says, "I've always wanted this mural to speak to the children who see it, and to say, 'Your dreams can come true.'"

ARTIST	LOCATION	TITLE
Hector Ponce	Los Angeles, California	"Immigrant"
Joshua Sarantitis	Philadelphia, Pennsylvania	"Reach High and You Will Go Far"
Paul Botello	Los Angeles, California	"A Shared Hope"
Allyn Cox	U.S. Capitol, Washington, D.C.	"Declaration of Independence, 1776"

It's interesting to note that when the artist repainted the mural seventeen years after it was originally completed, he changed one of the children from a boy to a girl. Much had changed over the years, and the artist wanted all children to know that girls can dream of flying model airplanes too. It is the artist's hope that over time the mural will inspire many of the children who see it to work hard and follow their dreams.

"Dreams of Flight," Los Angeles, California

Talking Walls

Cities, large and small, invite artists to paint special murals in public places for everyone to see. Murals are talking walls; they speak to the people.

Community murals tell stories of personal, political, and social beliefs of the local residents. Some murals inspire or amuse us, while others stir our hearts.

"Declaration of Independence, 1776" was painted by Allyn Cox in the United States Capitol, Washington, D.C.

From sea to shining sea, the artists who create art for the people are instrumental in reminding Americans everywhere of the freedoms that help our democracy work.

Muralists use scaffolding to reach large murals.

The "American Flag" mural was painted by Meg Saligman in Philadelphia, Pennsylvania. ▼

TEKS

3.13.A.1 Identify details or facts that support the main idea. **3.2.B.8** Locate details about other texts. **3.15.B.1** Locate specific information in graphic features of text. **Also 3.12.A.1, 3.12.A.2, 3.2.B.6, 3.2.B.9, 3.15.B.2.**

Envision It! Retell

Think Critically

1. In the story, the author uses a map to illustrate several mural locations in the United States. See if there is a mural in your city. If you were a muralist, where might you paint a mural? What would you paint a mural to celebrate? Text to Self

2. The subtitle of this selection is *Art for the People.* Why do you think the author used this subtitle? What topics does the author write about and why? Read "Meet the Author" on page 453 to find out. Think Like an Author

3. Look back at pages 448–449. What are the graphic sources on these pages? What information do they convey to the reader? Graphic Sources

4. What are the three most important ideas in the story? Explain your answers using evidence from the story. Important Ideas

5. **Look Back and Write** Look back at each artist and mural in the selection. Think about the reasons why the artists painted the murals. What do the murals represent, or stand for? Provide evidence to support your answer.

TEST PRACTICE Extended Response

Meet the Author

Katacha Díaz

Katacha Díaz grew up in Peru and immigrated to the United States when she was 15. She was one of seven daughters. Her parents moved to the United States so that the girls could get a good education. Moving to a new country as a teenager was hard. "My sister Ana María and I were the only Spanish-speaking students in our new school. There was a lot of peer pressure to get rid of the accent," she says.

Ms. Díaz wrote about murals because they have always fascinated her. She especially loves the murals by Paul and David Botello because they speak of education, immigration, and hope. These themes are a big part of her own life. "Education is important in my family," she points out.

Read more books about murals.

The School Mural
by Sarah Vázquez

Murals: Walls That Sing
by George Ancona

Use the Reader's and Writer's Notebook to record your independent reading.

TEKS

3.18 Write literary texts to express their ideas and feelings about real or imagined people, events, and ideas. **3.22.A.1.iii.1** Use descriptive adjectives in the context of reading, writing, and speaking.

Let's Write It!

Key Features of a Description

- explanation of something using sensory details
- is a written "picture" for the reader
- includes careful word choice

READING STREET ONLINE
GRAMMAR JAMMER
www.TexasReadingStreet.com

Descriptive

Description

A good **description** is an explanation of someone or something using careful word choice and sensory details. The student model on the next page is an example of a good description.

Writing Prompt Think about a piece of art that you know from the selection or your own life. Describe it using sensory details.

Writer's Checklist

Remember, you should . . .

☑ choose your words carefully.

☑ use details that appeal to different senses.

☑ use vivid, descriptive adjectives to help readers create a picture in their minds.

☑ express your ideas and feelings about the piece of art.

Description of "Reach High and You Will Go Far"

"Reach High and You Will Go Far" is a huge mural on the side of a building showing a girl holding her hands above her head. A twisty, beautiful tree with bright green leaves grows out of her hands and seems to burst right out of the top of the building. The tree looks so real that you feel like you can see leaves falling from it.

The girl in the mural looks up at the tree with a happy look on her face. **The roots of the tree are growing down over her arms, and they look like green veins.** She is surrounded by bright colors shaped like a stained glass window from a church. Behind the colors you can see the city street painted in the mural. This mural makes me feel happy and hopeful.

Writing Trait Word Choice Sensory details help readers picture the mural in their minds.

Genre A **description** explains something to a reader.

Combining sentences creates a smoother flow.

Conventions

Combining Sentences

Remember When you **combine sentences**, you join two sentences together. One sentence is joined with another using a comma and a conjunction.

TEKS

3.4.D.1 Identify playful uses of language. **3.4.D.2** Apply playful uses of language.

Genre
Palindromes

- A palindrome is a word or phrase that reads the same in both directions.

- Palindromes are a playful use of language created for fun many centuries ago.

- As you read "The History of Palindromes," try to think of other words that read the same in both directions.

THE HISTORY OF PALINDROMES

by Jeaninne Sage

The word palindrome is derived from the Greek *palíndromos,* meaning "a running back" (palín = BACK, + dromos = A RUNNING).

Some one-word palindromes are:

RADAR	DEED	LEVEL
ROTOR	POP	CIVIC
RACECAR	DID	MADAM

Palindrome Phrases:

Some phrases are also palindromes. Some palindrome phrases are:

Don't nod

Never odd or even

Too bad—I hid a boot

No trace; not one carton

Oozy rat in a sanitary zoo

A Man, A Plan, A Canal—Panama!

2D PALINDROMES
— SQUARES —

In these word squares, a word can be read in either direction in every row and column.

Here are a few palindrome squares.

The 2D palindrome square below dates back to ancient Roman times! It was inscribed on a stone tablet outside Rome, in Italy. It is the earliest known 2D palindrome.

Sator Arepo tenet opera rotas

It means: The sower Arepo works with the help of a wheel.

Let's **Think** About...

Try to create a 2D palindrome square that can be read in either direction in every row and column.
Palindromes

Let's **Think** About...

Reading Across Texts In *Talking Walls: Art for the People*, muralists express ideas on walls for the public to enjoy. How are palindromes similar? How are they different?

Writing Across Text Create a palindrome phrase.

TEKS

3.4.E.1 Alphabetize a series of words to the third letter. **3.4.E.2** Use a dictionary or glossary to determine meanings of unknown words. **3.16.A.1** Understand how communication changes when moving from one genre of media to another. **Also 3.3.A.1, 3.3.A.2, 3.29.A.1, 3.29.A.2, 3.29.A.3, 3.30.A.1, 3.30.A.2, 3.31.A.4, 3.31.A.5, 3.31.A.6.**

Let's Learn It!

READING STREET ONLINE
ONLINE STUDENT EDITION
www.TexasReadingStreet.com

Vocabulary

Unknown Words

Dictionary/Glossary Use a dictionary or glossary to find the meanings of unknown words. If a word has multiple definitions, choose the meaning that fits in the context of what you are reading.

 Choose three unknown words from *Talking Walls*. Put the words into alphabetical order, using the letters in the third or fourth place in each word if necessary. Look them up in a dictionary or glossary. Write the correct meaning of each word as used in the selection.

Fluency

Accuracy

The more accurately you read a text, the greater your understanding will be. As you read, focus on reading each word as it appears.

Practice It! With a partner, practice reading the story aloud. How many words did you misread? Reread the section. Did your accuracy improve?

458

Media Literacy

Use strategies— restate ideas and ask for clarification—to keep discussions going.

Talk Show

A talk show is hosted by a person who chats informally with guests who know about a subject or have done something noteworthy.

Practice It! Have a class talk show about the kind of murals you would paint and why. Take turns being the host, interviewing two classmates about their murals in front of the audience. How would communication change if the talk show were in an online format?

Tips

Listening ...

• Ask relevant questions and share your opinions.

• Listen attentively to others.

Speaking ...

• Speak loudly and clearly.

• Use appropriate verbal cues.

Teamwork ...

• Ask open-ended questions about the murals, and answer with detail.

TEKS

3.31.A.2 Participate in teacher-led discussions by answering questions with appropriate detail.
3.31.A.3 Participate in teacher-led discussions by providing suggestions that build upon the ideas of others.
Also 3.31.A.1.

Oral Vocabulary

Let's Talk About

Rules and Laws

- Describe why rules and laws are important.

- Offer suggestions for how people can stay safe by following laws.

- Pose and answer questions about keeping order, being safe, and doing the right thing.

READING STREET ONLINE
CONCEPT TALK VIDEO
www.TexasReadingStreet.com

Envision It! | **Prefixes to Know**

imperfect

prefix im-

incorrect

1+1=3

prefix in-

**READING STREET ONLINE
SOUND-SPELLING CARDS**
www.TexasReadingStreet.com

Phonics

Prefixes *im-, in-*

Words I Can Blend

im **passable**

im **practical**

in **convenient**

in **sensitive**

in **expensive**

Sentences I Can Read

1. The snow made the roads impassable.

2. It was impractical for me to come at such an inconvenient time.

3. Is it insensitive to ask if the price is inexpensive?

I Can Read!

My family was hiking in snowshoes through the woods. We stopped to rest at the bottom of a hill that we felt incapable of climbing.

My brother and dad became impatient, so they kept going. Suddenly, my mom pointed to a large brown animal, immobile and inaudible, watching us from behind a tree. Was it a bear? Impossible! Aren't bears supposed to be inactive during the winter?

I didn't wait to find out. I charged up the hill. My mom, in a moment of indecision and fear, froze. She stared, immovable, as the bear snorted in her direction. Then the bear turned and walked away. My mom was immeasurably grateful!

You've learned

🔵 Prefixes *im-, in-*

TEKS

3.5.A.1 Paraphrase themes of fables, legends, myths, or stories. **3.5.A.2** Paraphrase supporting details of fables, legends, myths, or stories. **3.8.B.2** Describe the interaction of characters, including changes they undergo. Also **3.8.A.1, 3.8.A.2, 3.8.A.3.**

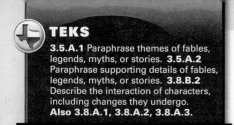

Envision It! | Skill Strategy

Skill

Strategy

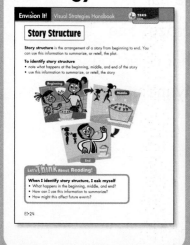

READING STREET ONLINE
ENVISION IT! ANIMATIONS
www.TexasReadingStreet.com

Comprehension Skill

Literary Elements: Plot and Theme

- The important events in the beginning, middle, and end of a story make up the plot.

- The theme is the "big idea" or lesson in the story.

- Use what you learned about plot and theme and a graphic organizer like the one below as you read "The Ant and the Beetle." Then write the theme of the story, using just one sentence.

Beginning → Middle → End

Comprehension Strategy

Story Structure

Good readers look for what happens in the beginning, middle, and end of a story. Authors usually write in time order, using sequence words to show the order of events.

464

The Ant and the Beetle

Adapted from Aesop's "The Fox and the Crow"

Annie Ant stole a piece of cheese from an abandoned picnic and scrambled up on a rock. She was about to eat the cheese when she noticed a beetle nearby. The beetle had a plan.

"My, my, I have never seen such a beautiful ant," flattered the beetle. "From the tip of your antennae to the end of your abdomen, you are simply gorgeous!"

"Finally, someone appreciates my beauty!" Annie thought.

"You must be delicate," continued the beetle. "Surely you are not strong enough to help the other ants."

"Hmph!" said the insulted ant. To show him, Annie set down the cheese and lifted a huge rock over her head.

The beetle grabbed the cheese and began to scurry away. "Yes, you are strong, but you are also foolish."

Strategy Note the time order clues *about to* and *when*. How did the author structure this story?

Skill Summarize the plot. What lesson did Annie learn at the end of the story?

Your Turn!

⏸ **Need a Review?** See the *Envision It! Handbook* for help with plot and theme and story structure.

▶ **Ready to Try It?** As you read *Two Bad Ants*, use what you've learned about plot, theme, and story structure to understand the text.

TEKS

3.4.A.1 Identify the meaning of common prefixes. **3.4.A.2** Know how prefixes change the meaning of roots. **3.4.A.3** Identify the meaning of common suffixes. **3.4.A.4** Know how suffixes change the meaning of roots.

Envision It! | Words to Know

crystal

discovery

scoop

disappeared

goal

journey

joyful

unaware

Vocabulary Strategy for

Prefixes and Suffixes *un-, dis-,* and *-ful*

Word Structure When you see a word you don't know, look for a prefix or suffix. The prefixes *un-* or *dis-* make the word mean "not ____" or "opposite of ____." The suffix *-ful* makes a word mean "full of ____." Use *un-, dis-,* or *-ful* to figure out the meanings of words.

1. When you see an unfamiliar word with a prefix or suffix, put your finger over the prefix or suffix.

2. Look at the base word. Put the base word in the appropriate phrase: "not____," "opposite of ____," or "full of ____."

3. Try the new meaning in the sentence. Does it make sense?

Read "How Ants Find Food" on page 467. Look for words that have a prefix or suffix. Use the prefix or suffix to help you figure out the meanings of the words.

Words to Write Reread "How Ants Find Food." Write about the jobs a worker ant does. Use words from the Words to Know list in your writing.

How Ants Find Food

Ants are social insects. Like wasps and bees, they live in large groups called colonies. The queen ant lays all the eggs, and the worker ants build the nest, look for food, care for the eggs, and defend the nest.

Ants that look for food are called scouts. Their goal is to find food and report the locations to the ants back at the nest. Suppose a scout ant makes this discovery: someone has left out a scoop of sugar. The scout carries a sugar crystal back to the nest. On its return journey, the scout ant also leaves a scent trail leading from the food to the nest. When the other ants realize that the scout has found food, they become very excited. They seem joyful about the news.

Many ants follow the scout's trail back to the food. They swarm over the sugar, picking up all the crystals. In a short time, all of the sugar has disappeared, and so have the ants. It happens so quickly that often people are unaware that ants were ever there at all.

Your Turn!

❚❚ Need a Review? For additional help with prefixes and suffixes, see *Words!*

▶ Ready to Try It? Read *Two Bad Ants*, pp. 468–485.

Two BaD AnTs

by Chris Van Allsburg

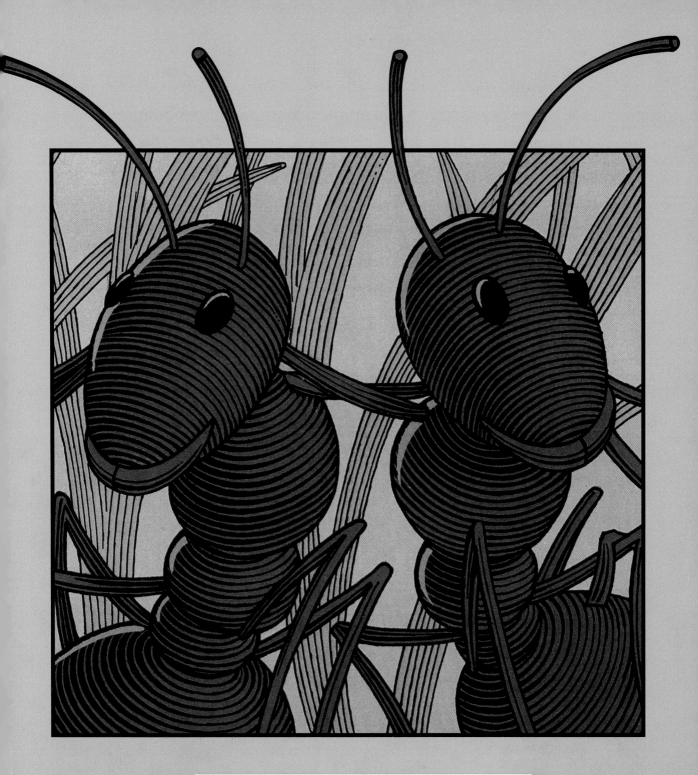

 Question of the Week
Why are rules and laws important to freedom?

The news traveled swiftly through the tunnels of the ant world. A scout had returned with a remarkable discovery—a beautiful sparkling crystal. When the scout presented the crystal to the ant queen, she took a small bite, then quickly ate the entire thing.

She deemed it the most delicious food she had ever tasted. Nothing could make her happier than to have more, much more. The ants understood. They were eager to gather more crystals because the queen was the mother of them all. Her happiness made the whole ant nest a happy place.

It was late in the day when they departed. Long
shadows stretched over the entrance to the ant kingdom.
One by one the insects climbed out, following the scout,
who had made it clear—there were many crystals
where the first had been found, but the journey was
long and dangerous.

They marched into the woods that surrounded their underground home. Dusk turned to twilight, twilight to night. The path they followed twisted and turned, every bend leading them deeper into the dark forest.

More than once the line of ants stopped and anxiously listened for the sounds of hungry spiders. But all they heard was the call of crickets echoing through the woods like distant thunder.

Dew formed on the leaves above. Without warning, huge cold drops fell on the marching ants. A firefly passed overhead that, for an instant, lit up the woods with a blinding flash of blue-green light.

At the edge of the forest stood a mountain. The ants looked up and could not see its peak. It seemed to reach right to the heavens. But they did not stop. Up the side they climbed, higher and higher.

The wind whistled through the cracks of the mountain's face. The ants could feel its force bending their delicate antennae. Their legs grew weak as they struggled upward. At last they reached a ledge and crawled through a narrow tunnel.

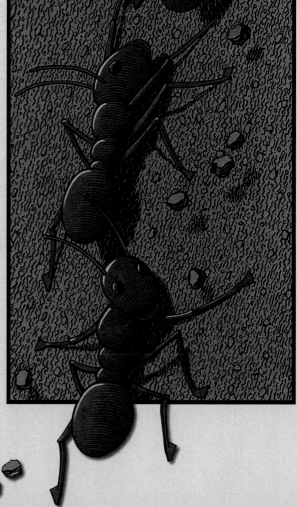

When the ants came out of the tunnel they found themselves in a strange world. Smells they had known all their lives, smells of dirt and grass and rotting plants, had vanished. There was no more wind and, most puzzling of all, it seemed that the sky was gone.

They crossed smooth shiny surfaces, then followed the scout up a glassy, curved wall. They had reached their goal. From the top of the wall they looked below to a sea of crystals. One by one the ants climbed down into the sparkling treasure.

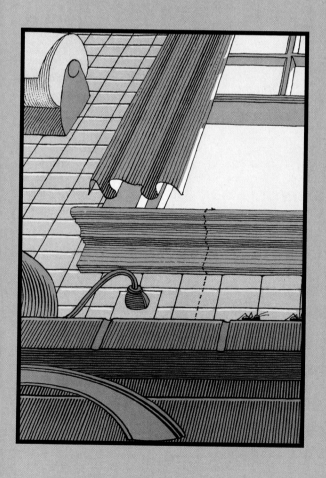

Quickly they each chose a crystal, then turned to start the journey home. There was something about this unnatural place that made the ants nervous. In fact they left in such a hurry that none of them noticed the two small ants who stayed behind.

"Why go back?" one asked the other. "This place may not feel like home, but look at all these crystals."

"You're right," said the other. "We can stay here and eat this tasty treasure every day, forever." So the two ants ate crystal after crystal until they were too full to move, and fell asleep.

Daylight came. The sleeping ants were unaware of changes taking place in their new-found home. A giant silver scoop hovered above them, then plunged deep into the crystals. It shoveled up both ants and crystals and carried them high into the air.

The ants were wide awake when the scoop turned, dropping them from a frightening height. They tumbled through space in a shower of crystals and fell into a boiling brown lake.

Then the giant scoop stirred violently back and forth. Crushing waves fell over the ants. They paddled hard to keep their tiny heads above water. But the scoop kept spinning the hot brown liquid.

Around and around it went, creating a whirlpool that sucked the ants deeper and deeper. They both held their breath and finally bobbed to the surface, gasping for air and spitting mouthfuls of the terrible, bitter water.

Then the lake tilted and began to empty into a cave. The ants could hear the rushing water and felt themselves pulled toward the pitch-black hole. Suddenly the cave disappeared and the lake became calm. The ants swam to the shore and found that the lake had steep sides.

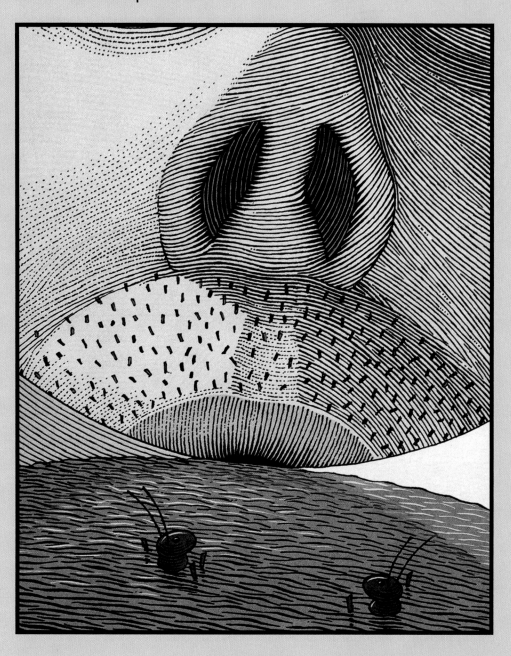

They hurried down the walls that held back the lake. The frightened insects looked for a place to hide, worried that the giant scoop might shovel them up again. Close by they found a huge round disk with holes that could neatly hide them.

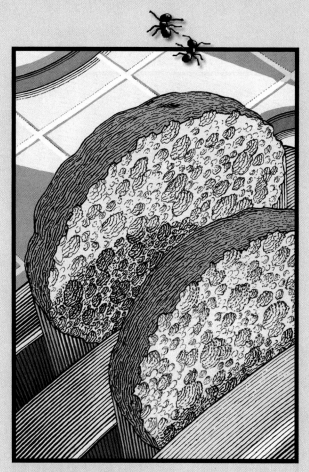

But as soon as they had climbed inside, their hiding place was lifted, tilted, and lowered into a dark space. When the ants climbed out of the holes, they were surrounded by a strange red glow. It seemed to them that every second the temperature was rising.

It soon became so unbearably hot that they thought they would soon be cooked. But suddenly the disk they were standing on rocketed upward, and the two hot ants went flying through the air.

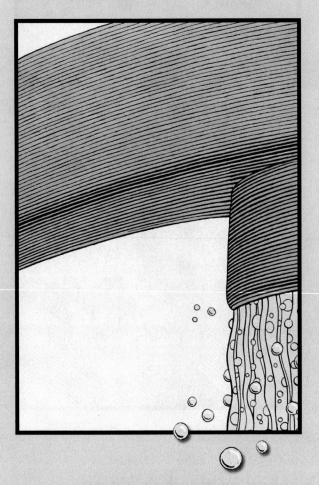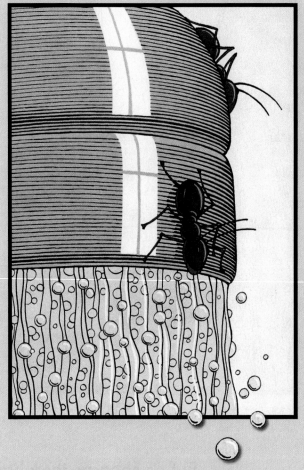

They landed near what seemed to be a fountain—
a waterfall pouring from a silver tube. Both ants had
a powerful thirst and longed to dip their feverish
heads into the refreshing water. They quickly climbed
along the tube.

As they got closer to the rushing water the ants felt
a cool spray. They tightly gripped the shiny surface
of the fountain and slowly leaned their heads into the
falling stream. But the force of the water was much
too strong.

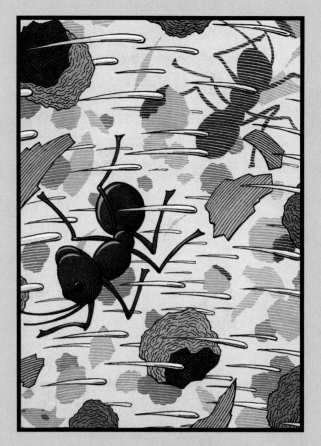

The tiny insects were pulled off the fountain and plunged down into a wet, dark chamber. They landed on half-eaten fruit and other soggy things. Suddenly the air was filled with loud, frightening sounds. The chamber began to spin.

The ants were caught in a whirling storm of shredded food and stinging rain. Then, just as quickly as it had started, the noise and spinning stopped. Bruised and dizzy, the ants climbed out of the chamber.

In daylight once again, they raced through puddles and up a smooth metal wall. In the distance they saw something comforting—two long, narrow holes that reminded them of the warmth and safety of their old underground home. They climbed up into the dark openings.

But there was no safety inside these holes. A strange force passed through the wet ants. They were stunned senseless and blown out of the holes like bullets from a gun. When they landed, the tiny insects were too exhausted to go on. They crawled into a dark corner and fell fast asleep.

Night had returned when the battered ants awoke
to a familiar sound—the footsteps of their fellow insects
returning for more crystals. The two ants slipped quietly to
the end of the line. They climbed the glassy wall and once
again stood amid the treasure. But this time they each
chose a single crystal and followed their friends home.

Standing at the edge of their ant hole, the two ants
listened to the joyful sounds that came from below. They
knew how grateful their mother queen would be when
they gave her their crystals. At that moment, the two ants
felt happier than they'd ever felt before. This was their
home, this was their family. This was where they were
meant to be.

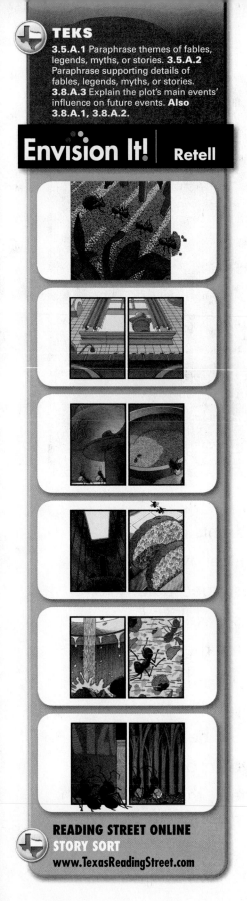
Think Critically

1. How is the ant world different from your world? How might ants describe a person? **Text to World**

2. How does the author and illustrator Chris Van Allsburg make you see the world the way ants see it? Use examples from the story in your answers. **Think Like an Author**

3. On page 476, the ants make a decision that leads to a huge problem for them. What is it, and how is it resolved? What can you learn from their adventures? Be sure to use details from the story to explain your answers. **Plot and Theme**

4. How did the author structure this story? What clue words help you know? **Story Structure**

5. **Look Back and Write** Look back at pages 477–479 to find "a boiling brown lake," "a giant scoop," and "a cave." Write a note to tell the ants what these things really are. Provide evidence from the story to support your answer. **TEST PRACTICE** **Extended Response**

Meet the Author and Illustrator

Chris Van ALLSBURG

Chris Van Allsburg won the Caldecott Medal for his books *The Polar Express* and *Jumanji*. He is one of the best known children's book illustrators working today.

Mr. Van Allsburg says that in elementary school other kids thought it was cool if you could draw. But in junior high, he stopped drawing. He gave in to the peer pressure. Suddenly learning how to play football seemed more important.

Thankfully, Mr. Van Allsburg changed his mind. In college he decided to take some art classes. That decision changed his life. "I had a fever again," he says, "a fever to make art." He loved his art so much that he sometimes forgot his other classes, but he was being true to his nature.

Mr. Van Allsburg says that good stories contain a moral truth. Does *Two Bad Ants* say something about being true to your own nature? Mr. Van Allsburg thinks it does.

Read more books by Chris Van Allsburg.

The Wreck of the Zephyr

Just a Dream

Use the Reader's and Writer's Notebook to record your independent reading.

487

TEKS

3.18.A.3 Write imaginative stories that contain details about the setting. **Also:** 3.23.C.1.ii.1, 3.23.C.1.ii.2, 3.23.C.1.ii.3, 3.23.C.1.ii.4.

Comic Book

In a **comic book**, drawings, or illustrations, are used to help tell the story. Characters' dialogue and any narration is included with the illustrations. The student model on the next page is an example of a comic book.

Writing Prompt Write a short comic book telling of a further adventure of these two ants.

Let's Write It!

Key Features of a Comic Book

- tells a story using a series of drawings
- characters' dialogue is part of the drawing
- sometimes uses narration

READING STREET ONLINE
GRAMMAR JAMMER
www.TexasReadingStreet.com

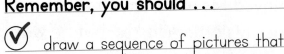

Writer's Checklist

Remember, you should . . .

✓ draw a sequence of pictures that show what the ants are doing.

✓ write dialogue in "word balloons."

✓ include details about the setting.

✓ tell a story with a beginning, middle, and end.

✓ use punctuation correctly, including commas in dates and in a series.

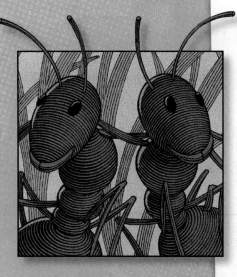

Two Bad Ants, Act II

Let's go back to the city.

Mmm....... Delicious crumbs.

She swept us into the waste basket. How do we get out?

April 12, 20__

Dear Ants,
We're stuck in a slippery place. Send scouts to find us!
Your friends,
Two Bad Ants

Commas, including the one in the date, are used correctly.

Writing Trait Conventions In a comic book, dialogue appears in a word bubble.

Genre A **comic book** is a series of drawings used to tell a story.

Conventions

Commas

Remember Commas separate words in a series. They also separate the month and day from the year in a date.

TEKS

3.16.A.1 Understand how communication changes when moving from one genre of media to another. **3.16.C.1** Compare various written conventions used for digital media. **Also 3.2.A.2, 3.2.A.4.**

21st Century Skills
INTERNET GUY

Evaluating Sources

Can you trust what you read on the Internet? You should always find out who wrote what you read. Can you believe that person? How can you tell? It is important always to check.

- Determine whether a Web site is reliable before you trust it. Web addresses that end in *.org* or *.gov* are usually reliable.

- Communication changes with different genres of media. Web sites use photos, colors, shapes, and other text features that wouldn't be on the radio or TV.

- Read "Hiking Safety Tips" to learn about evaluating sources. Compare the language used in the summaries of the Web sites. What tells you the first two sites won't be helpful?

Hiking Safety Tips

You are going on a camping trip. With camping comes freedom but also dangers. You must prepare a list of hiking safety tips. You decide to use the Internet to help you.

You type the keyword "hiking" into an Internet search engine. The first two sites probably won't help. But the third site looks promising, so you click on <u>Staying Safe on the Trail.</u>

| File | Edi |

http://www.url.here

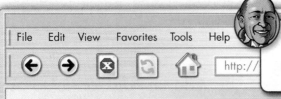

hiking | Search

<u>Hiking Clothes.</u> Outfit your family with these cute hiking shirts . . .

<u>Footwear.</u> We have 100% leather hiking boots, just what you're looking for . . .

<u>Staying Safe on the Trail.</u> Hiking is fun but beware of plants that . . .

File   Edit   View   Favorites   Tools   Help

http://

The list goes on. You print it out. Now you can enjoy the freedom of hiking safely.

STAYING SAFE

A few tips will help you enjoy the freedom of a safe family hike.

Drinking Water Don't hike anywhere without it, especially on hot days. Even the clearest stream water may not be safe.

Snacks Bring them to eat when you take breaks. Good hiking snacks include granola bars, trail mix, and crackers.

Poison Plants Beware of poison ivy and poison oak. Oil from the leaves can make you break out in a rash with blisters.

poison oak

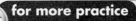

for more practice

Get Online!

www.TexasReadingStreet.com
Evaluate online sources about hiking safety tips.

21st Century Skills Online Activity

Log on and follow the step-by-step directions for evaluating reliable Web sites about staying safe while hiking.

TEKS

3.4.A.1 Identify the meaning of common prefixes. **3.4.A.2** Know how prefixes change the meaning of roots. **3.4.A.3** Identify the meaning of common suffixes. **3.4.A.4** Know how suffixes change the meaning of roots. **3.30.A.2** Speak coherently, employing eye contact, speaking rate, volume, enunciation, and the conventions of language to communicate ideas effectively. **Also 3.3.A.1, 3.3.A.2, 3.29.A.1, 3.29.A.2, 3.29.A.3, 3.30.A.1, 3.31.A.4, 3.31.A.5, 3.31.A.6.**

READING STREET ONLINE
ONLINE STUDENT EDITION
www.TexasReadingStreet.com

Vocabulary

Prefixes and Suffixes

Word Structure Remember that prefixes and suffixes change the meanings of words. The prefixes *un-* or *dis-* at the beginning of a word make the word mean "not___" or "the opposite of___." The suffix *-ful* at the end of a word makes a word mean "full of___."

 Add *un-*, *dis-*, or *-ful* to as many of the following words as you can: *usual, like, mouth, care, natural, tidy, like, comfort, care, scoop.* Make a list of the new words. Tell what each word means.

Fluency

Rate

Remember that when you read aloud, read as fast as you would normally talk. To do this, you might need to reread a story aloud a few times and practice some of the difficult words and phrasing.

Practice It! Practice reading aloud *Two Bad Ants*, page 477. Listen for places where your rate slows down. What can you do to read them at a faster rate?

492

Listening and Speaking

Speak loudly, clearly, and with expression.

Description

When giving a description, use words that tell how something looks, sounds, smells, tastes, or feels to create images in your listeners' minds.

Practice It! Describe your classroom from an ant's point of view. Begin with an exciting statement about what your classroom looks like. Then imagine the ant crawling to different areas in the room. Include details.

Tips

Listening . . .

- Comment about how effective the descriptions were.
- Paraphrase what the speaker says.

Speaking . . .

- Determine your purpose for speaking.
- Use expression.

Teamwork . . .

- Suggest creative ways to describe items.
- Build upon the ideas of others.

TEKS

3.29.A.2 Ask relevant questions.
3.30.A.1 Speak coherently about the topic under discussion.
3.31.A.3 Participate in teacher-led discussions by providing suggestions that build upon the ideas of others.

Oral Vocabulary

Let's Talk About

Keeping Freedom

- Offer suggestions for how people can keep their freedoms.

- Ask questions about the loss of freedom.

- Describe what freedom means to you.

READING STREET ONLINE
CONCEPT TALK VIDEO
www.TexasReadingStreet.com

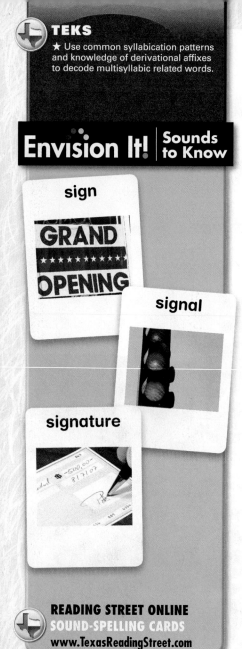

sign

GRAND OPENING

signal

signature

READING STREET ONLINE
SOUND-SPELLING CARDS
www.TexasReadingStreet.com

Phonics

↻ Related Words

Words I Can Blend

compete
competitor
competition

refresh
refreshment

Sentences I Can Read

1. Jenna is a strong competitor.
2. The three runners will compete in tomorrow's competition.
3. Let's refresh ourselves with some refreshment.

I Can Read!

Ms. Lara is the director of our school. Each day she directs the teachers and students to be the best that we can be. Her direction shows us how to make learning our number one goal.

My favorite part of the day is during science class. Sometimes we do scientific experiments in our lab. I want to be a scientist when I grow up, so I can help develop sources of energy. Our community has a favorable opinion of our school.

You've learned

 Related Words

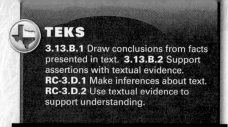

TEKS

3.13.B.1 Draw conclusions from facts presented in text. **3.13.B.2** Support assertions with textual evidence. **RC-3.D.1** Make inferences about text. **RC-3.D.2** Use textual evidence to support understanding.

Envision It! | Skill Strategy

Skill

Strategy

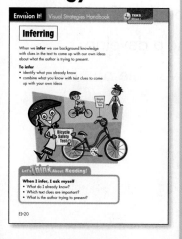

Comprehension Skill

🔄 Generalize

- A general statement, or generalization, tells how some things are mostly or all alike.

- Key words, such as *always*, *never*, and *most*, signal a generalization.

- Be sure you can support your generalization with facts and logic.

- Use what you learned about generalizing and a graphic organizer like the one below as you read "The Famous Thinker, Plato." Then write a short paragraph explaining your generalization and support it with details from the text.

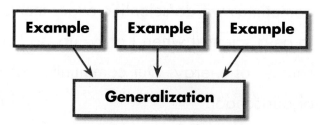

Comprehension Strategy

🔄 Inferring

Active readers use what they know and the ideas and clues in what they read to come up with their own ideas about what the author presents. Making inferences can help you understand the text better.

THE FAMOUS THINKER, PLATO

One of the most famous thinkers of the ancient world was Plato. He was a Greek man who lived about 2,400 years ago. Plato was a student of another famous thinker, Socrates. Some ideas about our world today started with Plato and Socrates.

How did Plato learn so much? Besides studying many writings, Plato traveled far. He observed much on his journeys. Then Plato began a school of science and philosophy. Philosophy is the study of how our minds gather knowledge. This school became a model for today's colleges.

Strategy Why do you think that the teachings of Plato are still popular today?

Many of Plato's writings have survived through history. He wrote mostly letters and dialogues. His writing covered many topics, including politics, nature, and happiness. In school, you will likely read some of Plato's famous writings. They have been part of many students' educations for hundreds of years.

Skill What generalization can you make about the writings of Plato? Use a key word, such as *always*, in your answer.

Your Turn!

❚❚ Need a Review? See the *Envision It! Handbook* for more information about generalizing and inferring.

▶ Ready to Try It? As you read *Atlantis: The Legend of a Lost City*, use what you've learned about generalizing and inferring to understand the text.

TEKS

3.4.B.3 Use context to distinguish among homographs. 3.4.C.3 Identify homographs. 3.4.C.7 Use homographs. **Also 3.4.E.2, 3.4.E.3, 3.4.E.4.**

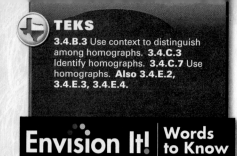

Envision It! Words to Know

aqueducts

crouched

pillar

content

guidance

honor

thermal

READING STREET ONLINE
VOCABULARY ACTIVITIES
www.TexasReadingStreet.com

Vocabulary Strategy for

🎯 Homographs

Context Clues Sometimes you may read a word you know, but the meaning doesn't make sense in the sentence. The word might be a homograph. Homographs are words that are spelled the same but have different pronunciations and meanings. For example, *lead* with a long *e* sound means to "go in front of," and *lead* with a short *e* sound means "a soft heavy metal."

1. If a word you know doesn't make sense in the sentence, it might be a homograph.

2. Look at the words around it. Can you figure out another meaning and pronunciation?

3. Try the new meaning in the sentence. Does it make sense?

Read "The Art of Architecture" on page 501. As you read, use context clues to find the meanings of homographs.

Words to Write Reread "The Art of Architecture." List the homographs and the other Words to Know, their pronunciations, including the syllables, and their meanings. Use a dictionary or glossary for help if needed. Then use those words to write a story about an ancient city.

THE ART OF ARCHITECTURE

The aqueducts of Paris, which are tunnels that carry water from one place to another, are an example of the ancient art of architecture. When Billy visited Paris with his grandmother, he crouched on his knees on the bank of the Seine to take a photograph of the famous structures, which were built centuries ago during Roman rule. Under his grandmother's guidance, Billy is learning more about architecture. Billy wants to be an architect when he grows up, which would honor the work of both his grandmother and grandfather who met in architecture school and designed many buildings in his hometown of Dallas. Ever since he could hold a crayon, he's been drawing houses with tall pillars and wide columns supporting giant roofs.

Now that Billy is older, he knows that architects do more than just draw fancy buildings. He feels a responsibility to conserve resources, and he has been reading about using thermal insulation to keep heating costs down. Even though he likes the idea of designing world-famous high rises, he knows that he will be happy and content with helping people make the best use of space and live better lives.

Your Turn!

❚❚ Need a Review?
For additional help with homographs, see *Words!*

▶ Ready to Try It?
Read *Atlantis: The Legend of a Lost City* on pp. 502–519.

ATLANTIS

THE LEGEND OF A LOST CITY

adapted and retold by Christina Balit

Genre

A **legend** is a traditional story about a people or land. The story may be based on truth but is mostly fiction. Read to find out why the author calls this story a legend.

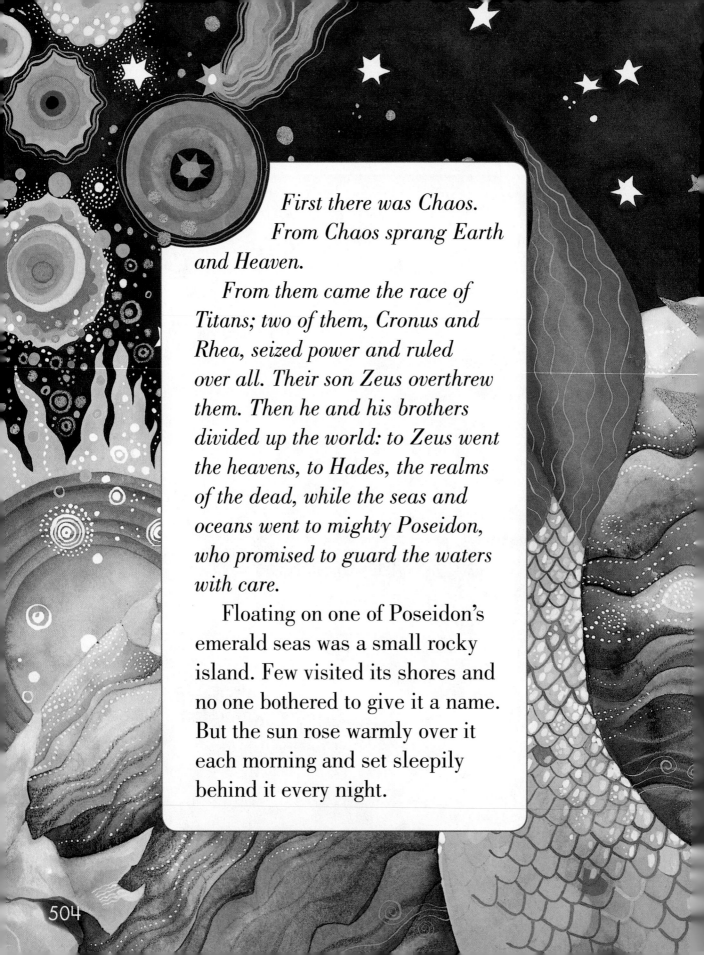

First there was Chaos.
From Chaos sprang Earth
and Heaven.

From them came the race of
Titans; two of them, Cronus and
Rhea, seized power and ruled
over all. Their son Zeus overthrew
them. Then he and his brothers
divided up the world: to Zeus went
the heavens, to Hades, the realms
of the dead, while the seas and
oceans went to mighty Poseidon,
who promised to guard the waters
with care.

Floating on one of Poseidon's
emerald seas was a small rocky
island. Few visited its shores and
no one bothered to give it a name.
But the sun rose warmly over it
each morning and set sleepily
behind it every night.

In the center of the island there stood a mountain, and at the foot of the mountain lived a man called Evenor and his wife, Leucippe. They lived happily together, working hard to tend the barren land, and brought up their daughter Cleito to honor all creatures.

Poseidon grew curious. How could they be content with so little? He took on human form and crouched unseen behind a rock to find out.

Each morning at daybreak, he watched Cleito walk over the pebbled ground, barefoot and smiling, to fill her water pot at the stream.

Seeing Cleito in all her beauty, Poseidon's heart grew tender, and one day he stepped out from behind the rock to talk to her. Day after day he came and slowly she began to return his love. Finally she agreed to become his bride. Her parents, unaware of Poseidon's divinity, blessed the union, and a simple wedding followed.

But a god cannot stay hidden. After the wedding, all the spirits of the sea rose to the surface to sing, and Poseidon assumed his divine form once more. He vowed to rebuild the island and make it fit for a king and his queen.

Poseidon used powers beyond human imagining to transform the isle into a paradise.

First, he arranged alternate circles of land and sea—three of land and three of water—to enclose the mountain. Within each circle of land a forest sprang up. Trees bloomed and grew heavy with fruits, and creatures multiplied.

Next, he made a network of canals, fed by waterfalls. Soon the island was yielding two crops each year—one watered by winter rains, the other irrigated by Poseidon's canals. The rich earth was carpeted with herbs and vegetables, and thick with healing roots; from its depths men dug out priceless yellow mountain copper. All things flourished on the sacred island.

Then, under Poseidon's guidance, the inhabitants built a palace fit for a god, with towers, gates, and parapets trimmed with gleaming brass and tin. In the center they set up a holy temple dedicated to Poseidon and Cleito, with pinnacles of silver surrounded by a wall of gold.

They built thermal baths and aqueducts, fountains and gardens— and even a huge racecourse.

It was a happy time for Poseidon and Cleito, and over the years Cleito gave birth to five pairs of twin sons. Their firstborn son they named Atlas. In the summer of his twentieth year he was crowned high king, and they named the island Atlantis in his honor.

Then Poseidon divided the island into ten parts, and gave his sons one-tenth each.

To ensure peace in his new island city, Poseidon set down laws in stone on a pillar of the temple. Chief among them was the commandment that no person should take up arms against another—with a terrible curse on anyone who disobeyed. Every five years, Atlas and the nine princes gathered by night beside the pillar to judge their people according to Poseidon's laws. The people of Atlantis became wise, gentle, and great-spirited. They were sober and kind, as the Creator had always wanted them to be. Above all, they lived in peace.

So Atlantis prospered. Its splendid docks were thronged with ships and merchandise, and behind them, a towering lighthouse lit the way for incoming boats bringing cargoes from other lands. The harbors hummed with trade. Bridges and an underground canal were built to connect the three circles of land around the mountain, as the people grew ever richer.

Poseidon, watching from the waves, was content and went away to his home at the bottom of the sea.

Many years passed, and Poseidon lay sleeping at the bottom of the ocean. The people of Atlantis began to change. Slowly, very slowly, the godlike part of their souls faded and their mortal, human natures took over. They started to argue. Gradually they lost the gift of goodness and became infected with ambition and power. Greed filled the citizens' hearts. The streets of Atlantis, once safe, became dangerous, as people began to steal, cheat, and lie.

514

One day Zeus, god of gods, who ruled according to the law of the Creator, looked down from the heavens above. He saw the city walls crumbling with neglect, the empty temple, and, worst of all, people fighting one another. He roared out his anger.

The sound of his fury woke Poseidon. Rising to the surface of the waves, the sea-god looked out over his once-perfect kingdom—and wept.

Now he had no choice: he must carry out his terrible curse.

Raising his trident, he stirred the seas into a wave that rose so high, it lashed the heavens. The wave vibrated with a roar that could be heard two thousand miles away, and the earth trembled in terror. Gathering its full force, the wave crashed upon the land, while burning rain and ashes blistered down from above.

In a single day and night, Atlantis was swallowed up by the sea.

Then there was silence. The city sank slowly to its new resting place on the ocean floor.

516

The people of Atlantis did not die. They continued to exist beneath the waves, but they never spoke or quarreled or fought again. As year followed year they paid a terrible penance, learning to live without gold or possessions in the cold depths. In time, they became little more than creatures of the water.

To this day, Atlantis has never been found. Some people believe that it is still there, under the sea, waiting to be discovered. . . .

Where was Atlantis?

People have suggested many different places where Atlantis might once have been. The oldest Greek legends describe Atlantis being out to the west, in the middle of the ocean—the ocean that is still named the Atlantic after Cleito's son. The people of Atlantis are said to have spread to other countries, founding settlements in Europe and Africa, and even in a land we now call America.

Some think Atlantis existed more or less as Plato described it, and that its people left traces behind them. Egypt has pyramids, Mexico has pyramids, so perhaps some Atlantean settlers built them in both places and their submerged homeland was midway between the two countries.

Others suggest that Atlantis was closer to America. The native inhabitants of the West Indies told early explorers that their islands were once part of a single landmass but that a disaster long ago shattered it. The fifth-century Greek philosopher Proclus, who wanted to convince his readers that Atlantis was real, writes, very mysteriously, as if he knew of the West Indies and their story.

Some people suggest that Atlantis was a part of Britain. Legend tells of a sunken land between Cornwall and the Isles of Scilly.

The theory taken most seriously is that the story is actually about the island of Crete, which was highly civilized and ruled over several smaller islands. One of them, Thera, was partially destroyed in about 1450 B.C.E. by a tremendous eruption, which also destroyed part of Crete, and its civilization never recovered.

With so much uncertainty, some argue that the story of Atlantis is not history at all but a myth warning us against conflict and power seeking. Yet the legend is so vivid that many will always believe Atlantis existed . . . somewhere.

TEKS

3.5.A.1 Paraphrase themes of fables, legends, myths, or stories. **3.5.A.2** Paraphrase supporting details of fables, legends, myths, or stories. **3.5.B.1** Compare settings in myths and traditional folktales. **Also 3.5.B.2, RC-3.D.1, RC-3.D.2.**

Envision It! | Retell

READING STREET ONLINE
STORY SORT
www.TexasReadingStreet.com

Think Critically

1. In the story, the author writes about the mythical lost city of Atlantis. Think about other myths you know, such as "Catch It and Run." How are the myths alike and different? Be sure to compare the settings; paraphrase the themes and supporting details; and describe the characters, their relationships, and the changes they undergo. **Text to Text**

2. The subtitle of this selection is *The Legend of a Lost City.* Why do you think the author used this subtitle? Why did the author use the word *legend* instead of *myth*? **Think Like an Author**

3. What generalization can you make about the gods in this story? What generalization can you make about people in this story? **Generalize**

4. Read page 514. What inference can you make about ambition and power? Explain your answer using evidence from the story. **Inferring**

5. **Look Back and Write** Look back at pages 518–519. Think about the reasons why the story was created. What does the story try to explain about the world? Provide evidence to support your answer.

TEST PRACTICE Extended Response

Meet the Author and Illustrator

Christina Balit

Christina Balit (pronounced "Ba-leet") was born in Manchester, England, but grew up in the Middle East. In her self-illustrated books, she uses Greek and Mediterranean art styles to create a way for young readers to visualize the stories.

As a young artist, Christina illustrated several books about mythology and fairy tales. Later, working with writer Jacqueline Mitton, Christina illustrated many books for young readers about constellations and our solar system. Christina's illustrations in these books help the characters from ancient worlds come to life.

Here are other books by Christina Balit.

Once upon a Starry Night: A Book of Constellation Stories

Zoo in the Sky

Reading Log

Use the Reader's and Writer's Notebook to record your independent reading.

521

TEKS

3.18.A.1 Write imaginative stories that build the plot to a climax. **Also 3.18.A.2, 3.18.A.3, 3.23.B.1.i, 3.23.B.1.ii, 3.23.D.1.**

Narrative

Historical Fiction

Historical fiction is realistic fiction that takes place in the past. The student model on the next page is an example of historical fiction.

Writing Prompt Write a historical fiction story about a voyage across the Atlantic Ocean.

Key Features of Historical Fiction

- set in the past
- events of the plot make sense
- characters, setting, or events may be based on historical fact

READING STREET ONLINE
GRAMMAR JAMMER
www.TexasReadingStreet.com

Writer's Checklist

Remember, you should . . .

☑ set your story in the past.

☑ include details about the characters and setting.

☑ build the plot to a climax.

☑ indent new paragraphs.

☑ capitalize geographical names and places, or historical periods.

To America!

My name is Sal Valle. I was only nine years old in 1910 when my family moved from Italy to America. We sailed on an enormous ship with hundreds of others. The journey took a very long time, and the conditions were harsh. The living quarters were stuffy and crowded, and there was little food. When I got scared or sad, my mother would say to me, "Soon we will live in the most wonderful place. It won't be long now."

Many people got very ill during the journey, including my mother. I worried about her as she got sicker and sicker, but there wasn't much anyone could do (there was no medicine). We just had to wait and hope for the best. After weeks, she showed signs of improvement.

Then one morning, I awoke to the voice of a man telling us that they had spotted land. Hurray! I ran to my mother's bed excitedly and leaned down to her and said, "Just like you said, Mother. It won't be long now. Land has been sighted!"

**Writing Trait
Word choice**
Specific adjectives create interest.

**Genre
Historical fiction** takes place in the past.

Quotations and parentheses are used correctly.

Conventions

• Quotations and Parentheses

Quotation marks ("") show the exact words of a speaker. **Parentheses** are punctuation marks inserted into a sentence around a word or group of words to
• explain something or give additional information.

523

TEKS

3.7.A.1 Explain elements of plot as presented through dialogue in scripts that are read, viewed, written, or performed. **3.7.A.2** Explain elements of character as presented through dialogue in scripts that are read, viewed, written, or performed. **Also 3.8.C.2.**

Social Studies in Reading

Genre
Drama

- Plays are a form of drama that use a cast of characters to perform a story.

- Plays use dialogue to create the beginning, middle, and end of plots and to show characters, their relationships, and how they change.

- The narrator tells the story to the audience from the third person (all knowing) or first person (his or her own) point of view.

- As you read and perform the play think about how the dialogue creates the plot and characters.

THE MONSTER IN THE MAZE
RETOLD FROM THE GREEK MYTH
by Walter Kirk

CHARACTERS

Theseus (THEE see uhs)
King Minos (MEYE nuhs)
Queen
Ariadne (air ee AD nee)
Guard
Monster

Scene 1

NARRATOR: *The island of Crete, in ancient times. In the great hall, King Minos, a cruel and mean ruler, and his Queen are seated on their thrones. Theseus bows before them. A Guard stands nearby.*

KING: Well, young man?

THESEUS: Great King Minos, I am Theseus, son of Aegeus (i GEE uhs), king of Athens.

KING: I know your father well. I beat him in a war, you know.

THESEUS: Yes, I know.

KING: What are you here for?

THESEUS: I've come to beg you to stop being cruel to our people and set them free.

QUEEN: You should listen to him, Minos.

KING: You don't need to be concerned with this, my queen. *(to Theseus)* And if I don't stop…what?

THESEUS: Why, I'll…I'll…find some way….

KING *(roars with laughter)*: You? You're just one little man. Here in my kingdom, I've got all the power.

THESEUS: People in power can afford to be merciful.

KING: Bah! I'll show you what power can do! Guard, take young Theseus's sword. *(The Guard does so.)* Now take him to the maze and lock him in.

GUARD: The maze, Your Majesty?

KING: You heard me. Do it! *(The Guard leads Theseus off.)*

QUEEN: Minos, do reconsider. Why the maze? He'll never make it out.

KING: Well, of course. That's what the maze is for.

QUEEN: But he's a king's son!

Let's **Think** About…

What do you know about each character so far? What problems are introduced on this page? **Drama**

Let's Think About...

Describe the King and Queen and their relationship. What questions would you ask them? **Drama**

KING: So what? I'm the one who won the war.

QUEEN: So you keep reminding me.

Scene 2

NARRATOR: *The hallway and entrance to the maze. The Guard leads Theseus along.*

THESEUS: What is this maze you're taking me to?

GUARD: Oh, it's a terrible place, terrible place. It's like a gigantic puzzle that you walk through. No one ever escapes.

THESEUS: What happens to them?

GUARD: See, there's a monster who lives there. A horrible beast with the body of a man but the head of a bull.

THESEUS: That's…that's awful!

GUARD: Oh, yeah. Awful enough. That's why they built the maze, just for him. So he couldn't get loose. The maze is so complicated, you see. You can't find your way out. Well, here we are. The maze. In you go. I'd tell you to have a nice day, but you won't. *(He starts to leave.)*

THESEUS: No, wait! At least tell me…. *(But the Guard has gone.)* Well, here I am.

Let's Think About...

What do you think will happen to Theseus and the people? **Drama**

ARIADNE: *(whispering from the shadows):* Theseus! Over here!

THESEUS: What? Who's that? Why, it's a young woman! Who are you?

ARIADNE: I'm Ariadne, King Minos's daughter.

THESEUS: But what are you doing here? Isn't it dangerous?

ARIADNE: I don't think the monster ever found its way this far out. The maze really is complicated. And I'm here to save your life.

THESEUS: But you don't even know me.

ARIADNE: No, but I'm just sick of Father being so terrible to people, just because he's king and wants to show off.

THESEUS: I hear there's a monster.

ARIADNE: Yes. I've never seen him, but I've heard him howling, some nights. But here, I brought you a sword. You can kill the monster.

THESEUS: But what if I get lost in the maze?

ARIADNE: I've thought of that. Here.
(She hands him a ball of string.)

Let's **Think** About...

Pretend that you are inviting a friend to the play and she asks you what the play is about. How would you summarize the plot for her so far? **Drama**

527

THESEUS: What's this? It looks like a ball of string.

ARIADNE: That's what it is. Listen, tie one end of the string to a pillar. Then as you go through the maze, unwind the ball. After you've killed the monster, just follow the string back here. Then I'll call the guard to set us both free.

THESEUS: You know, that might work! All right. I'll do it!

ARIADNE: Good luck. Come back a hero!

Scene 3

The maze. Theseus ties one end of the string to a pillar and starts into the maze. He crosses and recrosses the stage several times.

THESEUS: They were right. This maze is gigantic, and it is complicated. I've lost track of the number of turns I've made. Thank goodness for Ariadne and her string, or I'd never find my way back out. I haven't seen any sign of a monster yet, though. *(A terrible roar is heard from offstage.)* Unless…. *(Another roar)* Now that sounds like a monster. But I wonder where…?

Let's **Think** About…

Is the narrator of this play first person or third person?
Drama

MONSTER *(appearing):* Ha! Who dares to come into my home?

THESEUS: Oh, there he is! And they're right. He is a monster!

MONSTER: Am I? To me, you're the monster. Who are you?

THESEUS: My name is Theseus, Prince of Athens.

MONSTER: A prince, huh? I wonder if you'll taste any richer than my usual fare.

THESEUS: Well, you won't get a chance to find out! *(He draws his sword.)*

MONSTER: We'll see about that! Say, what's that?

THESEUS: It's called a sword, and it's for killing… monsters!

(The monster roars, terribly. They fight. Theseus kills the monster, and then he follows the string back to Ariadne. By bravely killing the monster and escaping the maze, Theseus and Ariadne have set the people free.)

Let's **Think** About…

Summarize the plot of this play. In your own words, what is the theme of this play? Support your answer with details from the text.
Drama

Let's **Think** About…

Reading Across Texts Use a Venn diagram to compare and contrast the setting in this myth with the setting from "Catch It and Run!"

Writing Across Text Use the Venn diagram to write a paragraph about how the settings in myths are alike and different.

TEKS

3.4.B.3 Use context to distinguish among homographs. **3.4.C.3** Identify homographs. **3.4.C.7** Use homographs. **3.6.A.1** Describe characteristics of various forms of poetry. **3.6.A.2** Describe how the characteristics of various forms of poetry create imagery. **3.31.A.6** Participate in student-led discussions by providing suggestions that build upon the ideas of others. **Also 3.3.A.1, 3.3.A.2, 3.29.A.1, 3.29.A.2, 3.29.A.3, 3.30.A.1, 3.30.A.2, 3.31.A.4, 3.31.A.5.**

Let's **Learn** It!

READING STREET ONLINE
ONLINE STUDENT EDITION
www.TexasReadingStreet.com

Vocabulary

Homographs

Context Clues Homographs are words that are spelled the same, but have different meanings and pronunciations. You will need to use clues in the context of the word to understand which meaning and pronunciation is correct.

Practice It! Using a sheet of paper, write down two different definitions for each of the following homographs: *produce, lead, tear, invalid, moped.* Then write a sentence for each homograph.

Fluency

Expression

When you are reading aloud, change your voice to match the mood of what you are reading. Changing your volume, tone, emotion, and rhythm helps you express the meaning of the story. This makes the story more interesting and understandable.

Practice It! With a partner, read aloud page 516 of *Atlantis*. How should you use expression to make this page sound interesting?

Song

Songs are words sung to music. Songs have rhythm and sometimes rhyme. Their purpose is usually to express emotions or feelings.

Practice It! Look back at *Atlantis: The Legend of a Lost City.* Write a song that tells a story about the lost city of Atlantis. Set your lyrics to music or just speak them to the class. Listen when your classmates speak or sing their lyrics.

Tips

Listening . . .

- Face the speaker.
- Listen attentively to the lyrics.

Speaking . . .

- Have good posture and make eye contact.
- Use expression to show the mood of your song.

Teamwork . . .

- Give suggestions for writing lyrics.
- Build upon the ideas of others.

Poetry

- **Free verse poems** have little or no **rhyme** or regular **rhythm,** but they can use many comparisons and sensory words. In some free verse poems, the lines do not start with a capital letter.

- **Imagery** is one of the most important elements of any kind of poem. Sensory words help you to see, hear, feel, taste, or smell in your mind what is being described.

- **Lyrical poems** usually rhyme and use **cadence,** or rhythm that repeats itself. Lyrical poems have the form and musical quality of a song. (The words to songs are called "lyrics.")

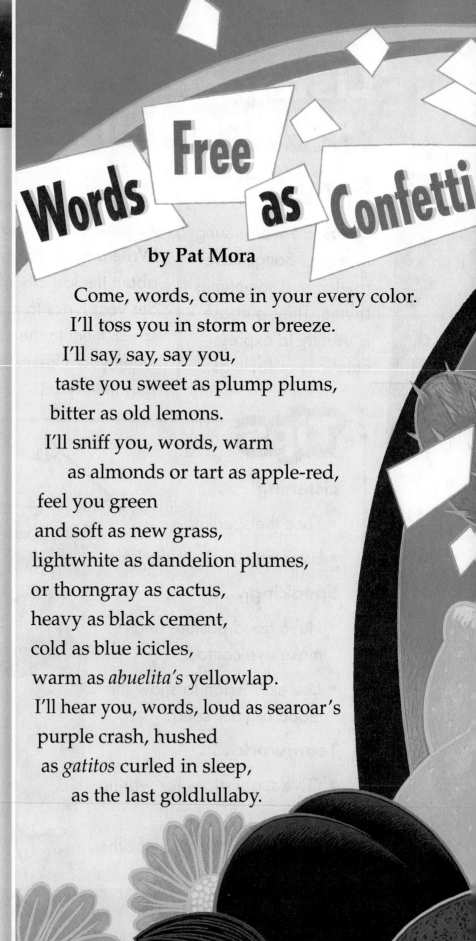

Words Free as Confetti

by Pat Mora

Come, words, come in your every color.
I'll toss you in storm or breeze.
I'll say, say, say you,
taste you sweet as plump plums,
bitter as old lemons.
I'll sniff you, words, warm
as almonds or tart as apple-red,
feel you green
and soft as new grass,
lightwhite as dandelion plumes,
or thorngray as cactus,
heavy as black cement,
cold as blue icicles,
warm as *abuelita's* yellowlap.
I'll hear you, words, loud as searoar's
purple crash, hushed
as *gatitos* curled in sleep,
as the last goldlullaby.

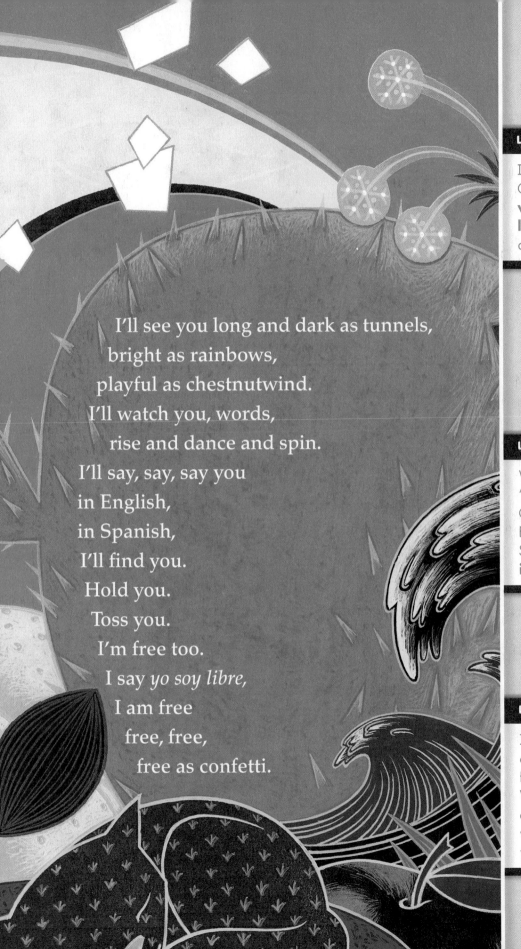

I'll see you long and dark as tunnels,
   bright as rainbows,
   playful as chestnutwind.
I'll watch you, words,
   rise and dance and spin.
I'll say, say, say you
in English,
in Spanish,
   I'll find you.
   Hold you.
   Toss you.
   I'm free too.
   I say *yo soy libre*,
   I am free
      free, free,
         free as confetti.

Let's **Think** About...

Is "Words Free as Confetti" a **free verse** poem or a **lyrical** poem? How do you know?

Let's **Think** About...

Why do you think "Words Free as Confetti" uses both English and Spanish to create **imagery**?

Let's **Think** About...

Identify examples of sensory language for all five senses. What comparisons create graphic visual images for you?

The Star-Spangled Banner

by Francis Scott Key

Oh say, can you see, by the dawn's
    early light,
What so proudly we hailed at the twilight's
    last gleaming—
Whose broad stripes and bright stars,
    through the perilous fight,
O'er the ramparts we watched were so
    gallantly streaming!
And the rocket's red glare, the bombs
    bursting in air,
Gave proof through the night that our flag
    was still there;
Oh! say, does that star-spangled banner
    yet wave
O'er the land of the free, and the home
    of the brave!

I Watched an Eagle Soar

by Virginia Driving Hawk Sneve

Grandmother,
I watched an eagle soar
high in the sky
until a cloud covered him up.
Grandmother,
I still saw the eagle
behind my eyes.

How to Use This Glossary

This glossary can help you understand and pronounce some of the words in this book. The entries in this glossary are in alphabetical order. There are guide words at the top of each page to show you the first and last words on the page. A pronunciation key is at the bottom of the following page. Remember, if you can't find the word you are looking for, ask for help or check a dictionary.

The entry word is in dark type. It shows how the word is spelled and how the word is divided into syllables.

The pronunciation is in parentheses. It also shows which syllables are stressed.

Part-of-speech labels show the function or functions of an entry word and any listed form of that word.

a·dore (ə dôr′), *VERB.* to love and admire someone very greatly: *She adores her mother.* ❑ *VERB.* **a·dores, a·dored, a·dor·ing.**

Sometimes, irregular and other special forms will be shown to help you use the word correctly.

The definition and example sentence show you what the word means and how it is used.

Aa

air·port (âr′pôrt′), *NOUN.* an area used regularly by aircraft to land and take off: *An airport has buildings for passengers and for keeping and repairing aircraft.*

airport

aq·ue·duct (ak′wə dukt), *NOUN.* a large pipe or channel for bringing water from a distance.

at·tic (at′ik), *NOUN.* the space in a house just below the roof and above the other rooms.

av·er·age (av′ər ij), *NOUN.* the quantity found by dividing the sum of all the quantities by the number of quantities. The average of 3 and 5 and 10 is 6 (because 3 + 5 + 10 = 18, and 18 divided by 3 = 6).

Bb

bak·er·y (bā′kər ē), *NOUN*. a place where bread, pies, cakes, and pastries are made or sold.

bakery

bas·ket·ball (bas′kit bȯl), *NOUN*. **1.** a game played with a large, round ball between two teams of five players each. The players score points by tossing the ball through baskets hanging at either end of the court. **2.** the ball used in this game.

batch (bach), *NOUN*. a quantity of something made at the same time: *a batch of cookies.*

board (bôrd), *NOUN*. **1.** a broad, thin piece of wood for use in building: *We used 10-inch boards for shelves.* **2.** a group of people managing something; council: *a board of directors.*

boil (boil), *VERB*. to cause a liquid to bubble and give off steam by heating it: *He boiled some water for tea.* ❑ *VERB* **boils, boiled, boil·ing.**

bou·quet (bü kā′), *NOUN*. a bunch of picked or cut flowers: *He picked a bouquet of wildflowers for his mother.*

bow (bou), *VERB*. to bend the head or body in greeting, respect, worship, or obedience: *The people bowed before the queen.* ❑ *VERB* **bows, bowed, bow·ing.**

braid·ed (brād′ed), *ADJECTIVE*. woven or twined together: *The warm, braided bread was delicious.*

Cc

card·board (kärd′bôrd′), *NOUN*. a stiff material made of layers of paper pulp pressed together, used to make cards, posters, boxes, and so on.

a in *hat*	ėr in *term*	ô in *order*	ch in *child*	ə = a in *about*
ā in *age*	i in *it*	oi in *oil*	ng in *long*	ə = e in *taken*
â in *care*	ī in *ice*	ou in *out*	sh in *she*	ə = i in *pencil*
ä in *far*	o in *hot*	u in *cup*	th in *thin*	ə = o in *lemon*
e in *let*	ō in *open*	u̇ in *put*	ᴛʜ in *then*	ə = u in *circus*
ē in *equal*	ȯ in *all*	ü in *rule*	zh in *measure*	

cel·e·brate (sel′ə brāt), *VERB.* to do something special in honor of a special person or day: *We celebrated my birthday with a party.* ❑ *VERB* **cel·e·brates, cel·e·brat·ed, cel·e·brat·ing.**

celebrate

cel·lar (sel′ər), *NOUN.* a room or rooms under a building where things are stored: *She went down to the cellar to get a can of peaches.*

chill·y (chil′ē), *ADJECTIVE.* cold; unpleasantly cool: *It is a rainy, chilly day.*

chore (chôr), *NOUN.* a small task or easy job that you have to do regularly: *Feeding our pets is one of my daily chores.* ❑ *PLURAL* **chores.**

cir·cus (ser′kəs), *NOUN.* a traveling show in which clowns, acrobats, and trained animals perform: *His favorite part of the circus was the elephant parade.* ❑ *PLURAL* **circuses.**

clutch (kluch), *VERB.* to grasp something tightly: *I clutched the railing to keep from falling.* ❑ *VERB* **clutch·es, clutched, clutch·ing.**

con·tent¹ (kon′tent), *NOUN.*
1. contents, all the things inside a box, a house, and so on: *An old chair and a bed were the only contents of the room.* **2.** chapters or sections in a book: *A table of contents gives a list of the sections in this book.*

con·tent² (kən tent′), **1.** *VERB.* to satisfy; please: *Nothing contents me when I am sick.* **2.** *ADJECTIVE.* satisfied; pleased: *Will you be content to wait till tomorrow?* ❑ *VERB* **con·tents, con·tent·ed, con·tent·ing.**

con·tin·ue (kən tin′yü), **1.** *VERB.* to keep up; keep on; go on: *The rain continued all day.* **2.** *VERB.* to go on with something after stopping for a while: *The story will be continued next week.* ❑ *VERB* **con·tin·ues, con·tin·ued, con·tin·u·ing.**

cot·ton (kot′n), *ADJECTIVE.* cloth made from soft, white fibers that grow in fluffy bunches on the cotton plant: *Light-colored cotton clothes keep me cool in hot weather.*

crouch (krouch), **1.** *NOUN.* a crouching position. **2.** *VERB.* to stoop over with the legs bent: *She was crouched beside the table.* ❑ *VERB* **crouch·es, crouched, crouch·ing.**

crown (kroun), *NOUN.* a head covering of precious metal worn by a royal person, such as a queen or a king.

crys·tal (kris′tl), *NOUN.* a hard, solid piece of some substance that is naturally formed of flat surfaces and angles: *Crystals can be small, like grains of salt, or large, like some kinds of stone.*

crystal

cur·i·ous (kyür′ē əs), *ADJECTIVE.* strange; odd; unusual: *I found a curious, old box in the attic.*

cur·rent (kėr′ənt), **1.** *NOUN.* a flow or stream of water, electricity, air, or any fluid: *The current swept the stick down the river.* **2.** *ADJECTIVE.* of or about the present time: *current events.*

cus·tom·er (kus′tə mər), *NOUN.* someone who buys goods or services: *Just before the holidays, the store was full of customers.*

Dd

deep (dēp), *ADJECTIVE.* going a long way down from the top or surface: *a deep cut; a deeper pond; the deepest trench in the ocean.* **deep·er, deep·est.**

de·li·cious (di lish′əs), *ADJECTIVE.* very pleasing or satisfying; delightful, especially to the taste or smell: *a delicious cake.*

depth (depth), *NOUN.* the distance from the top to the bottom: *The depth of the well is about 25 feet.*

de·scribe (di skrīb′), *VERB.* to tell in words how someone looks, feels, or acts, or to record the most important things about a place, a thing, or an event: *The reporter described the awards ceremony in detail.* ❑ *VERB* **de·scribes, de·scribed, de·scrib·ing.**

des·ert (dez′ərt), *NOUN.* a dry, sandy region without water and trees: *In North Africa there is a great desert called the Sahara.*

dif·fi·cult (dif′i kult), *ADJECTIVE*. hard to make, do, or understand: *The math test included some easy problems and some difficult ones.*

dis·ap·pear (dis′ə pir′), *VERB*. to vanish completely; stop existing: *When spring came, the snow disappeared.* ❑ *VERB* **dis·ap·pears, dis·ap·peared, dis·ap·pear·ing.**

dis·ease (də zēz′), *NOUN*. a sickness; illness; condition in which a bodily system, organ, or part does not work properly: *Diabetes is a disease.*

dis·cov·er·y (dis kuv′ər ē), *NOUN*. something found out: *One of Benjamin Franklin's discoveries was that lightning is electricity.*

dough (dō), *NOUN*. a soft, thick mixture of flour, liquid, and other things from which bread, biscuits, cake, and pie crusts are made.

dough

drown (droun), *VERB*. to die or cause to die under water or other liquid because of lack of air to breathe: *We almost drowned when our raft overturned.* ❑ *VERB* **drowns, drowned, drown·ing.**

Ee

ech·o (ek′ō), *VERB*. to be heard again: *Her shout echoed through the valley.* ❑ *VERB* **ech·oes, ech·oed, ech·o·ing.**

en·cour·age (en kėr′ij), *VERB*. to give someone courage or confidence; urge on: *We encouraged our team with loud cheers.* ❑ *VERB* **en·cour·ag·es, en·cour·aged, en·cour·ag·ing.**

e·rupt (i rupt′), *VERB*. to burst out violently: *Lava and ash erupted from the volcano.* ❑ *VERB* **e·rupts, e·rupt·ed, e·rupt·ing.**

erupt

ex·pres·sion (ek spresh′ən), *NOUN.* the act of putting into words or visual medium: *freedom of expression.*

Ff

fare·well (fâr′wel′), *ADJECTIVE.* parting; last: *a farewell kiss.*

feast (fēst), *NOUN.* a big meal for a special occasion shared by a number of people: *The breakfast that she cooked was a real feast.*

fes·ti·val (fes′tə vəl), *NOUN.* a program of entertainment, often held annually: *a summer music festival.*

festival

fierce (firs), *ADJECTIVE.* wild and frightening: *The fierce lion paced in its cage.*

fierce

flight (flīt), *NOUN.* a set of stairs from one landing or one story of a building to the next.

fool·ish (fü′lish), *ADJECTIVE.* without any sense; unwise: *It is foolish to cross the street without looking both ways.*

fo·reign (fôr′ən), *ADJECTIVE.* outside your own country: *She travels often in foreign countries.*

freeze (frēz), *VERB.* **1.** to become hard from cold; turn into a solid. **2.** to become unable to move: *I froze in my tracks when I saw the bear.* ❑ *VERB* **freez·es, froze, freez·ing.**

Gg

goal (gōl), *NOUN.* something desired: *Her goal was to be a scientist.*

grace·ful (grās′fəl), ADJECTIVE. beautiful in form or movement: *He is a graceful dancer.*

guard (gärd), **1.** NOUN. (in basketball) a member of the backcourt. **2.** NOUN. a person or group that protects or watches. **3.** VERB. to watch over someone or something; keep safe; defend: *The dog guarded the child.* ❏ VERB **guards, guard·ed, guard·ing.**

guid·ance (gīd′ns), NOUN. helpful advice or instruction: *a teacher's guidance.*

gul·ly (gul′ē), NOUN. a ditch made by heavy rains or running water.

Hh

hand·ker·chief (hang′kər chif), NOUN. a soft, usually square piece of cloth used for wiping your nose, face, or hands.

handkerchief

home·sick (hōm′sik′), ADJECTIVE. very sad because you are far away from home.

hon·or (on′ər), **1.** NOUN. knowing what is right or proper and always doing it: *A person of honor always keeps his or her promises.* **2.** VERB. to show respect to someone: *We honor our country's dead soldiers on Memorial Day.* ❏ VERB **hon·ors, hon·ored, hon·or·ing.**

Ii

in·gre·di·ent (in grē′dē ənt), NOUN. one of the parts of a mixture: *The ingredients of a cake usually include eggs, sugar, flour, and flavoring.* ❏ PLURAL **in·gre·di·ents.**

Jj

jour·ney (jėr′nē), NOUN. a long trip from one place to another: *I'd like to take a journey around the world.*

joy·ful (joi′fəl), ADJECTIVE. causing or showing joy; glad; happy: *joyful news.*

Ll

la·bel (lā′bəl), VERB. to put or write a name on something: *She labeled her backpack with her name and address.* ❏ VERB **labels, labeled, label·ing.**

lib·er·ty (lib′ər tē), *NOUN.* freedom: *In 1865, the United States granted liberty to all people who were enslaved.*

lo·cal (lō′kəl), *ADJECTIVE.* about a certain place, especially nearby, not far away: *I go to a local doctor.*

Mm

med·al (med′l), *NOUN.* a piece of metal like a coin, given as a prize or award, usually with a picture or words stamped on it: *She received two medals in gymnastics.* ❑ *PLURAL* **med·als.**

medal

mem·or·y (mem′ər ē), *NOUN.* a person, thing, or event that you can remember: *One of my favorite memories is my seventh birthday party.* ❑ *PLURAL* **mem·or·ies.**

mix·ture (miks′chər), *NOUN.* a mixed condition: *At the end of the move, I felt a mixture of relief and disappointment.*

mod·el (mod′l), *NOUN.* a small copy of something: *A globe is a model of the Earth.* ❑ *PLURAL* **mod·els.**

Nn

narrow (nar′ō), *ADJECTIVE.* not wide; having little width; less wide than usual for its kind: *a narrow path.*

na·tive (nā′tiv), *ADJECTIVE.* belonging to someone because of that person's birth: *The United States is my native land.*

nib·ble (nib′əl), *VERB.* to bite something gently or to eat with small, quick bites: *The rabbits were nibbling the lettuce in the garden.* ❑ *VERB* **nib·bles, nib·bled, nib·bling.**

Oo

out·run (out run′), *VERB.* to run faster than someone or something else: *She can outrun her older sister.* ❑ *VERB* **out·runs, out·ran, out·run·ning.**

Pp

pace (pās), *NOUN.* a step: *He took three paces into the room.* ❑ *PLURAL* **pac·es.**

pale (pāl), *ADJECTIVE.* not bright; dim: *a pale blue.*

peak (pēk), NOUN. the pointed top of a mountain or hill: *We saw the snowy peak in the distance.*

perch (pėrch), VERB. to come to rest on something; settle; sit: *A robin perched on the branch.* ❑ VERB **perch·es, perched, perch·ing.**

pier (pir), NOUN. a platform that extends over water, used as a landing place for ships and boats: *The boys sat at the end of the pier and watched the boats on the lake.*

pier

pil·lar (pil′ər), NOUN. a slender, strong upright support used either to support or to decorate a building: *There were pillars on either side of the front door.* ❑ PLURAL **pil·lars.**

pitch·er (pich′ər), NOUN. a player on a baseball team who pitches to the catcher. A batter tries to hit the ball before it gets to the catcher.

pop·u·lar (pop′yə lər), ADJECTIVE. liked by most people: *a popular sport; a popular song.*

Rr

rain·drop (rān′drop′), NOUN. the water that falls in drops from the clouds. ❑ PLURAL **rain·drops.**

rec·i·pe (res′ə pē), NOUN. a set of written directions that show you how to fix something to eat: *Please give me your recipe for bread.*

reed (rēd), NOUN. a kind of tall grass that grows in wet places: *Reeds have hollow, jointed stalks.* ❑ PLURAL **reeds.**

reeds

rhythm (riŦH′əm), NOUN. the natural, strong beat that some music or poetry has: *Rhythm makes you want to clap your hands to keep time.*

ru·in (rü′ən), *VERB.* to destroy or spoil something completely: *The rain ruined our picnic.* ❑ *VERB* **ru·ins, ru·ined, ru·in·ing.**

Ss

scoop (sküp), *NOUN.* a tool like a small shovel used to dip up things: *A cuplike scoop is used to serve ice cream.*

scoop

scram·ble (skram′bəl), *VERB.* to make your way, especially by climbing or crawling quickly: *We scrambled up the steep, rocky hill, trying to follow the guide.* ❑ *VERB* **scram·bles, scram·bled, scram·bling.**

set·tle (set′l), *VERB.* to set up the first towns and farms in an area: *The English settled New England.* ❑ *VERB* **set·tles, set·tled, set·tling.**

snug (snug), *ADJECTIVE.* fitting your body closely: *That coat is a little too snug with a sweater under it.*

soar (sôr), *VERB.* to rise, fly, or glide high in the air: *The hawk soars above the treetops.* ❑ *VERB* **soars, soared, soar·ing.**

soar

so·cial (sō′shəl), *ADJECTIVE.* concerned with human beings as a group: *Schools and hospitals are social institutions.*

spare (spâr), **1.** *ADJECTIVE.* extra: *a spare tire.* **2.** *VERB.* to show mercy to someone; decide not to harm or destroy: *He spared his enemy's life.* ❑ *VERB* **spares, spared, spar·ing.**

sport (spôrt), **1.** *NOUN.* A game or contest that requires some skill and usually a certain amount of physical exercise. **2.** *PLURAL* **sports,** *ADJECTIVE.* of, about, or suitable for sports: *sports clothes, sports medicine.*

stamp (stamp), **1.** *NOUN.* a small piece of paper with glue on the back; postage stamp: *You put stamps on letters or packages before mailing them.* ❑ *PLURAL* **stamps. 2.** *VERB.* to bring down your foot with force: *He stamped his foot in anger.* ❑ *VERB* **stamps, stamped, stamp·ing.**

stir (stėr), *VERB.* **1.** to mix something by moving it around with a spoon, stick, and so on: *Stir the sugar into the lemonade.* **2.** to move something: *The wind stirred the leaves.* ❑ *VERB* **stirs, stirred, stir·ring.**

stoop (stüp), *NOUN.* a porch or platform at the entrance of a house.

stroke (strōk), *NOUN.* **1.** the act of hitting something; blow: *I drove in the nail with several strokes of the hammer.* **2.** a single complete movement made over and over again: *He rowed with strong strokes of the oars.*

stroke 1.

stud·y (stud′ē), **1.** *NOUN.* the effort to learn by reading or thinking: *After an hour's study, I knew my lesson.* **2.** *VERB.* to make an effort to learn: *She studied her spelling words for half an hour.* ❑ *PLURAL* **stud·ies.** ❑ *VERB* **stud·ies, stud·ied, stud·y·ing.**

sup·port (sə pôrt′), *VERB.* to help; aid: *Parents support and love their children.* ❑ *VERB* **sup·ports, sup·port·ed, sup·port·ing.**

swal·low (swäl′ō), *VERB.* to make food or drink travel from your mouth down your throat: *Swallow your food before you talk.* ❑ *VERB* **swal·lows, swal·lowed, swal·low·ing.**

sweep (swēp), *VERB.* to move or pass over a wide area: *A crow swept over the field.* ❑ *VERB* **sweeps, swept, sweep·ing.**

swoop (swüp), *VERB.* to come down fast on something, as a hawk does when it attacks: *Bats are swooping down from the roof of the cave.* ❑ *VERB* **swoops, swooped, swoop·ing.**

sym·bol (sim′bəl), *NOUN.* an object, diagram, icon, and so on, that stands for or represents something else: *The dove is a symbol of peace.*

Tt

tab·let (tab′lit), *NOUN.* a small, flat surface with something written on it.

ter·ri·ble (ter′ə bəl), *ADJECTIVE.* causing great fear; dreadful; awful: *The terrible storm destroyed many homes.*

thatch (thach), *NOUN.* plant material, such as straw or reeds, that is used to make or cover a roof.

ther·mal (thėr′məl), *ADJECTIVE.* of or about heat: *They wear thermal socks when they go hiking in cold weather.*

tide (tīd), *NOUN.* the rise and fall of the ocean about every twelve hours that is caused by the gravitational pull of the moon and the sun.

torch (tôrch), *NOUN.* a long stick with material that burns at one end of it.

torch

treas·ure (trezh′ər), *NOUN.* any person or thing that is loved or valued a great deal: *The silver teapot is my parents' special treasure.*

Uu

un·a·ware (un′ə wâr′), *ADJECTIVE.* not aware; unconscious: *We were unaware of the approaching storm.*

un·for·get·ta·ble (un′fər get′ə bəl), *ADJECTIVE.* so good or so wonderful that you cannot forget it: *Winning the race was an unforgettable experience.*

un·veil (un vāl′), *VERB.* to remove a veil from; uncover; disclose; reveal: *The bride unveiled her face.* ❑ *VERB* **un·veils, un·veiled, un·veil·ing.**

Vv

val·ley (val′ē), *NOUN.* a region of low land that lies between hills or mountains: *Many valleys have rivers running through them.* ❑ *PLURAL* **val·leys.**

Ww

wa·ter·fall (wȯ′tər fȯl′), *NOUN.* a stream of water that falls from a high place: *The canoe turned back before it reached the waterfall.*

waterfall

547

Unit 4

The Man Who Invented Basketball

English	Spanish
basketball	* básquetbol
disease	enfermedad
freeze	congelar
guard	alero
popular	* popular
sports	deportes
study	* estudio
terrible	* terrible

Hottest, Coldest, Highest, Deepest

English	Spanish
average	promedio
depth	profundidad
deserts	desiertos
erupted	tuvo erupciones
outrun	correr más rápido que
peak	cima
tides	mareas
waterfalls	cascadas

Rocks in His Head

English	Spanish
attic	* ático
board	consejo
chores	quehaceres
customer	cliente
labeled	rotuló
spare	de repuesto
stamps	* estampillas

America's Champion Swimmer: Gertrude Ederle

English	Spanish
celebrate	* celebrarán
continued	siguió
current	corriente
drowned	se ahogó
medals	* medallas
stirred	revolvió
strokes	brazadas

* English/Spanish Cognate: A **cognate** is a word that is similar in two languages and has the same meaning in both languages.

Fly, Eagle, Fly!

English	Spanish
clutched	agarraron
echoed	resoné
gully	barranco
reeds	juncos
scrambled	luchó por salir
thatch	paja
valley	* valle

Unit 5

Suki's Kimono

English	Spanish
cotton	algodón
festival	* festival
graceful	elegante
handkerchief	pañuelo
paces	* pasos
pale	claro
rhythm	ritmo
snug	ceñido

I Love Saturdays y domingos

English	Spanish
circus	* circo
nibbling	picando
bouquet	ramo
difficult	* difícil
pier	muelle
swallow	tragar
soars	vuela alto

Good-Bye, 382 Shin Dang Dong

English	Spanish
airport	aeropuerto
cellar	sótano
curious	* curiosa
delicious	* deliciosa
described	descrito
farewell	despedida
homesick	nostálgico
memories	* memorias
raindrops	gotas de lluvia

Jalapeño Bagels

English	Spanish
bakery	panadería
batch	hornada
boils	hierva
braided	trenzado
dough	masa
ingredients	* ingredientes
mixture	mezcla

Me and Uncle Romie

English	Spanish
cardboard	cartón
feast	festín
fierce	feroz
flights	tramos (de escalera)
pitcher	lanzador
ruined	arruinado
stoops	pórticos
treasure	tesoro

Unit 6

The Story of the Statue of Liberty

English	Spanish
crown	corona
liberty	* libertad
models	maquetas
symbol	* símbolo
tablet	lápida
torch	antorcha
unforgettable	inolvidable
unveiled	descubrió

Happy Birthday Mr. Kang

English	Spanish
bows	inclina
chilly	frío
foolish	tonto
foreign	extranjero
narrow	estrechas
perches	se posa
recipe	receta

Talking Walls: Art for the People

English	Spanish
encourages	anima
expression	* expresión
local	* locales
native	nativo(s)
settled	se asentaron
social	* sociales
support	apoyar

Two Bad Ants

English	Spanish
crystal	* cristal
disappeared	desapareció
discovery	descubrimiento
goal	meta
journey	viaje
joyful	alegres
scoop	cucharilla
unaware	no se dieron cuenta

Atlantis

English	Spanish
aqueducts	* acueductos
content	* contenido
crouched	agachados
guidance	orientación
honor	* honor
pillar	* pilar
thermal	térmico

Text

Grateful acknowledgment is made to the following for copyrighted material:

28: From "The Man Who Invented Basketball: James Naismith and His Amazing Game" by Edwin Brit Wyckoff. Copyright © 2008 by Enslow Publishers, Inc. Published by Enslow Publishers, Inc. Berkeley Heights, NJ. Used by permission. All rights reserved.

46: From "My Turn at Bat: The Story of My Life" by Ted Williams as told to John Underwood. Copyright © 1969, 1988 by Ted Williams and John Underwood. Used by permission of Simon & Schuster, Inc. All rights reserved.

49: WWW.SPORTINGNEWS.COM/ ARCHIVES/WILLIAMS/TIMELINE.HTLM. Copyright © 2002 SportingNews.com. Used by permission The Sporting News.

51: "Baseball Hall of Fame Information and Baseball Card Statistics for Ted Williams" from http://www.baseballhalloffame.org/hofers/ detail.jsp?playerId=124341. From National Baseball Hall of Fame (NBHOF)

62: From *Hottest, Coldest, Highest, Deepest* by Steve Jenkins. Copyright © 1998 by Steve Jenkins. Reprinted by permission of Houghton Mifflin Company. All rights reserved.

94: *Rocks in His Head* by Carol Otis Hurst. Text copyright © 2001 by Carol Otis Hurst. Illustrations © 2001 by James Stevenson. Used by permission of HarperCollins Publishers.

124: *America's Champion Swimmer: Gertrude Ederle*, text copyright © 2000 by David A. Adler, illustrations copyright © 2000 by Terry Widener, reprinted by permission of Harcourt, Inc.

126: From "Women in History: Wilma Rudolph biography." Lakewood Public Library. http:// www.lkwdpl.org/wihohio/rudo-wil.htm. Reprinted by permission of Women in History, Lakewood, Ohio.

158: From *Fly, Eagle, Fly!* by Christopher Gregorowski, illustrated by Niki Daly. Text copyright © 2000 by Christopher Gregorowski, illustrations copyright © 2000 by Niki Daly. Reprinted with permission of Margaret K. McElderry Books, an imprint of Simon & Schuster Children's Publishing Division. All rights reserved.

176: *Purple Coyote* by Cornette, illustrated by Rochette. Copyright © 1997 by L'Ecole des Loisirs, Paris. First American edition 1999—Originally published in France by Pastel, 1997. English translation copyright © 1999 by Random House, Inc. Published by arrangement with Random House Children's Books, a division of Random House, Inc., New York, New York. All rights reserved.

185: "Written at the Po-Shan Monastery" by Hsin Ch'i-chi, translated by Irving Yucheng Lo, from *Sunflower Splendor: Three Thousand Years of Chinese Poetry* by Wu-Chi Liu (Author), Irving Yucheng Lo (Editor), published by Indiana University Press, 1990. Reprinted by permission of Indiana University Press.

186: "Me with apologies to Joyce Kilmer ("Trees")" from *Because I Could Not Stop My Bike* by Karen Jo Shapiro. Text copyright © 2003 Karen Jo Shapiro. Illustrations copyright © 2003 by Matt Faulkner. Used with permission by Charlesbridge Publishing, Inc. All rights reserved.

187: "By Myself" from *Honey, I Love* by Eloise Greenfield. Text copyright © 1978 by Eloise Greenfield. Used by permission of HarperCollins Publishers.

198: *Suki's Kimono*, written by Chieri Uegaki and illustrated by Stéphane Jorisch is used with the permission of Kids Can Press Ltd., Toronto. Text © 2003 Chieri Uegaki. Illustrations © 2003 Stéphane Jorisch.

230: From *I Love Saturdays y domingos* by Alma Flor Ada. Text copyright © 2002 by Alma Flor Ada. Reprinted with permission of Atheneum Books for Young Readers, an Imprint of Simon & Schuster Children's Publishing Division. All rights reserved.

250: From *Scott Foresman Social Studies Communities*, 2003. Copyright © 2003 Pearson Education, Inc. Reprinted by permission of Pearson Education, Inc.

262: Reprinted with permission of the National Geographic Society from *Good-Bye, 382 Shin Dang Dong* by Frances Park and Ginger Park. Copyright © 2002 Frances Park and Ginger Park. Illustrations © 2002 Yangsook Choi.

284: The Lois Lenski Covey Foundation, Inc., for "Sing a Song of People' from *The Life I Live* by Lois Lenski. Copyright © 1965 by The Lois Lenski Covey Foundation, Inc. Reprinted by Permission of Licensor. Copyright © Renewed 1993, no. RE 615-252.

296: From *Jalapeño Bagels* by Natasha Wing.

552

Text copyright © 1996 by Natasha Wing. Reprinted with permission of Atheneum Books For Young Readers, an imprint of Simon & Schuster Children's Publishing Division. All rights reserved.

314: Excerpts from *Viva Mexico! The Foods* by George Ancona (Benchmark Books). Copyright © 2002 by George Ancona. Reprinted with permission of Marshall Cavendish Corporation.

328: From *Me and Uncle Romie: A Story Inspired by the Life and Art of Romare Bearden* by Claire Hartfield, illustrated by Jerome Lagarrigue, copyright © 2002 by Claire Hartfield, text. Copyright © 2002 by Jerome Lagarrigue, illustrations. Used by permission of Dial Books for Young Readers, A Division of Penguin Young Readers Group, A Member of Penguin Group (USA) Inc., 345 Hudson Street, New York, NY 10014. All rights reserved.

360: "My Friend in School" from *Deshawn Days*. Text copyright © 2001 by Tony Medina. Permission arranged with Lee & Low Books, Inc., New York, NY 10016.

362: "Lunch Survey," from *Swimming Upstream: Middle Grade Poems* by Kristine O'Connell George. Text copyright © 2002 by Kristine O'Connell George. Reprinted by permission of Clarion Books, an imprint of Houghton Mifflin Company. All rights reserved.

363: "Saying Yes" by Diana Chang is reprinted by permission of the author.

374: *The Story of the Statue of Liberty* by Betsy C. Maestro, illustrations by Giulio Maestro. Text copyright © 1986 by Betsy Maestro. Illustrations copyright © 1986 by Giulio Maestro. Used by permission of HarperCollins Publishers.

390: From *Scott Foresman Social Studies: Communities*, 2003. Copyright © 2003 Pearson Education, Inc. Reprinted by permission of Pearson Education, Inc.

402: From *Happy Birthday Mr. Kang* by Susan L. Roth. Copyright © 2001 Susan L. Roth. Reprinted with permission of the National Geographic Society.

468: *Two Bad Ants* by Chris Van Allsburg. Copyright © 1988 by Chris Van Allsburg. Reprinted by permission of Houghton Mifflin Company. All rights reserved.

502: "Atlantis: The Legend of A Lost City" by Christina Balit. Text and illustrations copyright © 1999 by Christina Balit. Used by arrangement with Henry Holt and Company, LLC.

532: "Words Free as Confetti" from *Confetti: Poems for Children*. Text copyright © 1996 by Pat Mora. Permission arranged with Lee and Low Books, Inc., New York, NY.

535: "I Watched an Eagle Soar" from *Dancing Teepees: Poems of the North American Indian Youth* by Virginia Driving Hawk Sneve. Copyright © 1989 by Virginia Driving Hawk Sneve. Reprinted from *Dancing Teepees* by permission of Holiday House, Inc.

Every effort has been made to locate the copyright owner of material reproduced in this component. Omissions brought to our attention will be corrected in subsequent editions.

Illustrations

Cover: Leo Timmers
EI•1–EI•15 Mike Lester
80–82 James Madsen
113 Larry Jones
230–244 Claudia Degliuomini
284 Remy Simard
296–309 Antonio Castro
332–344 Jerome Lagarrigue
362 Laurie Keller
532 Stephen Daigle
W•2–W•15 Nomar Perez.

Photographs

Every effort has been made to secure permission and provide appropriate credit for photographic material. The publisher deeply regrets any omission and pledges to correct errors called to its attention in subsequent editions.

Unless otherwise acknowledged, all photographs are the property of Pearson Education, Inc.

Photo locators denoted as follows: Top (T), Center (C), Bottom (B), Left (L), Right (R), Background (Bkgd)

18 (C) ©Joel Sartore/Getty Images, (B) ©Rebecca Emery/Getty Images
20 (BR) ©Hans Neleman/zefa/Corbis, (BL) ©Yellow Dog Productions/Getty Images
26 (B) ©Roy Dabner/epa/Corbis, (C) ©Dennis Macdonald/PhotoLibrary Group, Ltd., (TL) Jupiter Images

WORDS! | Vocabulary Handbook

Antonyms

Synonyms

Base Words

Prefixes

Suffixes

Context Clues

Related Words

Compound Words

Multiple-Meaning Words

Homographs

Homonyms

Homophones

Dictionary

Thesaurus

Antonyms

Antonyms are words that have opposite meanings. *Same* and *different* are antonyms.

Same

Different

Antonyms can be used to contrast two things. Antonyms help readers understand differences.

Synonyms

Synonyms are words that have the same meaning or similar meanings. *Loud* and *noisy* are synonyms.

Loud

Knowing and using synonyms can help make your writing more interesting. Look in a thesaurus to find synonyms.

Noisy

Base Words

A base word is a word that cannot be broken down into smaller words or word parts. *Cover* and *motion* are base words.

Cover

Motion

Knowing the meaning of a base word can help you understand the meanings of longer words.

Prefixes

A prefix is a word part that can be added to the beginning of a base word. In the word *uncover*, *un-* is a prefix.

Cover

Uncover

Knowing the meaning of a prefix can help you figure out the meaning of a new word.

Common Prefixes and Their Meanings

un-	not
re-	again, back
in-	not
dis-	not, opposite of
pre-	before

Suffixes

A suffix is a word part added to the end of a base word. In the word *motionless*, *-less* is a suffix.

Motion

Motionless

Common Suffixes and Their Meanings

-able	can be done
-ment	action or process
-less	without
-tion	act, process

Knowing how a suffix changes a word can help you figure out the meaning of a new word.

Context Clues

Read the words before and after a word that you don't know to help you make sense of it.

I couldn't decide what to wear! The red, blue, green, or fuchsia dress?

Related Words

Related words are words that have the same base word. *Sign, signal,* and *signature* are related because they all have the base word *sign*.

Sign

Signature

Signal

If you know the base words, you may be able to figure out the meanings of words related to it.

W•8

Compound Words

Compound words are words made of two smaller words. *Sandbox* and *ladybug* are compound words.

sand + **box** = **sandbox**

Look for smaller words that you already know in unfamiliar words.

lady + **bug** = **ladybug**

Multiple-Meaning Words

Multiple-meaning words are words that can have different meanings depending on how they are used.

Homographs

Homographs are words that are spelled the same but have different meanings. They may be pronounced the same way or differently.

Lead

Lead

Read the words before and after a homograph to discover its meaning and pronunciation. Check a dictionary to be sure.

Homophones

Homophones are words that sound the same, but they
are spelled differently and they have different meanings.

Homonyms

Homonyms are words that are spelled the same and sound the same, but they have different meanings.

Seal

Seal

You can figure out the meaning of a homonym by reading the words around it.

Homophones

Homophones are words that sound the same, but they are spelled differently and they have different meanings.

Hair

Hare

Homophones might be confusing when you hear them being read aloud. Pay attention to the words before and after the homophone to find its meaning.

Understanding
Homographs, Homonyms, and Homophones

	Pronunciation	Spelling	Meaning
Homographs	may be the same or different	same	different
Homonyms	same	same	different
Homophones	same	different	different

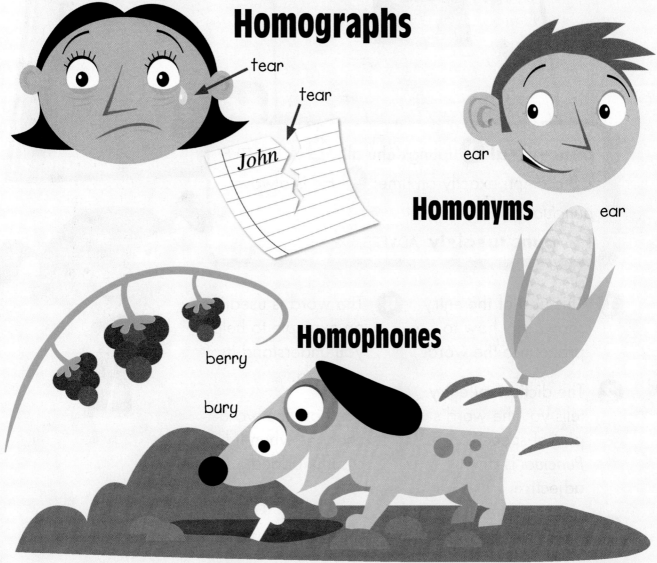

Homographs

tear

tear

John

Homonyms

ear

ear

Homophones

berry

bury

Dictionary

A dictionary is a book that explains the words of our language. The words in a dictionary are in alphabetical order.

punc•tu•al ❶ (pungk'chu al), ❷ *ADJECTIVE*
❸ prompt; exactly on time: ❹ *He is always punctual to the minute.*
❺ -**punc'tu•al•ly** ADVERB.

❶ This part of the entry shows you how to pronounce the word.

❷ The dictionary entry tells you the word's part of speech. *Punctual* is an adjective.

❸ Here is the word's definition.

❹ The word is used in an example to help you understand its meaning.

❺ See how the word changes when it has a suffix added.

Thesaurus

A thesaurus is a book of synonyms. The words in a thesaurus are in alphabetical order.

cute
adjective
attractive, appealing, amusing, charming, adorable, enchanting

Keep a thesaurus handy when you write. It can help you find just the right word.

Spot is so cute!